The Independent Consultant's Brochure and Letter Handbook

HERMAN HOLTZ

John Wiley & Sons, Inc.

New York • Chichester • Brisbane • Toronto • Singapore

IBM® is a registered trademark of International Business Machines Corp.
WordPerfect® is a registered trademark of WordPerfect Corporation.
Microsoft® Word for Windows is a trademark of Microsoft Corporation.

This text is printed on acid-free paper.

REQUIREMENTS:
An IBM PC family computer or compatible computer
with 256K minimum memory, a 3.5" high-density floppy drive,
PC DOS, MS DOS, or DR DOS Version 2.0 or later, and a printer.

Copyright© 1995 by Herman Holtz
Published by John Wiley & Sons, Inc.

Library of Congress Cataloging-in-Publication Data:
Holtz, Herman
    The Independent Consultant's Brochure and Letter Handbook / by Herman Holtz,
        p.   cm.
    Includes index
    ISBN 0-471 59734-1 (cloth)   ISBN 0-471-59733-3 (paper)

Printed in the United States of America

10 9 8 7 6 5 4 3 2 1

PREFACE

WHAT WILL THIS BOOK DO FOR YOU?

Despite the overwhelming ubiquity of the computer today, despite communications satellites and message-carrying cables circling the earth, despite the decades-long promises of a paperless society, paper is more in evidence than ever. There is still no acceptable substitute for paper. There is still mainly reliance on the postal service to deliver the bulk of our daily messages and other communications.

A large share of this paperbound communication is created and propagated in the interest of marketing. That is as true in general for the independent consultant as it is for the corporation and supercorporation. Perhaps it is even more true for the independent consultant, because we must look to the most effective and inexpensive means for marketing services. Words on paper are the means of choice.

There is, of course, no question that success as an independent consultant depends on success in marketing. Perhaps this is even more critical in the case of independent consultants, since we must be the marketers, in addition to handling many other duties. In any case, supporting this need to market effectively is the principal concern of these pages, despite this book's resemblance to others of the "business writing" genre.

There are a great many "business writing" books, manuals, tapes, cassette programs, and training courses. Why another one? What has this book to say that has not already been said?

This is not one of those general how-to-write books. Discussions of grammar, punctuation, and "composition" (which we ought to call "organization") will appear only as the occasion mandates. They will be inspired by reminiscences of the common errors I have encountered in more than 50 years of writing experience and my efforts to guide others away from these faults. This book is really not about how to write at all; if anything, it is about *what* to write. It is about how to achieve purposes, about success as an independent consultant. This book is about how to create the marketing and sales tools that do what you want them to do; to present you and your services properly, to act as effective instruments for closing sales, and to help you solve the problems that can be solved via written tools.

One of the premises on which this book is based is that writing well does not really come easily, to even those professional writers who achieve the highest acclaim. (And there is a definite relationship between how hard the writer works and the quality of the product.) The logical inference to be drawn is that with enough hard work anyone can learn to write well—reasonably well, at least. Even if that is true, why should you, as a consultant, devote a great deal of time to composing letters and brochures? Would you not be better off devoting your time to consulting work that clients pay you for? Of course you would. The main objective of this book is not to teach you how to write letters and brochures of professional quality, but to provide you with an instrument that will enable you to produce high-quality letters and brochures. I will impart all the little tricks of the trade I know that will make it easier for you to create effective marketing tools.

If the focus of this book is not as much on how to write as it is on what to write, it is also about how to solve the many problems that arise in writing. It's about planning the solution before attempting to write, instead of floundering about trying to find a thread of logic and hoping that somehow a coherent product will result. This book will provide you with representative models of the various letters and brochures needed for various applications, models you can tailor to your needs.

Today's office tools—desktop computers, word processors, and even sophisticated electronic typewriters—make it relatively easy to produce simple diagrams, so that professional illustrators are not required. You should learn to prepare and use such aids.

You may reasonably expect from all this that this is not a text on grammar and "composition," although I reserve the right to present a few basics of usage later, strictly as a refresher.

Nor is this a training program, although it does include frequent tutorials. Learning that results from use of this book, however desirable, is not a major purpose.

Finally, this is not a complete set of models for each and every occasion, despite the large number of models offered for a great number of situations and applications. In today's complex society, it would be futile to attempt anyting approaching a complete set of models for all occasions.

Those are some things this book is not. It is, however, a reference—a book or program. It is to be referred to as necessary. The models are representative, not total, but they are complete for all possible needs. This book includes a number of illustrations that you may emulate or adapt as models. Many were drawn by computer, using the WordStar word processor. It is also something more, reflecting a somewhat more sophisticated goal, a model and set of patterns from which you can construct a complete system of your own, tailored to your own needs. (I urge you to do so!)

The tutorials were written with that in mind, to explain the models and their uses, and to enable you to create your own, custom-designed models to suit your own needs.

I hope that you will install this system in your own desktop computer as a complete set of files from which you can readily summon the models you need to create.

Overall, the purpose of this system is to ease your burden and save your time. It is also to enable office organizations to turn over many of the writing chores to secretaries, assistants, and aides.

Herman Holtz
Wheaton, Maryland

INTRODUCTION

Brochures, sales letters, releases, newsletters, broadsides, circulars, flyers, and other such written and printed materials are essential to the conduct of all businesses, from the tiniest one-person, home-based enterprise to the largest industrial corporation. Such items are at the heart of the marketing and sales efforts of business, but they are also necessary to the management, administration, and general conduct of a business venture.

Many of these items of business literature serve both marketing and general management/administrative needs. You will write letters to respond to customers' queries, but you will also write sales letters seeking business. You will create or have created for you brochures to explain your services and offers or to seek contracts. Even if printed materials play the most minor role in your marketing, you are expected to have a business card and at least one general brochure.

Writing, in general, is a task many people shrink from. Little by little, as I gained experience in the world of business and industry, that simple truth became more and more apparent. As I worked in the world of engineering, I saw that most engineers were not at all well disposed to writing as one of their daily duties. They, too, disliked—perhaps feared—writing, which was and is an inescapable responsibility of most career professionals. Their dislike of it showed up in the quality of their written prose—not too surprisingly. It is not easy to do well at something one does not want to do at all.

Thus it was that, with recognition of this truism, I was inspired a number of years ago to write a how-to article for engineers on technical writing. I submitted it to an engineering trade journal for publication, sure that the editor would welcome this helpful piece.

To my dismay, the editor quickly rejected it, returning it to me with dazzling speed. Never did the U.S. Postal Service perform more promptly.

I was dismayed, convinced that the article offered sound advice and would provide a most useful service to the beleaguered engineer. I was sure that it would be worthwhile reading for the readers of that journal. Why would the editor not want to offer it to his readers?

I pondered and analyzed the problem, and then the light dawned. I perceived what I concluded was the weakness of that article, and resubmitted it with a new lead of two sentences:

> "Mr. Engineer, much as you dislike writing, as many engineers do, our profession requires it of us. Here are a few tips on how to make the job of writing much less painful."

The editor who had rejected the article a few days earlier now bought it with dazzling swiftness. He suddenly understood why it was an article his readers would grasp and appreciate.

There are two important messages in this little anecdote:

1. What was, and is, true for those engineers is true for you. You cannot conduct a consulting practice without writing, and the ability to write effectively is not inconsequential; it is a critically important asset. You *need* to be able to write coherent letters, brochures, and reports.

   There are no magic formulas to make writing easy, but there is information I can provide to make the job easier and models you can adapt to your needs. I also hope to impart some deeper understanding of the common problems of writing in general and how to overcome them. I therefore, present a variety of model letters and some "lectures" on the art of writing effectively—not "well," for we are not dealing here with efforts to create great literature, but *effectively,* which means clearly and to the point. That is what general business literature ought to be.

2. I initially failed to sell my article because I assumed that the editor would understand why his readers should and would welcome it. I knew that my premise that his readers would be glad they had read the article was correct. However, my assumption that the editor would understand that was wrong; he did not grasp that idea immediately or, more likely, was too busy to think about it. He needed me to point it out to him, just as anyone you write to does, especially clients and prospective clients. They all need to be told *why* they should read what you have written, why they need your services or products, and what your services will do for them. Far too much literature, whether aimed directly at making sales or at serving other needs of your practice, talks about the author—you—and what *you* want, when it ought to talk about the reader and what the *reader* needs and wants—i.e., what you will *do* for the reader.

Bear that always in mind as you progress through these pages and, especially, later, as you write. Whenever you explain what and who you are and what you do, always explain it in terms of why it is beneficial to the reader to know this. That is what persuasion is: showing the other party how to gain important benefits by doing what you suggest.

BROCHUREMANSHIP

It seems that almost every independent consultant decides that the first sales tool he or she requires is a calling card and the second one is a brochure. A poor business, indeed, is the one that does not have a brochure or two. Nor is there any other sales tool that has a greater number of transformations and permutations. The brochure appears in many physical forms and formats—as a single sheet, folded and printed on each of the resulting four or more panels; as a set of several sheets folded and stacked within each other; as a bound pamphlet or booklet; as something as small as 3 or 4 inches on a side to something as large as 12 or more inches on a side; and with even more ramifications than those, such as process color illustrations and hard covers.

Brochures are tools for different purposes—for example, general descriptive brochures, special-services brochures, product brochures, mini-catalogs, capability brochures, and still others. Some are so simple and inexpensive that they are distributed freely, while others are so costly that they are distributed only on a carefully restricted basis to those qualifying as prime prospects. Many beginning entrepreneurs place their faith in their brochures, mailing out thousands and brooding in puzzlement verging on indignation when the addressees do not respond immediately with enthusiastic proffering of contracts. In fact, the subject of brochures is far more complex than most consultants even imagine.

Brochures appear in countless forms for an infinity of uses. Despite all this, really good brochures—that is, brochures that are truly effective in achieving their purposes—are relatively rare. We will be examining the common faults and shortcomings of brochures, using the four broad classes into which almost all brochures fall:

- The *general* brochure, used in much the same manner and with much the same casual distribution as a business card, that is, as a general introduction to one's business.

- The *specialty* brochure, focused sharply to present, describe, and explain some specific services and/or related products.

- The *capability* brochure (also referred to as a "capability statement"), serving as a kind of generalized proposal to demonstrate technical and general qualifications for inclusion on bidder's lists—for example, to be invited to submit quotations, bids, and proposals for contracts. This brochure can be critically important to many consultants, especially those pursuing large contracts. However, it is also useful as a general brochure in certain circumstances.

- The *showcase* brochure, intended to act as almost its own public relations or special promotion. For example, the entertainer or public speaker seeking new professional engagements tends to feel the need for such an elaborate presentation when he or she is not already a well-known figure.

Each of these classes has its subclasses, and there are also hybrids among them, of course. We will explore many of these at some length.

CONTENTS

PART I

BROCHUREMANSHIP

FIRST STEPS TO CREATING YOUR OWN BROCHURE

You can hire someone to do almost anything for you that you do not wish to do. There are, however, some things that no one can do for you quite as well as you can do them for yourself. Explaining to others what you do professionally that would be of value to them is probably one of those things.

EVERYTHING, EVEN WRITING, HAS ITS OWN RULES

So you are not a writer or do not consider yourself to be one. A great many people, professionals and others, find writing to be a chore they would prefer to leave to others.

That doesn't mean that you can't or shouldn't write your own brochures and related sales tools. It isn't really a writing job, anyway; it's much more a marketing job, one of selling yourself. It is sales effectiveness, not literary excellence, that makes a brochure effective at doing what it was intended to do. Still, you can get help with it if you wish.

Dave Voracek is a marketing consultant who offers clients 3-hour training courses in developing brochures and other marketing tools, such as newsletters and direct mail packages. He uses a rather striking but simple 8- x 11-inch presentation as his own brochure for announcing his courses. (See Figure 1-1.) It enables him to use a large headline that wouldn't work in a small brochure. It is a legitimate approach, of course, for no law or rule of practice dictates that a brochure must be folded, of any given size, or structured to any preconceived format. Dave's innovative presentation illustrates the independent and creative nature that he puts into his clients' service.

Anyone can learn to create an effective brochure by following a few simple rules and making an energetic effort. Easy? no, I didn't say it would be easy. Few things that are worth doing are easy. But there is a logical sequence to follow, and the first step is to decide how important your brochure is to you. Is it important enough:

- To go to some trouble to get it right?
- To work hard at making it maximally definitive of the message you want to project?
- To labor over painting your image as you want it painted?
- To spend the time and effort to keep complete and total control over the process?

The answers to those and related questions—"yes" answers, I hope—should settle for you the question of whether you will surrender the writing of your marketing appeals or do your own. This does not mean that you should not consider having some qualified person act as editor to ensure that your copy is grammatical, punctuated properly, spelled correctly, and with the oversight of other mechanics of usage attended to competently. Nor does it preclude the use of a graphic arts service—an illustrator or designer—to aid you in achieving an effective layout. Certainly, there are professionals who can help you immeasurably in achieving the results you want. Still, the final decision in all matters must be yours. The specialists can propose, but you must dispose.

In substance, I would assume that even if you choose to hire a writer or an advertising agency to develop your brochures, you still wish

CHECK IT OUT!

**3 Courses That Can Improve
Your Marketing Effectiveness**

Tell a Friend !!!

Dave Voracek Announces Fall '93 Classes

Dave Voracek teaches these popular 3-hour courses downtown and out in the Virginia suburbs, plus conducts specially-tailored talks to associations & business groups.

Pick one of the convenient dates and call the appropriate organization to register (phone numbers on the back) . . . or call Dave at (703) 824-8787.

◆

How to Write, Design & Produce an Effective Brochure

Nearly every organization needs a brochure...from simple to fancy. At last, here's a class that walks you through the *entire process* of making one happen.

You'll learn the important steps you must go through to write brochures that really *sell*. You will see examples of the 15 basic design rules which improve reader comprehension, plus examine the importance of paper, color & other graphic elements.

You will hear how to cost-effectively work with outside writers and designers. Plus you'll get the formulas for figuring budget and production schedules, and tips for saving money at the printers. This useful class tells you how the *professionals* do it, and gets your ready to tackle your next brochure.

This one-session course lasts about 3 hours and is offered on the dates listed on page two.

To Register...

Please see dates and locations on page two. Sign up early...to assure your place in class !

Figure 1-1. The Voracek Brochure

How to Get *Results* With Business-to-Business Direct Mail

Here's everything you ever wanted to know about doing a direct mailing piece...to generate sales or get inquiries for your sales force to follow up.

You'll learn how to set realistic objectives and measure mailing success...how to buy lists...advice about writing copy that really pulls responses...how often and when to mail...how to work with designers, printers, and letter shops...how to set a schedule and budget for mailing...and all the details about postal permits and postage fees.

Plus you'll see numerous examples of all kinds of mailing formats and analyze the tricks which increase success. Corporate marketers, fundraisers, and association directors have all found this class to be extremely informative and *very* helpful.

This one-session course lasts about 3 hours and is offered on the dates listed on page two.

◆

How to Use a Marketing Newsletter to Gain & Retain Customers

The focus is on how companies, service firms, stores, professionals, consultants, non-profits and others can create an informative, promotion-oriented newsletter to generate added revenues from current clients...and increase awareness among prospects.

This is **not** a computer how-to class. Rather, you will learn the overall approach to what kind of articles to use (and not use) in your publication...easy ways to find and

(over, please)

to be in control and able to judge whether the product being developed for you is satisfactory. No one can know your business or what you want to say about it quite as well as you. To do so, you must work closely with anyone you hire for the job, review the work in draft stages and, later, approve or disapprove it. In fact, a conscientious specialist will want to be sure that you are completely satisfied. Thus, even if you choose to have someone else do the actual writing, it is appropriate to study what follows to serve you as a standard for passing judgment.

Brochure is a broad and general term. It can be and is applied to quite a wide variety of materials, from simple leaflets of a few hundred words to slender folders that may be inserted in an ordinary number 10 business envelope to quite elaborate bound publications of many thousands of words, and even to "broadsides"—folded advertising enclosures that unfold to 11- x 17-inches or 17- x 23-inches and even larger size "flats." Brochures may be bound with staples; spiral wire or plastic spines; commercial binding posts or similar fasteners; or by having their spines glued with "hot melt," in what is called "perfect" binding, the way rack-displayed paperback books are bound. However, if brochures are a diverse and loosely related family of printed materials in their sizes and other physical characteristics, they are almost equally diverse and loosely related to each other in the purposes and objectives for which they were created.

The term *brochuremanship* was coined to refer to the practice of gilding the lily when writing any kind of descriptive paper about a subject. This assumes that every brochure is written to sell something—to indoctrinate and persuade, if not to sell in the literal sense. That is not always the case, although every brochure should be developed to pursue a clear and specific goal. Many brochures are created simply to inform, advise, reinforce, or record information, as in the case of brochures written to document and make official an organization's personnel policies and purchasing procedures or to describe the symptoms of a common disease. Even in the case that most concerns us, brochures used to support your marketing, not all brochures make a direct effort to sell because consulting is normally not a "one-call business," but requires multi-step marketing to close most sales. A brochure may be written to describe what you offer, present your credentials, and describe your resources, but you may find it advisable to have a separate brochure for each of these and perhaps still others for new or special services.

Before you proceed to design and write your first brochure, you need to examine your motives and objectives closely. Writing a brochure ought not to be motivated by the fact that "everyone needs a brochure." Rather, ask yourself, as objectively as possible, why you want the brochure:

- What do you expect the brochure to do for you?
- How, exactly, do you expect to use it?
- To whom do you expect to distribute it?
- What do you expect its impact to be?

You will get "school solutions" to answer these questions, as we proceed, but these will be generalities, the primary purpose of which is to stimulate your thinking and inspire you to find your own answers. You will be served much better to seek your own answers appropriate to your own situation, than to accept my answers without question. But let's go on to describe how to create a general brochure.

THE GENERAL BROCHURE

Figure 1-2 illustrates the front and back panels of Barbara Brabec's general brochure. Brabec is a successful small business specialist who lectures, publishes a quarterly periodical, and writes books about home-based business, with a significant concentration on home-based crafts. (Her now-classic *Home Made Money*, published by Writer's Digest Books today, after acquiring the original publisher, Betterway, is about to be released in its fifth edition.) This brochure is in an 8- x 11-inch format, printed on an 11- x 17-inch sheet that is folded and then folded again to a final 8- x 5-inch size. It opens to its 8- x 11-inch format for three remaining panels.

Still another general brochure, that of a consultant specialist in telecommunications, is offered as Figure 1-3. This is an example of basic copy for a general brochure. (Note that this is copy only, and does not suggest a format, layout, or other ideas in re the physical product.)

Here, the promise is that of getting rapid results in what is a new and highly technical industry. The sales strategy is to first help the prospect understand why outside help is needed and is in the client's interest. This is an example of educating the client, on the assumption that the client probably does not know just how complex and specialized the telecommunications industry is today, nor how much opportunity

↖ Special Offer Inside ↗

**HELP
for Your
Growing
Homebased
Business**

Barbara Brabec

P.O. Box 2137
Naperville, IL 60566

Address Correction Requested

70,000 Copies in print!

Creative Cash
How to sell your
Crafts,
Needlework,
Designs & Know-how
by Barbara Brabec

Sequel to *Creative Cash*
A Treasure Trove of
**Crafts Marketing
Success Secrets**
by Barbara Brabec

Special Help For Those In Craft Businesses

"There's a good reason why over 70,000 copies of this book are in print; it is truly outstanding."
--The New Careers Center Catalog

This is a collection of profit-oriented ideas which adds to the information in *Creative Cash*.

This is a book for beginning craft sellers. Here, the emphasis is on selling through retail outlets, at crafts fairs, by mail, and to special needlework and design markets. Book includes beginning legal and financial information, advertising and publicity guidelines, insight on copyrights, patents and trademarks, as well as tips on how to make money from writing, self-publishing, teaching, designing and kit manufacturing.

A 300-listing RESOURCE CHAPTER rounds out the book. $11.95 ppd.

Says *The Crafts Report*: "Barbara Brabec has a knack for laying her hands on a whole lot of very helpful information and gathering it all between the covers of a book. Here is another such project which she carries off effectively."

Topics include selling at fairs, to shops/galleries, wholesaling, marketing through trade shows, party plans, holiday boutiques, co-ops, and craft organizations.

Includes five special RESOURCE LISTS. $10.95 ppd.

☆ Says *Family Circle* magazine: "Barbara Brabec is a...master networker. Her first book, *Creative Cash*, is considered a kitchen-table classic in its field. Satisfied readers credit it with changing their lives."

Figure 1-2.   A General Brochure

**MARKETING SERVICES
FOR THE TELECOMMUNICATIONS INDUSTRY
How to Get Rapid Results in This Dynamic New Industry**

Why Hire Outside Services?

There are at least three good reasons for going outside your own organization for marketing support:

To gain objectivity. The outside consultant or contract specialist brings a fresh and unbiased view to your situation and needs, something those who are "close" to the problem have difficulty in achieving.

To avoid undue staff pressures. Requiring your own staff to mount extra effort when they already bear a full workload is not in the best interests of your management, for they do not produce their best work under such pressure. The outside consultant is able to concentrate full attention on the problem.

To bring special skills to bear. Telecommunications, especially in the modern sense with all the high-tech developments of recent years, is highly specialized. It's a job for a specialist who has no conflicting duties.

Why Choose George Watkins?

With a background of 20 years as sales and marketing manager for six well-known manufacturers of telecommunications equipment, I have full knowledge of the field in terms of technology, equipment, markets, and competition. (Details of this experience available on request.) This is the kind of expert help I provide.

How I Work

Every job I undertake is a custom job, tailored to my client's needs and convenience. Following are typical arrangements, depending on the circumstances of the individual case:

A Defined Project. In this arrangement we agree on what is to be done, end-product(s), schedules, and costs. (We work together to identify your need and we reach an agreement.)

Open-Ended Assignment. In this arrangement you retain my services, on a daily or hourly basis and on your premises or mine, for as long as you perceive the need. You may terminate those services at any time on minimum notice.

Task Assignment. You may retain my services on a task-by-task basis or for single tasks as you see the need. We negotiate each task informally.

General Retainer. In this arrangement you are assured of priority demand for my services by paying me a monthly retainer (which accumulates, if not used each month) for some minimum number of hours or days per year.

Figure 1-3. Another General Brochure—Text Only

awaits in that new industry. (*New* in the sense that it is today completely revolutionary, as compared with telecommunications of only a few years ago.)

The second approach is to sell the consultant as the specific outside help needed by citing his credentials as an expert. The third step is to propose several specific options, making it clear that the client remains in control, but showing evidence of an organized, thought-out service, and true professionalism.

OFFERING PROOF OF YOUR CAPABILITIES

One thing you must think about in developing brochures (or other elements) to go into a direct-mail package is how much motivation and proof (selling) do you need?

It is another case of, "The more you tell, the more you sell." A simple one-page letter brought me in enough $6 orders for a manual to encourage me to continue, but adding a four-page brochure to the letter more than tripled the orders. There is no doubt that the combination of the one-page letter and the four-page brochure were more effective than a five-page letter or five-page brochure alone would have been. "The more you tell . . ." does not refer to number of words alone, but to the general impact of the brochure.

Motivation: Fear and Greed

There are many kinds of motivation, but all fall into just two broad classes: fear and gain. (I like to think "fear and greed" and use it in my seminar presentations because it is a more dramatic expression and probably more accurate, but the connotation of "greed" is that of a cynical and offensive characteristic, and I really mean gain, rather than greed.) One's self-interest is always in terms of something to be desired as a gain or in terms of something to fear. Picture something highly desirable that one would wish earnestly to gain or something highly undesirable that one would wish earnestly to avoid. You will get attention if you can make the prospect identify with one of those emotions. Everyone wants to be rich, attractive, happy, successful, secure, and less burdened with taxes, to name just a few of the things that usually get attention when you can offer them. But most of us have fears too, and are interested to learn how we can avoid disasters of any and all kinds; that is what sells insurance, burglar alarms, locks, and whatever else makes us feel a bit more protected and secure. In practice, the motivational element may or may not be starkly and glaringly apparent, but it must be there and clear in the copy. Without it, the copy has little chance of success. Prospects do not buy what they really do not want, and the job of marketing is to find those prospects who want what you are selling or those who *can be persuaded to want what you are selling.* The first time I bought a new automobile, I had decided consciously that I did not want it, but was "just looking." I suppressed my desire because I didn't think I could afford a new automobile.

A highly capable salesman persuaded me to decide that I wanted it. More literally, he suspected that I really was interested but afraid to risk the investment. He went to work on me to explain the easy financing, and I became convinced I could handle it. He also made it clear that I did not have to wait, but could drive my new car home and leave my old jalopy there on his lot, which was itself a powerful motivation and clinched the deal. The immediacy of the promised reward was simply too much for me to resist. Immediacy of reward is itself a powerful motivator. People prefer and will be drawn to whatever is or appears to be (is promised as) the fastest way to lose weight, smooth their skin, or get whatever is the promised benefit.

I bought the salesman's promises when he showed me evidence that proved what he said and handed me the keys to my brand new automobile. That is usually the case: Customers buy a promise when they are given evidence that the promise is valid and will be kept. Thus my explanation of advertising and sales—really the same thing—is made up of just two elements: proof and promise. That needs some examination and explanation.

The Promise

If you wish to subscribe to a diet plan and you begin to survey the many diet plans offered, how do you decide which is the one for you? It's a difficult decision because each seller of diet plans claims that his or her plan is the best. Suppose one insists that his plan is not only the easiest one, but the quickest one, so you decide to buy the quick diet plan.

Ostensibly, you bought a diet plan, but what you really bought was losing weight quickly, a *fast* diet plan. But wait; how do you know it's fast? Well you know because the advertiser told you so. He *promised* it and persuaded you that his promise was sincere and would be kept. So what you really bought was not a fast diet plan, but the *promise* of a fast diet plan.

In fact, that is what customers almost invariably buy. I buy some things by mail, and not long ago I bought a program for my computer that promised to speed up operations for me. It had a number of other useful and attractive features, but it was solely the increased speed—the *promise* of increased speed—that I bought.

Perhaps you bought a certain watch because the jeweler *promised* you that it was 18-karat gold. Perhaps you bought a certain automobile because the dealer *promised* you that you were getting it for less than dealer cost. True, you saw the watch, automobile, or whatever it was, but you accepted the assurances—promises—that satisfied you as to quality, value, fair price, or whatever you needed to believe.

What is Proof?

Of course, you are not naive. You needed more than simple assurance that the car was offered you for less than dealer cost. Today, the law requires that lit costs be posted on new cars in the showroom. Dealers offering low prices often promise to show you the invoice. Sometimes the mere offer to present the invoice is evidence enough for the customer, and the dealer is never required to actually produce it.

Do you accept the assurance that the watch is 18-karat gold or do you need some *proof*? If you turn the watch over and there is a statement on the back that says "18-karat gold," you will probably accept that as proof. We may have our doubts about the validity of claims made in print or in broadcasts, but we tend to believe what purport to be statements of fact stamped into a product.

There are other kinds of evidence you might accept. If the store was Cartier or Tiffany's, you would probably reason that such a store would not handle anything that was not quality merchandise. Any jewelry store that has the right "front" is likely to find that most customers accept what the salesperson says because the ambience of the emporium—an elegant store, with deep carpets, expensive furnishings, and a hushed atmosphere—is reassuring. There are many kinds of evidence acceptable by most customers as proof.

My wife collects dolls, collectors' items in limited editions by well-known artists. How does she know they are limited editions? Because the manufacturer swears it is so and furnishes a unique number for each doll sold, with a certificate. There is the law about truth in advertising and other statutes designed to protect the consumer, and that also affords the prospect a bit of comfort as assurance—proof. Proof is whatever the customer will accept—testimonials, certificates, guarantees, logical argument, "front," authority, or any of many other things. Most of us, ordinary citizens that we are, are honest enough and we accept what merchants say if they merely *appear* to be honest and sincere.

Truth and Perception, or Is It Verisimilitude?

Anything in writing, such as a brochure, may also convey a message beyond what the words say. The choice of language and methods of expression themselves can have the ring of truth—or lack it. It is one reason that hyperbole often backfires: We have become fairly sophisticated in this modern era, and we are suspicious of superlative self-appraisals. Understatement is often far more persuasive than hyperbole because it has more of a ring of truth, an air of quiet self-assurance that is not a bad image for a consultant to project. *Reporting* is also far more persuasive than *claiming* or *alleging* statements to be fact. One highly effective way to achieve credibility is by quantifying in precise numbers (e.g., not "thousands of successful projects," but "more than 3,768 projects completed on schedule"). Reporting, like beauty, lies in the eyes of the beholder. The reader will judge what is reporting of facts and what is claim of superiority, but the art of writing includes providing persuaders to induce the reader to the beliefs you wish to establish.

There are probably many kinds of truth, but there are at least two kinds of truth that concern us here: yours and the client's. Your truth does not count; the client's truth does count, very much so.

One highly regarded professional copywriter refers to verisimilitude, the *appearance* of truth, as the "magic word" in copywriting. Maybe it is the magic word, but the client's perception of truth is more than mere appearance; it *is* his or her truth, and the success or failure of your brochure rests on that perception. There are many kinds of evidence that a client may accept as truth and, therefore, proof. They range from simple logical argument to testimonials and documentary evidence.

Using Testimonials as Proof

Testimonials are usually good evidence, not only because they tend to prove the claims and promises, but because most people tend to follow the crowd. There is a certain degree of faith in what many others do as something worth doing. The old pitch man selling snake oil from the back of his wagon understood that quite well and hired shills to make the first few purchases, which others found reassuring and encouraged them to buy the product also. It helps greatly when you can include testimonials you have gotten from clients. The brochure copy of a mythical publication, *Merchandising Today*, is bolstered by including the testimonials of Figure 1-4.

In many cases, only a single, simple brochure is required. Two such simple brochures are offered as Figures 1-5 and 1-6. Again, as in the preceding cases, only text is provided here. Of course, while many brochures are simple folders containing nothing but text and headlines, many others are quite elaborate with drawings, photographs, multi-color printing, and even special effects, such as die-cut windows and foldouts, which attract attention. (That, however, should not be allowed to distract from the text, which is the message.)

The brochure copy of Figure 1-5 makes a clear promise in its headline: It promises to provide the software necessary to satisfy the special needs of the reader's profession. Here again, an effort is made to educate the client in areas where he or she is presumably not especially knowledgeable. It is reasonable to assume that the reader is unaware that there is special software that has been developed to match the individual, often unique, needs of each profession.

There is both gain and fear motivation in these two brochures. There is the promise of gains to be made as the principal motivational strategy. Yet, it is not unlikely that the reader may infer the hazard of remaining ignorant and suffering thereby, and so there is fear motivation in that implication, although that is secondary; gain is the intended main motivation, quite clearly.

It isn't difficult to turn this around and make fear the main motivation, as illustrated by Figure 1-6. Note that even fear motivation can be done on a positive note. Here, the motivational note was the fear of becoming antiquated before one's time, but other fear-based sales strategies are possible. One appeal might be to the fear of being bogged down solving minor problems, promising a product that does the work with a theme along the lines *We Make Your Computer Do the Work for You* or *We Free You up to Attend to the More Important Things*.

WHAT DELIGHTED USERS HAVE TO SAY
ABOUT *MERCHANDISING TODAY*

(Original correspondence on file in our offices and available for inspection.)

"Boosted sales 32%."—*RBF, Halifax, NS*

"I get at least two good ideas a month from this great newsletter, and most of those ideas either save me money or produce extra sales."—*GG, Topeka, KS*

"Merchandising Today paid for itself and showed me a profit with the very first issue. I never knew how much I didn't know about merchandising!"—*HS, Philadelphia PA*

"One item in last month's issue of your newsletter alone was worth the entire year's subscription price and reading time."—*PG, San Francisco, CA*

"Please renew my 'Merchandising Today' subscription for three more years. If you had a lifetime subscription rate I'd subscribe for it."—*BS, Pocatello, ID*

"Enclosed is payment for four additional subscriptions for my four store managers. I couldn't begin to teach them how to retail as well as your newsletter does."—*HGH, New York, NY*

"A friend of mine sent me a copy of "Merchandising Today," and I fell in love with it at once. Why shouldn't I, when it has so many priceless ideas in it? Enclosed is payment for my two-year subscription."—*BB, Olean, NY*

"Sorry I didn't subscribe sooner. Please send as many back issues as possible and bill whatever it costs."—*HH, Bakersville, PA*

Figure 1-4. Testimonials as "Proof"

PROFESSIONAL SOFTWARE PROGRAMS ARE DIFFERENT;
THEY ARE TAILORED TO THE SPECIAL NEEDS
OF YOUR PROFESSION

PROFESSIONAL SOFTWARE specializes in programs carefully designed to meet the special needs and solve the special problems of physicians, lawyers, architects, engineers, dentists, and other independent professionals. Among the many general classes of programs we have available for your personal computer systems are those that do such things as the following:

- Conventional word processing, with special technical dictionaries available for each profession.
- General accounting and payroll systems.
- Inventory management and reporting systems.
- Establishment and maintenance of patient and client records.
- Automatic billing.
- Generation and sending of statements.
- Sending out late notices and collection letters.
- Communication with central databases, such as the National Library of Medicine's MEDLARS and the Department of Education ERIC systems.
- Maintenance of library files.
- Indexing and cataloging systems.

In most cases we have special programs (as listed in enclosed catalog) for each profession, so that the word processor for physicians lists thousands of medical terms in its built-in dictionary/speller, while that for architects lists construction and building design terms, and that for lawyers lists legal terms.

The same principle applies to the communications programs, library programs, and other special programs. Each of our programs is designed for a specific profession. You no longer need adapt your way of doing things to the software programs available; we adapted the programs to your needs. But we have gone even beyond that: We offer many programs designed for specialists within a profession, such as obstetricians and surgeons in the medical profession, and corporate lawyers and criminal lawyers in the legal profession.

All programs are available in a variety of PC and PC-compatible formats, and fully supported via our toll-free number. That is what makes these programs different: You are never stuck because of technical or applications difficulties. Our specialists are available every day, all day, to take your call and help you solve your problems.

We guarantee it, as we do our products.

Figure 1-5. Another Simple, General Brochure—Text Only

PROFESSIONAL SOFTWARE PROGRAMS ARE DIFFERENT;
THEY ARE DESIGNED TO KEEP YOU "UP WITH THE TIMES"

Everyone today, especially independent professionals—physicians, lawyers, architects, engineers, dentists, and others—struggles to fight early obsolescence in this high-tech era. The old country doctor and others who served their communities could practice for many years before they became "old fashioned." Not today. Now, if you are doing what you did five years ago, you are already losing touch. If ten years, you are already antiquated.

PROFESSIONAL SOFTWARE tailor programs to keep you abreast and doing things by the latest and most efficient software for all functions, including these:

- Conventional word processing, with special technical dictionaries available for each profession.
- General accounting and payroll systems.
- Inventory management and reporting systems.
- Establishment and maintenance of patient and client records.
- Automatic billing.
- Generation and sending of statements.
- Sending out late notices and collection letters.
- Communication with central databases, such as the National Library of Medicine's MEDLARS and the Department of Education ERIC systems.
- Maintenance of library files.
- Indexing and cataloging systems.

We have special programs (as listed in enclosed catalog) for each profession, so that the word processor for physicians lists thousands of medical terms in its built-in dictionary/speller, while that for architects lists construction and building design terms, and that for lawyers lists legal terms. The same feature appears in our communications, library, and other special programs. You need no longer make your systems conform with general software programs available; we have tailored the programs to your needs, as they exist *today*.

All programs are available in a variety of PC and PC-compatible formats, and fully supported via our toll-free number. That is what makes these programs different: You are never stuck because of technical or applications difficulties. Our specialists are available every day, all day, to take your call and help you solve your problems.

The best news is that we offer reasonably priced upgrades to all software frequently: *We won't let you get "old fashioned."*

Figure 1-6. Using Fear Motivation In a Brochure—Text Only

THE EVOLUTIONARY PROCESS OF
BROCHURE WRITING

There may be cases where a brochure is born or conceived in a sudden flash of brilliant insight, but that would be the rare and unusual case. Not even the most talented and experienced professional copywriter or advertising expert expects such a thing to happen. The brochure normally evolves, as other written works do, step by step, from a single idea, and progresses through the laborious development of many ideas, and usually with many rewrites and refinements. Still, let's not discount the possibilities of insights that are not entirely the result of conscious analysis and synthesis. Insights can play a part.

The Creative Phenomenon

Studies of creativity, many based on interviews with inventors and scientists, reveal rather clearly a three-step sequence of invents, as rationalized by many interviewees in explaining how they get their ideas and make their breakthrough discoveries. The three steps are:

Step 1. *Concentration.* Concentration is explained as the direct effort to solve a problem via intense conscious effort. You ponder the problem, trying out ideas, for as long as you are able to conjure up new and different ideas. That may be a step of a few minutes, many hours, or even many days. It ends when you can no longer think creatively about the problem.

Step 2. *Incubation.* Having reached that dead end, with no hope of doing more, at least for the time being, you abandon the effort. You put it out of your mind, and go on to other matters. You permit the problem to incubate in your subconscious. (More on this in a moment.)

Step 3. *Inspiration.* At some later time, often when you are enjoying relaxation with little of importance on your mind, you are suddenly inspired with an insight, a brilliant solution.

The Creative Process

Can you bank on this happening? Certainly not; it is not a guaranteed result. It may or may not work, but it is how, many inventive and creative people agree, you can often find the solutions to difficult problems. Here is an example of that, in the form of an experience most of us have occasionally:

You are unable to think of a name, telephone number, and address, or something else that you ordinarily have securely installed in your memory and are usually able to recall instantaneously. Why can't you recall it now? Who knows why you are blocked; it simply happens to all of us now and then. You twist and turn, mentally, but the name won't come to you. Never mind; forget it and go on to something else.

Minutes later—perhaps hours or days later—that name is suddenly clear in your memory: It has come to you.

The accepted explanation for this is that your subconscious mind, which is unlike your conscious mind in that it never forgets anything, came to your rescue. You turned the problem over to your subconscious by concentrating and incubating the matter. When you relaxed, you opened the communications gateway, and your subconscious passed on the information that you wanted.

For some reason, your conscious and subconscious minds can communicate only when you are in a relaxed state, as when you are hypnotized. But it requires first the concentration to alert your subconscious to your need for a solution, incubation to permit your subconscious to work on the problem, and a relaxed state to permit your subconscious to send on suggestions for solution.

Does this smack of the metaphysical? the arcane? perhaps, but it does seem to be the explanation of the creative process favored by recognized creative individuals. It does have the ultimate virtue that it works surprisingly often, often enough to be well worth taking seriously and putting it to work in your own behalf.

Applying Creativity to Brochure Writing

Support for the validity of the concept may be found in the accepted processes of writing brochures and most other things. It is, in fact, inherent in the writers' platitude that all good writing is actually rewriting. The typical professional writer accepts the idea that few, if any, of us write a really good first draft. Even the best of us usually rewrite our initial draft several times before we even begin to become satisfied with our product. We write that first draft, our conscious ideas, but hours, days, even weeks and months later, we return to rewrite—to reorganize, revise, polish, sometimes incessantly, over many cycles. We have concentrated and we have incubated, and often we do not accept our latest rewrite as final until we are convinced that it is the inspiration we have been looking for from the beginning.

Accept that as fact. Your first draft is mere concentration, and perhaps your next few rewrites are still part of concentration, not yet ready for incubation. In fact, accept that your first draft does not, or should not, even begin as a brochure design. It begins/should begin as a persuasive message, polished to its maximum, and only then designed to fit a brochure format. Still, it is necessary to have at least a rough idea of size, and probably the most commonly used and most convenient size is that of an 8- x 11-inch sheet printed on both sides. Let's use that as an example in discussing principles.

FORMATTING YOUR BROCHURE

A single sheet of paper or light card stock can hold up to about 1500 words in a readable type size, although you will probably not want to crowd that much text into a small brochure, nor is it necessary to. The sheet can be folded in half to present a brochure of four panels, but the six-panel brochure (Figure 1-7) made up of an 8- x 11-inch piece of paper that will be printed on both sides and folded twice is much more convenient and functional: It fits easily into a purse, jacket pocket, or a number 10 business envelope. As the figure shows, the righmost panel of the front side is panel one, and that is folded back to reveal its reverse side, which is the second panel to be read. Let's assume that you will want to use about two-thirds of the available space—four panels—for text passages, and the remainder for other purposes, such as graphics of some kind or a form, depending on your final design.

First Questions

What You Sell: Think about what you sell in the client's terms, not yours, and focus on what is or can be made to appear special: Just what is special about your services? Are there only a few consultants who can offer what you offer? Do only a few have some special skill or experience that is of special value to clients? Are you in a special position to help clients in some way? What is it you *do* for your clients? How do you *help* them? That is the key.

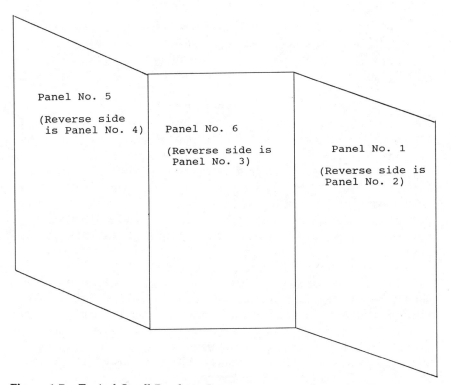

Figure 1-7. Typical Small Brochure Layout

Objective: It should not be exactly a revolutionary idea that you must first decide what the objective of the brochure is to be. Ask yourself, what is your brochure supposed to do: Is it something to hand out to people you meet so they will remember you and know who and what you are? Is it to be a tool for prospecting—to find sales leads? Is it to explain your general areas of expertise and services or to highlight some special area of concentration? Is it to get attention? Do you think that you are expected to have a brochure as you are expected to have a business card, and so the brochure is obligatory, but not of any real importance?

For Whom Intended: Who do you want to reach with your brochure: computer managers? general executives? marketing managers? accountants? everyone and anyone? This is a most important consideration because the brochure will be effective only insofar as it talks the reader's "language" (i.e., addresses the reader's problems in terms with which the reader identifies, and which your services address). That individual whom you had in mind as the object of the message in your brochure must, logically, be that individual you would expect to want to retain you as a consultant—the one to whom you would be most likely to be able to sell your services.

The Message

The message can be written only after you have answered the earlier questions. If you are a financial consultant, you want to talk to either the top executives or the comptrollers. Lower-level managers and managers of other functions, such as production and inventory, are not concerned with the company's financial needs and problems. On the other hand, if you are pursuing top corporations, your approach and language is going to be considerably different than if you are pursuing small start-up businesses.

Of course, you must understand the needs and problems of the individuals you address. If you are a computer consultant and you specialize in spreadsheets or database management software, you must understand who in the companies you address is concerned with these and what set of terms he or she will best understand. You may be able to be highly technical with computer managers in your target organizations, but your brochure will go nowhere fast with executives who know virtually nothing of computers except the rote keypress routines.

The Theme

Every message needs a theme, if it is to have any impact or even any significance. How to arrive at a theme without first asking and answering the above questions is a poser. I certainly could not do so. A theme is what you should decide on before you start writing copy. The theme should be summed up as briefly as possible and with as much impact as possible up front, at the start of your brochure.

Every example shown had such a theme. For my own brochure announcing one of my proposal seminars I used the theme shown in Figure 1-8. It told the reader what I represented the seminar to be—what I promised to deliver, in fact. And if the word *proposalmanship* was new and strange, for I had coined it, the second line explained what it meant.

In spite of this, many start out with the message, having only a vague idea, if any, of the intended reader and what the brochure is supposed to accomplish. It is perhaps not surprising, then, that so many

Proposalmanship
The Graduate Course in Proposal Writing

Presented by
Government Marketing News
0000 Connecticut Avenue, NW
Washington, DC 20036

Figure 1-8. Brochure with Theme On Cover

begin by writing what amounts to their personal resumes to fill the space. The case of Michael Barnard is probably fairly typical.

Mike is an independent TV producer and writer in Burbank, California. Although he was getting his business by word of mouth, Mike felt the need for a brochure, but rejected the idea of what he regarded as the conventional brochure, full of extravagant language claiming superiority and pledges of satisfaction. He did know that he wanted a tri-fold, six-panel brochure. Probably it never occurred to Mike that the decision on size and format was premature, since he had not answered the other questions—had not even asked them, in fact.

He drafted copy that began with the question, "What does a producer do?" on the front flap, illustrated by a drawing of a man asking the question, and then went on to describe what a producer does indirectly by presenting a series of short paragraphs summarizing some of his clients, their needs, and what he did to solve them. He ended by summarizing the services he provides and a cartoon of someone (himself) "tooling around Hollywood in a sports car." Still unsure that this is what he wanted or should have, however, he appealed to a group of other consultants for their suggestions.

He got critiques, comments, and suggestions in abundance. He was advised that his copy read more like a resume than a brochure, that it was just fine as he had conceived it, but that he ought to do a video brochure, or just be entirely unconventional, etc. Some of the ideas included specific recommendations of copy.

In the end, Mike used some of the ideas, but not all, as Figures 1-9 and 1-10 show. He changed his front flap to "Television Production For Your SPECIAL Needs," and went on to discuss TV on the first inside panel, commenting briefly on its many uses, and concluding by explaining that Michael R. Barnard Productions makes TV work for the client. From that point on, he used his original copy of summarizing several projects, and then went to the back cover to summarize what he can do for the reader in re TV production.

Mike's theme was, finally, the right one for him. In his place, I would have opted for a stronger opening, making a promise of a benefit of some sort, at least by broad implication. I would have used something such as "How to Get That Special Impact for Your Message" as a headline, following it with a reinforcing blurb making it clear that I was talking about TV production, and then identifying my business at the bottom of that front panel. I would have tried this to get the reader interested in Michael R. Barnard Productions. The idea is to try to arouse

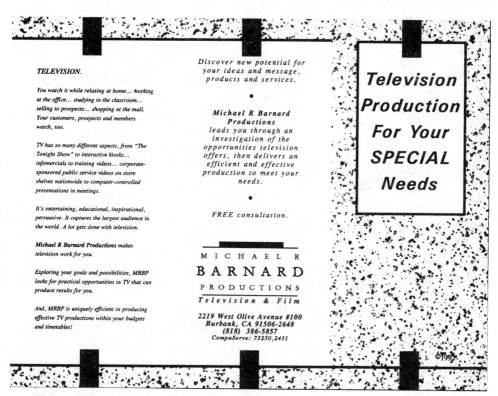

Figure 1-9. First Side of a Six-Panel Brochure

the interest of those who are not conscious of a want for TV production, as well as those who are already looking for such a service.

If you are developing a brochure as a marketing tool, remember the alternative marketing problems and decide which one you wish to address:

1. The client who already buys or wants to buy the kind of services and/or products you sell. That client does not have to be persuaded to want the kind of services you offer, but does need to be persuaded to buy them from you, and not from your competitors.

2. The client who has not yet bought what you sell and doesn't have a conscious want for those services. That client has to be made to feel that want, and then persuaded to have you, rather than someone

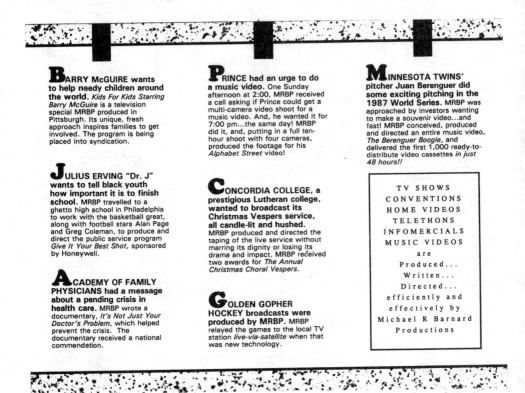

BARRY McGUIRE wants to help needy children around the world. *Kids For Kids Starring Barry McGuire* is a television special MRBP produced in Pittsburgh. Its unique, fresh approach inspires families to get involved. The program is being placed into syndication.

JULIUS ERVING "Dr. J" wants to tell black youth how important it is to finish school. MRBP travelled to a ghetto high school in Philadelphia to work with the basketball great, along with football stars Alan Page and Greg Coleman, to produce and direct the public service program *Give It Your Best Shot,* sponsored by Honeywell.

ACADEMY OF FAMILY PHYSICIANS had a message about a pending crisis in health care. MRBP wrote a documentary, *It's Not Just Your Doctor's Problem,* which helped prevent the crisis. The documentary received a national commendation.

PRINCE had an urge to do a music video. One Sunday afternoon at 2:00, MRBP received a call asking if Prince could get a multi-camera video shoot for a music video. And, he wanted it for 7:00 pm...the same day! MRBP did it, and, putting in a full ten-hour shoot with four cameras, produced the footage for his *Alphabet Street* video!

CONCORDIA COLLEGE, a prestigious Lutheran college, wanted to broadcast its Christmas Vespers service, all candle-lit and hushed. MRBP produced and directed the taping of the live service without marring its dignity or losing its drama and impact. MRBP received two awards for *The Annual Christmas Choral Vespers.*

GOLDEN GOPHER HOCKEY broadcasts were produced by MRBP. MRBP relayed the games to the local TV station *live-via-satellite* when that was new technology.

MINNESOTA TWINS' pitcher Juan Berenguer did some exciting pitching in the 1987 World Series. MRBP was approached by investors wanting to make a souvenir video...and fast! MRBP conceived, produced and directed an entire music video, *The Berenguer Boogie,* and delivered the first 1,000 ready-to-distribute video cassettes *in just 48 hours!!*

TV SHOWS
CONVENTIONS
HOME VIDEOS
TELETHONS
INFOMERCIALS
MUSIC VIDEOS
are
Produced...
Written...
Directed...
efficiently and
effectively by
Michael R Barnard
Productions

Figure 1-10.   Reverse Side of a Six-Panel Brochure

else, satisfy it. (If you want to sell lemonade, you have to make your prospects thirsty.)

You must decide which is the marketing problem in your case, and work to solve it. In my case, I compiled a list of companies who write and submit proposals, so my marketing problem was the first one: I had to convince them that I had something special to reveal and teach in the way of proposal techniques and tactics. In some subsequent brochures I would promise to teach the reader things that he or she would not be likely to get anywhere else, such how to *appear* to be the low bidder, whether that client was or was not actually so, and how to maximize the technical score of his or her proposal. These gave me an exclusive, even unique position.

DEVELOPING THE GENERAL BROCHURE

In general then, don't think about the brochure as a brochure first, but about the copy. Think about answering the questions posed in the preceding paragraphs. What is it you sell precisely, and how can you make something special of it, especially something unique or exclusive? Once you find that, you can build the brochure around it. Think carefully about your work and how you work with clients. Find that "unique selling proposition," that very special item that advertising specialists seek so earnestly. Find it and find the way to express it simply, clearly, and in only a few words. Be sure that in doing so you are talking about the client—what your special thing means to the client, not to you. Think as insurance salesman Frank Bettger (first member of the "million dollar roundtable" of insurance salespeople) did when he created a unique selling point and said to his clients, "I can now do something for you that no one else in the world can do." *That* is an attention-getting statement.

I asked you earlier to decide who you wish to address with your brochure. That was actually backwards. In fact, you don't decide who you *want* to address, but whom you *must* address. Once you have decided what it is that is special about your services—that powerful sales argument you can make—it dictates to you who your prospects are. If your service helps clients solve financial problems, for example, you want to address the individual responsible, and that might be the comptroller, financial vice president, or chief executive officer.

Assuming a six-panel brochure as illustrated in Figure 1-7, you might approach it along the following general lines:

Panel 1: Theme statement, with blurb, possibly with lead-in copy, and identification of your company.

Panels 2–3: Expansion from first panel, presenting some details of what you do and how you do it, to support the theme statement.

Panels 4–5: Credentials of your company, including your personal qualifications, since you are the chief, and perhaps the only, service provider. Include names of clients and testimonials, if possible.

Panel 6: Summary and proposed follow up, invitation for client to call, offer to make a full presentation, or other proposed action.

Of course, these discussions can be varied considerably, but all these elements ought to be present:

- A powerful theme statement, representing a promise of substantial benefit to the client.
- Explanation of what you do in enough detail to support the promise and flesh it out.
- Your credentials, both as a business entity and as an individual who will deliver the services.
- A definite follow-up strategy. The matter must not be left hanging in the air, waiting hopefully for the prospect to call.

Figure 1-11 is another excellent example of the small, six-panel brochure.

Are you prepared to make all the right choices when it comes to marketing?

There's just so much to know, and it takes years of experience to learn it all. A few poor marketing decisions can cost you a lot, maybe even your family's savings. But good, well-informed decisions can win you more business, fuel your company's growth, and position you for success.

Starting and running a business means wearing many hats

National Marketing Federation, Inc.
"On call, on target marketing solutions"

1-800-2 SOLVE IT (800-276-5834)
301-681-6626 FAX 301-681-0227
324 Pinewood Avenue
Silver Spring, MD 20901

National Marketing Federation - professional liability is limited to a full refund of the cost of the call
© National Marketing Federation, Inc.

National Marketing Federation, Inc.
1-800-2 SOLVE IT

Figure 1-11.   Front Side of National Marketing Federation Brochure

Top Marketing Minds Provide Affordable Advice

Quality marketing guidance used to be priced out of reach for most of America's small and home-based businesses due to the high fees and minimums charged by traditional marketing consulting firms and advertising agencies. Now, National Marketing Federation is the first organization to provide top-quality guidance in a revolutionary and affordable new way—by *telephone*. By calling our toll-free number, you have access to advice from some of the country's most experienced marketing consultants.

If you are a small or home-based business owner, or an entrepreneur developing a new venture, we'll help you win new business, create an effective company image, position against your competitors, and conduct cost-efficient marketing programs. We can even walk you step-by-step through proven tactics for making cold or warm calls, building prospect lists, or closing sales.

On Call, On Target Marketing Solutions

Most other "advisors" have a conflict of interest. They stand to make money if you take their advice—by selling you ad space, software, design services, printing, and more. National Marketing Federation sells no products and takes no commissions. We offer a totally independent and objective analysis of your situation and recommend solutions for your day-to-day marketing challenges.

Affordable pricing and convenient access from any telephone means you may call National Marketing Federation as often as you need, when you need to, and receive as much or as little advice as you require. The first time you call, we'll talk with you about your company and specific needs. Then you'll work with a professional marketing consultant with expertise in your area.

Your consultant will listen carefully to your concerns, understand your unique situation, and offer the best solutions to help you succeed. And when you need quick advice, such as how to find a unique mailing list or directory, or an unbiased second opinion on a proposal from a printer, designer, or other vendor, you can always count on us for help.

Business Owners Call For Answers to Tough Questions Like These...

"I don't have much time to spend on marketing. What can I do to cultivate new business?"

"My competitors have big budgets for brochures and advertising. How can I create a successful image on a small budget?"

"What are the most important components of an effective direct mail package...and what's missing from my pieces?"

"Where can I get a good direct mail list?"

"I've written the copy for my new company brochure. Before I spend money having it typeset and printed, can you tell me if it will motivate my prospects?"

"How can I get leads and build lists of prospective clients?"

"What are the best ways to get PR for my business?"

"There are three or four newspapers in my area. Which one should I advertise in?"

"Cold calls make me uncomfortable. How can I keep potential clients on the phone without sounding like just some salesman?"

"With thousands of potential customers for my services, how can I reach the right ones without spending a fortune?"

Free Analysis of Your Marketing Materials

Before your first consultation, fax or mail us your brochures, flyers, ads, plans, or proposals. We'll review them for discussion completely free. You'll pay only for the time it takes to answer your questions during your consultation. In fact, most calls average just ten to twenty minutes.

When you call, you'll be asked to provide a Visa or MasterCard to charge the cost of the consultation. Charges are based on the length of the call, $3.45 per minute, with the first minute free.

Your Quality Guarantee

Founders Kim T. Gordon and Stephen Mizner created National Marketing Federation in response to requests from small and home-based business owners who were searching for quality, affordable marketing guidance. Both are respected marketing strategists whose views have appeared in media nationwide, including *ABC News with Peter Jennings*, Wall Street Journal Radio network, *Business Marketing, Home Office Computing, Independent Business,* and *Nation's Business* magazines. Gordon is the noted author of *Growing Your Home-Based Business* (Prentice Hall), and a top-rated seminar leader.

National Marketing Federation guarantees quality service. And if during your telephone consultation you ever feel you are wasting your time, we'll write off the cost.

> *"We want you to be successful and we intend to prove it each and every time you call."*
> Kim T. Gordon and Stephen Mizner

So if you think your "Marketing Director" hat doesn't fit, call us. We'll make it look great on you. For more information on how National Marketing Federation will work for you, call toll-free **1-800-2 SOLVE IT** or **301-681-6626** in the Washington, D.C. area.

Figure 1-12. Reverse Side of National Marketing Federation Brochure

The right-hand copy of Figure 1-11 presents the front-panel information of the brochure and suggests a typical problem of small business, the need to do it all. The theme of the brochure, that the reader does not have to do it all but can call on National Marketing Federation, Inc. for help, is thereby established, and the remaining copy follows that line up, explaining it. Finally, the text makes an offer of a free analysis of the reader's marketing materials, concluding with a summary on a back panel. The brochure is on a smooth light card stock, printed in green ink, with captions in another, light and bright color.

DON'T GET KLEVER: KLEVERNESS KILLS KOPY

If you are not a clever writer you are already many points ahead of many professionals. Professional copywriters sometimes permit their egos to interfere with getting the job done. Too often, they tend to become so intent on creating clever copy that they seem to forget their mission, which is, of course, to *sell* something. They work so hard at producing what I call Klever Kopy and Kute Kopy that they resort to a variety of clever puns, alliteration, humorous ideas, literary allusions, immortal quotations, and other evidence of erudition and wit.

For example, AT&T, marketing their own facsimile machine, advertised, "We stand behind the fax," a meaningless statement in terms of sales appeal, distracting the reader with the sophomoric play on "fax" and "facts," so that the reader will probably not get the real message, which is that good, old reliable AT&T is now offering customers its own fax machine. *Of course, you can depend on good, old reliable AT&T to back up anything they sell with a dependable guarantee,* they appear to be saying between the lines. What's wrong with stating their case in those terms? If you did not immediately grasp that main message, that simply demonstrates the weakness of the copy. As in this case, by far the bulk of the "kleverness" in "kopy" consists of puns and other double entendres.

Marketing is a serious business, and making prospects smile does not make them more likely to buy; it only makes them less likely to understand your message or to take it seriously if they do get it. Concentrate on selling, which means "doing it by the book" or conforming to sound principles of selling: commanding attention, arousing interest, motivating, convincing, and urging buying action.

Commanding Your Reader's Attention

Mystery writers, hopefully, get your attention by opening the story or play with something that is either rivetingly dramatic or so novel that your curiosity is immediately piqued. (It is not for nothing that this is called "the hook.")

When copywriters attempt to get attention by a device such as that, they often use something connected with the subject rather nebulously or not really connected with it at all. Or they use something that is clever, but so subtle that the average reader doesn't get it and is merely mystified. (I am myself deeply puzzled by many TV commercials: I just do not understand the message at all.)

Subtle advertising rarely works. Subtlety is completely out of place in most advertising. One computer consultant, for example, used a blurb that told readers he did interesting things with ones and zeros. Even if the reader knew enough of computers to understand that "ones and zeros" referred to the binary machine language of computers and, even more indirectly, to computer programming, there would be no reason for the reader to be impressed or intrigued by the idea expressed. Would it not be simpler, clearer, and certainly more appealing to the reader's interests to say, "We write computer programs that solve your problems"? No, that is not poetic and it is not subtle, so it is not clever. It simply tells the reader in simple language why he or she should be interested. That is exactly what headlines and captions in brochures and elsewhere ought to do. The headline must lead the reader to the body copy, to want to know what the body copy says about the subject introduced by the headline. Every line must coax the reader into reading the next line. The advertisement with a mystic headline is almost certain to fail because the reader may pause and frown, and then does not read the body copy.

The best way to get anyone's attention is to make a direct appeal to his or her direct interest, especially self-interest of an emotional nature. The novel or dramatic opening of a story is such an appeal: The subject wants to be entertained, of course, and that opening delivers an immediate promise that what is about to follow will be entertaining. Entertainment and mystery are out of place here and hamper the achievement of useful goals. What the reader of a brochure wants to find out is simple enough, it's "What's in it for me? How are my interests involved?" Entertaining and novel copy may get attention and may even be remembered, but that can produce the opposite result of the desired one.

Sometimes, the distraction is accidental and totally unforeseen. Every so often, for example, a slogan or a line used in advertising catches on with the public as amusing or intriguing in some way. Some years ago, a commercial caused millions of people to mimic the actress who protested to her always interfering mother, "Please, Mother, I'd rather do it myself!" I recall that clearly, as did many people for months after, and used it in jest as many did. The humor actually distracted one's attention from the sales message, and the humor itself did not sell anything, it rarely does. People usually remember the slogan, but not the product as in this case. French sculptor Auguste René Rodin made that point when the hands of one of his figures drew special admiration. Outraged, he chopped the hands off the figure because he would not permit the part to be greater than the whole (i.e., to distract attention from the figure overall).

More recently, a character in a TV commercial uttered the memorable and humorous growl soon to be repeated everywhere, "Where's the beef?" as she displayed a tiny hamburger hidden in a huge bun. Again, the line was amusing and caught on with a great many people, but as advertising it left something to be desired, probably because it focused on criticizing the competition instead of focusing on something positive about the advertiser and his product.

Effective advertising motivates the prospect to buy, and the most effective advertising is that which incorporates the most effective motivation. The most effective motivation turns out to be, not too surprisingly, whatever is the most effective appeal to the prospect's self-interest.

OPTIONS

You can include graphics, of course. but be careful that they are not frivolous. Some sobersided clients will decide that you are not to be taken seriously if your brochure is illuminated with humorous sketches. That makes the use of cartoons a bit risky. Think carefully about this.

You may include terms (e.g., rates and related matters), but it is probably a bad idea. In fact, one of the accepted principles in selling is to never volunteer the price. There is a psychological advantage in waiting to be asked, but there is also the tactical advantage of using that query as an excellent indication of the prospect's interest, that the prospect is probably satisfied with what you offer and your credentials, and is now weighing the cost of doing business with you. It is thus time to shut up about the marvels of what you offer. It's equally valid in written sales techniques.

REFERENCES

You do not have to go to great expense to print your brochures with decorative, eye-catching backgrounds and graphics. There is an increasing number of companies offering special papers and light card stock designed especially for printing your brochures and other sales materials on your own computer printer. Here are three companies who offer such materials and have extensive catalogs available for the asking:

Paper Direct
205 Chubb Avenue
Lyndhurst, NJ 07071

BeaverPrints
Main Street
Bellwood, PA 16617

Quill Corporation
100 Schelter Road
Lincolnshire, IL 60069-3621

For an outstanding bimonthly publication devoted to desktop print-ing, with an abundance of useful information about laser printers and toners, write Walter Jeffries at the following address:

Flash Magazine
RR 1 Box 2G
West Topsham, VT 05086-9988

2

CREATING FLEXIBLE, ADAPTABLE BROCHURES

If you can count on nothing else in an uncertain world, you can count on the inevitability of change. It is a fact of business life as well as a fact of life in general.

THE NEED TO PLAN

The certainty of change mandates planning to avoid being overwhelmed by the future, but the uncertainty of what the changes will be and when they will come makes planning a most difficult art. Unfortunately, many, and probably most, independent consultants begin their ventures with little, if anything, in the way of a plan. That was the way I started, too. Like so many, I never set out to be a consultant, nor did I even have a distinct career plan. I did think myself to be a writer quite early in life. That probably explains why I chose the consulting specialty I did. Once involved with major engineering firms in defense contracting, years later, I discovered that I had a penchant for technical writing and proposal writing. I enjoyed great success in winning contracts for my employers with the proposals I had written as one of my technical writing responsibilities. Before long, acquaintances who had proposal responsibilities were asking for my help. That soon grew to such a large number of requests that I could no longer accommodate them, so I was forced to begin refusing my help, rather apologetically, since I was truly pleased that my services were so valued. That unavoidable refusal led quite soon to offers of compensation for my time, and soon enough I found myself to be a proposal consultant, not quite sure how it had happened or where it was to lead me.

Consulting as a government-marketing/proposal-development specialist soon proved to have its own problems as a full-time undertaking. Government marketing and proposal writing, it soon was apparent, were rather seasonal activities, with distinct peaks and valleys of demand. That was especially true of proposal writing for government contracts, which represented the bulk of the market for proposal specialists. It paid me well enough when I was busy, but there were long slack periods when it paid me not at all because the demand for proposal help was almost nonexistent. Obviously, I had to do something about those valleys, if I were to continue specializing as an independent proposal consultant.

That need to fill in the slack times led me eventually to giving seminars, writing newsletters, and, later, books. That was after I sat down to confront the base problem of a feast-or-famine business and try to devise tactics and techniques—new initiatives, that is—to develop *plans* to overcome this inherent disadvantage of proposal consulting. In a nutshell, I began planning my future career as what one might call a mini-conglomerate. The proposal-writing business had to be regarded as a marketing service in broader terms than the face to face, one client at a time, personal services applied directly to the production of individual proposals. I needed a broader base for my practice. I therefore had to decide what else other than writing, counseling, and related services on specific contract marketing initiatives I ought to offer my clients as a proposal specialist.

Developing a Business Plan

I began to draft ideas, but I didn't call the ideas I was drafting a business plan. The underlying concepts of the business plan are simple enough.

Begin your venture by setting yourself goals and objectives, technical and financial. You set these on the basis of estimates and assessments made on what you know from experience and have been able to learn from research. You then plan your routes to the goals and objectives, with timetables. Difficult? yes, indeed, it *is* difficult because many of the estimates are really nothing more than guesstimates, and even those are often based on the most flimsy of hard data. (Even experience is not always reliable because it is often only yesterday's wisdom, and not necessarily today's wisdom.) That is why a business plan is never chiseled in stone. It is always penciled in and highly susceptible to revision, frequently at first and less frequently as accumulating experience enables you to fine-tune your estimates, assessments, and projections and make them ever more accurate. These are never final because at best, they are based on today's conditions, with your best guesses and appraisals on what tomorrow's conditions will be.

But what has all this to do with writing brochures? The answer is that your business will change, and that change will inevitably affect your brochure. Want evidence of that? Turn over the sheets of a few scratch pads and discover how many are the blank sides of stationery, forms, and brochures that are no longer useful in their original form. Note how many letterheads, brochures, and business cards have a label or inked correction presenting a new address, and sometimes even a new business name, covering or changing the original. Your brochure must be flexible enough to accommodate the changes in your consulting business.

Estimates and Educated Guesses

You made some initial estimates and projections upon which you based the establishment of your venture, no matter how informally you made them. You didn't start without some idea of where you were at the start and where you planned to go, no matter how offhandedly you thought these things out. It is possible that those early premises and projections you made will prove to be so uncannily accurate that you will never vary from your original business plan and never offer more or different services than the basic ones you started with. It is possible, as are all things, but it is not at all likely. It is not at all likely for more than one reason: Change, in its inevitability, is based on a number of factors, many of which are entirely beyond your control.

Where You Start Is Not Necessarily Where You Finish

First of all, it is most unlikely that you will have gauged with absolute precision those services that will be most appealing to those you regard as prospective clients, and therefore that you will never make substantial changes to what you offer to do for them. The truth is that most of us—almost all of us—start out as somewhat generalized consultants because we are still feeling our way and trying to maximize our chances for success through being a "general store" of consulting services within our chosen general field. Most of us do not yet have a clear vision of our markets and prospects, when we start. It should not therefore be a great surprise that most of us, in time, find ourselves doing and selling something quite different than that with which we started or planned to start.

There are more than enough examples to illustrate this. Here are a few:

- Walter A. Sheaffer, of the famous white-dot fountain pen marketed by the W. A. Sheaffer Pen Company, started out selling music organs.
- The W. H. Hoover Company was manufacturing leather saddles, harnesses, and similar goods before the company became the best known manufacturer of vacuum cleaners.
- John Deere was a village blacksmith before he began to manufacture the plows and other farm tools and machines for which the company is famous today.

There are various reasons that we wind up far differently than we began, but usually it is either because circumstances compel us to change, if we are to survive, or because unexpected opportunities arise and we decide to take advantage of them. The changes we feel forced to make may be because we did not gauge prospective clients' desires accurately. Perhaps we miscalculated the needs of most prospects. That's easy enough to do, and we do write business plans with the full knowledge that we base them in large part on assumptions that have to be somehow validated. We fully expect to return to the business plan periodically and revise it with the 20/20 hindsight of experience.

But there are other factors:

- Perhaps there have been recent or currently occurring changes in the field in which we specialize, especially if we are in a super-dynamic field such as computers. W. H. Hoover found the demand for saddles and harnesses declining sharply, as people began to buy automobiles, and village blacksmith John Deere designed his first plow to help his customers overcome the problem of current plows that could not cope with soil that clung obstinately to their plow blades.

- Perhaps there have been recent or currently occurring changes in the economic picture and the markets that we did not know of or pay enough attention to. For example, in a time of recession, the factor of price becomes more important to clients and prospective clients, and can greatly influence buying habits. Those who fail to recognize this new factor inevitably experience their own declines in business, sometimes extinction.

- Then there are many cases of failed beginnings and repeated tries before encountering success. One such case is that of Elisha T. Otis, whose many ventures failed for one reason or another until he invented the safety device that converted freight hoists into passenger elevators and so founded the elevator company that bears his name today. Or that of Milton Hershey, whose career evolved in much the same fashion, through a procession of failed candy company ventures before he started his successful chocolate candy business in Lancaster, Pennsylvania. In fact, a stream of failures preceding eventual success is almost characteristic of those who achieve great successes. Milton Reynolds was another who was up and down more than once before he launched his successful aluminum business.

Some change happens to or is forced upon almost everyone entering into business of any kind. Every new business is based on estimates and premises, all of which have yet to be tested in the marketplace by the final arbiters, the clients. It would be quite amazing if many of us were so fortunate or so prescient as to gauge the future with 100 percent accuracy. In the end, *only your clients can tell you what they want,* at the time. If you want to do business, you must pay close attention to what clients are telling you via their buying habits—via their reactions to your marketing initiatives—and what overall conditions are telling you about market changes. Markets are rarely static for long. You must sell to today's market, not yesterday's, and be as prepared as you can be for tomorrow's market.

Forces for Change Are Both Short- and Long-Term

Even that is not all of it, however. If we did estimate with unparalleled accuracy or adjust almost instantaneously to the current realities of the marketplace, those short-term or dynamic forces for change, there are other forces beyond our control and beyond our vision or ability to predict: There are the long-term forces that bring about gradual changes. These are changes that take place continuously, but slowly, so that we may not be conscious that changes have taken place until it is too late. It is the kind of change that has in recent years brought IBM so much grief, as they failed to appreciate the seminal changes taking place in the computer field, with the lowly PC threatening the majestic mainframe. (The statistics reveal that the mainframe market is still declining today, while the PC market is still growing.)

The lessons of that kind of change are plain enough: Hardly anyone can sell today exactly what they sold ten years ago. The products and services of even five years ago are likely to be on the edge of obsolescence today. In any venture, one must stay abreast of the times and respond to the winds of change. Only ten years ago, for example, fax machines were a novelty, they produced copy that was not very good, and no one expected you to have a fax of your own. Today, even as a one–person business based in your own home, you are badly out of step if you do not have a fax or access to one. As little as five years ago, if you invested heavily in the Beta type of videocassette recorder, you would have come to grief as the VHS models pushed the Beta models into a corner and virtually into Valhalla. Who could have predicted it? no one. There seems to be a consensus that the Beta machines were technically superior, but that is not always a market factor. In the computer business, for example, technical experts could have made (and often did make) a case for the technical superiority of many other mainframe computers than those of IBM, but that had no effect on IBM's dominating position in the computer market. In one year, Remington-Rand, who brought the digital computer to the commercial market, set itself a goal of becoming "a better number two" (to IBM, that is).

Technical superiority is not always a factor in marketing, and a focus on technical superiority, even if based on absolute fact, may be only a distraction from the real issue of popular appeal. Do not confuse technical considerations with marketing considerations; they are not the same.

In the very short time of a scant decade, desktop computers and printers have made the conventional typewriter all but obsolete. In an even shorter time, laser printers have made most other types of printers all but obsolete. These changes affect the way in which you conduct your business. You would hesitate to send out correspondence prepared on a manual typewriter or even an electric one today, if you even have an electric typewriter.

The Growth of the Super-Specialist

Frequently, the independent consultant discovers that among the array of services he or she provides, one or more stand out from all as the most popular and most in-demand services. Martin Schiff, a computer consultant in Maitland, Florida, super-specializes in both his technical area and his market. The bulk of his practice is with banks in his service area, and he works primarily with the FoxPro computer software.

This is by no means atypical. Most of us start with a broad spectrum of services in our field. A freelance writer seeking custom writing jobs is likely to seek and accept almost any kind of writing, but in time has become somewhat specialized as a speech writer, newsletter specialist, writer of direct marketing materials, or any of many other specialties within his or her career field.

Of course, one rarely starts with that highly specialized, or narrow, an area of services and markets, but usually selects and grows into his or her favored specialties as experience directs. I did not start out or make a conscious decision to be a proposal writer-consultant. I was a writer, tending to specialize in technical writing, for a long time. I also wrote resumes and training programs, as opportunities presented themselves. I responded, eventually, to a market demand for proposal writing for government contracts, from that to an opportunity to write a book on that subject, and then to a market demand for how-to business and professional books. It was largely serendipity, true, but it was a market change that happened along at the time.

Still Another Reason for Change: Business Growth

There is still at least one other influence for change that grows out of experience. Most of us eventually discover not only a *need* for change, as we gain experience with our ventures, but we find *opportunities* for profitable and desirable changes. That is, we make totally arbitrary changes as *additions* to our services. My own consulting projects were profitable enough, for example, but I found a good market for seminars on the subject, and ultimately a newsletter, followed by publishing a series of related monographs and, eventually, by a book, and then by other books on the subject. This is not an unusual series of developmental steps, and you can go on to the development of audiotapes and videotapes, and even to a busy speaking career. Many independent consultants develop broad-based businesses in this manner. They usually find, too, that these various activities are mutually supporting: Each one additional activity creates market opportunities and visibility for the other activities, with added income, rather than added marketing costs.

HOW CHANGES AFFECT YOUR BROCHURE NEEDS

These forces are significant in two ways, as far as your brochures are concerned:

1. Your original, general brochure is most likely to undergo change from time to time, as your practice takes form and evolves, and as conditions force change. Your brochure(s) must reflect your practice, of course. You should expect that evolution and prepare for it as you develop your first brochure. Know that it is the first version only.

2. If you develop additional specialties, whether they are specialties of service or involve products, expect to encounter a need for new and separate brochures, one for each. It is usually a mistake to try to sell completely different things in a single presentation.

   The first situation requires little discussion, except to point out that the difficulties and uncertainties of making those assessments and estimates for your initial business plan have their counterpart in the difficulties and uncertainties of the most effective brochure presentation.

How to Ask Prospects What They Want: Testing Your Copy

In the direct-mail field it is an accepted premise that testing is the only reliable way to determine how well your offer, copy, price, and other aspects of your campaign will work. You may apply logic, or what you think is logic, as did one man who did a satisfactory volume of business advertising an item for $3. Since the markup on the item was quite great—it was that type of item—so that it would still be profitable at $2, he decided that he could greatly increase sales and make even more money by dropping the price to $2. To his dismay, at $2 sales fell off. Probably his readers did not believe the product could be any good at only $2. In fact, he might have done more business by raising the price to $4. There is an optimal price always, and too low a price can be as big a mistake as too high a price can be. The "trick" is to be able to estimate what the typical buyer thinks the price *ought* to be. A much better "trick" is to find out what the typical buyer thinks by testing various prices.

Of course, it is quite difficult to understand the mind of the buying public or to anticipate how that public will respond to any proposition. Even when the public has demonstrated overwhelming acceptance or rejection of a product or service, we are rarely able to determine with any great accuracy why it did so. The hula hoop was an overwhelming success—for six weeks. Then it died and was heard of no more. The Pet Rock endured for one season, a holiday season at that, and then expired. Rubik's Cube was another short-lived success, great as its success was during that short life. I can recall the time when the yo-yo was a novelty that was sweeping the country as a fad.

That is typical of novelties, and while some novelties become staples, most perish in time. We can guess how the public will react, but that is only a guess; we can be sure only of what it does, not what we think it will do.

Prospects often judge value by price, for example, but how can we know that price is "right" in this respect? We can guess, and we can often make what we believe to be expert estimates, based on experience. However, the point here is that all estimates and premises need to be tested. It is when we think we have a foolproof formula that we are headed for disaster. There is no way to know with any certainty what is the "right" price, proposition, or copy. You can learn that only by asking the clients, for only they know. You ask them by testing to see how they react. For example, run three ads or make three mailings at $2, $3, and $4 to find out which price the customers prefer. Do the same for your copy, and any other element you believe needs to be tested.

It's fairly easy to test a mail order idea in this manner because there are short-term results you can use as direct indicators, but it is not easy to test a brochure this way. Brochures rarely produce short-term results in adequate quantity to deliver messages unless you specifically design them to do so. On the other hand, it takes far too long to determine by long-term experience whether your first idea was a good one or not. You could become the most senior citizen of all while waiting to compile significant results through general experience alone. To get more immediate results, and thus an indication of your brochure's effectiveness, you need to devise something that will induce a more immediate response from readers of the brochure.

Testing a Brochure

To test brochure copy you must do something that will provoke an immediate response from the reader, such as inviting the reader to respond to a request for something you are offering. That could be some kind of small information piece (e.g., "Ten Ways to Increase Your Tax Deductions" or "How to Write More Effective Help-Wanted Advertisements"). It might be to offer a free survey or inspection (e.g., "A FREE security survey of your premises" [That is especially good, since it gets you on the premises talking to the prospective clients about what you sell]). You might offer a free mini-seminar (e.g., a one-hour presentation—on the prospect's premises, in which you impart useful information and answer the prospect's questions directly, while you are making what is really a sales presentation).

What you offer would be related to what you do, so that an expression of interest by a reader indicates not only that the brochure has been read, but the interest suggests that he or she is a good sales lead to be followed up. It doesn't really help to offer a calendar or even tax tips, unless the tax tips are related to your business somehow (e.g., tax lawyer or accountant). The idea in offering something free is to help you identify good sales prospects, so you must design your offer to be attractive to only those you think to be good prospects.

You can test your brochure's appeal and readers' reactions as you would test prices by varying the brochure's contents and the offers you make to invite responses from readers. That can help you in finding out what works best. You can enclose a postage-paid response card, on which you ask the reader to check off a few things to give you more information, information you can use to start or add to a database marketing file, while you are refining your brochure.

Recognizing and Using All Test Data

Although you should devise specific methods for getting feedback from clients to gauge the impact and effectiveness of your brochure (e.g., a postage-paid response card or envelope) some data will come to you as spontaneous responses from readers. You must, however, recognize these responses as useful data. They will arrive in somewhat random fashion. To make them useful as definitive feedback, they will require analysis of some sort.

For example, what kinds of questions and comments do you get from readers of your brochure? Are they questions indicating that your brochure has inspired interest and thus a desire to know more or are they responses reflecting readers' difficulties in understanding your copy? That is, do readers want to know more or do they want to know what your copy means? The difference is quite significant and quite important. Are they complaints of some sort, suggestions, general comments? All of these can be revealing too.

For all the data to be maximally useful, you must collect it all, sort it out, classify it, and analyze it. The occasional case is not significant overall; only the typical response, one made by many respondents, has general significance. You must find the trends to determine what to keep, what to change, and how to change it. Those occasional questions and comments, however, should not be discarded without thought. There is an excellent possibility that they furnish information worth inserting into the individual's record in your marketing database.

How Many Copies to Print

One other point with regard to that first brochure: Printing a large quantity of your first brochure is quite likely to be a great mistake. It is true that nowhere is economy of scale more significant a cost factor than it is in printing: The cost of each copy of your brochure plummets sharply with increases in quantity. At the same time, gaining that lower unit price by printing great quantities is a false economy if you find it necessary to revise your brochure relatively soon after printing it, thereby mandating the trashing of all the remaining copies. Moreover, unless you are using brochures up in large quantities (e.g., by mass mailings) the economies of scale in printing are not significant because the overall cost is not significant.

Mike Barnard avoided the problem by printing copies of his brochure on his own laser printer. (You can also use a copier, of course.) He found that a practicable approach because he needed only limited quantities. Of course, that limits him to a single color of ink and to small quantities, but that was his choice and probably a wise one. However, he used a special brochure "blank," "Atrium," available from companies selling such items. (Several sources were cited at the end of Chapter 1.) This gave him a brochure form with color and design. In fact, a quite enormous number and variety of choices are available to you for brochures, letterheads, forms, and many other items, not only in blank forms of many designs, but in other items, such as foils that enable you to add color.

Doing your own laser printing to make copies, as Barnard did, is not a disadvantage, but in fact, an advantage. Unless you are going to do mass mailings, it is not likely that you will use more than a few hundred copies of your brochure before you will want to revise it. Ergo, you probably would do well to print not more than about 500 to 1,000 copies, at most, even if you go to a nearby print shop to have it printed on a press. That should give you a reasonable per-copy cost without an excessive inventory, which itself might inhibit change when change ought to be made and so become the tail wagging the dog. Printing in limited quantities is a way of keeping your options open.

THE SPECIALTY BROCHURE

In the waiting rooms of many professional offices are racks of brochures. A law office handling cases for individuals may specialize—in accident cases, for example—but many handle a variety of cases and thus may have separate brochures discussing legal services with regard to wills, accidents, divorce, lawsuits, and other discrete legal activities. A plastic surgeon might have one brochure on changing the shape of one's nose—rhinoplasty—another on breast reduction or enlargement, another on liposuction, and still others on various procedures. It is not at all uncommon for an independent professional to have a series of brochures, each offering a different service.

It is quite frequently that we find consulting, writing, and public speaking to be major activities of an individual. If you read a public speaker's periodical, such as *Sharing Ideas*, published by the well-known Dottie Walters, you find that a great many full-time public speakers are also writers and consultants. Some also have their own speakers bureaus, and act as brokers to book other speakers for clients. There are even those who make and sell products, such as newsletters, audiotapes, videotapes, books, and other items. When the individual regards him- or herself primarily as a consultant, the basic brochure will reflect that, and the specialty brochures will present the ancillary services that the individual offers.

This is where it is helpful to have some sort of overall business identity that serves as an umbrella for several major activities. You may then use a subtitle, slogan, or blurb in each brochure, under that title, to clarify and define the service that the brochure is about.

In my own case, I decided to create a corporate entity, "HRH Communications, Inc." deliberately choosing a name that could accommodate various and diverse subordinate entities. Within that corporate umbrella, I write books as a principal activity, but I also publish and sell, by mail, a number of monographs, do some custom writing under contract, lecture occasionally, and market an artistic creation my wife manufactures. Each of these activities is a separate entity with its own literature and marketing. Occasionally, I accept a consulting assignment or custom seminar presentation, and treat these, again, as separate ventures with their own identities. "HRH Communications, Inc." is the common factor, but otherwise the literature for each activity is quite separate and distinct, focusing quite clearly on that activity.

Maintaining Your Image Is a Consideration

When you add income centers by presenting your clients and prospective clients other offerings than your basic consulting services, you introduce, along with that new activity, the consideration of your professional image. If you want to remain best known to your clients as a consultant, you must be careful to avoid blurring that image. When you create new and different or supplemental income centers, they become almost separate businesses. To try to present all your offerings (e.g., direct consulting services, a newsletter, and a seminar) in a single brochure is to invite confusion. The average client can't handle that, and your image becomes diffused if you are not careful. We think in terms of specialties and specialists today, and so many clients will mentally slot you in only one category. They may not associate you with those other services and functions at all if you rely on a single brochure to explain all. Even a client who had once been an employee did not realize that as a technical publications group, we had illustrators, as well as writers, on staff, and went elsewhere seeking art services, as we had been supplying him only writing and editing services. I started as a consultant and later added seminars, and my seminar brochures made it as clear as I could that I was a consultant. Still, attendees at my seminars constantly sought me out to ask if I also did consulting. It seems that it is rather difficult for many people to understand that you may offer several, disparate services, without any service compromising your ability to provide the others in a competent and professional manner.

Aside from that problem, lumping all these activities together in a single brochure may very well tend to negate in the client's mind the very idea that you are a consultant and thus a specialist by appearing to say that you do everything. If you pursue several income centers, you do well to make each stand on its own feet, and thus merit its own literature.

Note that large corporations, even those that are not conglomerates, recognize this by establishing separate departments, divisions, companies, or corporations. The General Electric Company, for example, manufactures consumer goods of many types, as well as military goods, the latter in separate divisions. They long ago split their work for the Department of Defense into a Heavy Weapons Division and a Light Weapons Division. When they began to manufacture jet engines, that also became a separate company. When they decided to support NASA in its work in space, they created still another division for that. Of course, as a one-person venture, you are not going to split into several companies; that would be a bit too ambitious an undertaking, but it is not overly ambitious to create separate brochures to describe and explain each major income-producing activity as a separate entity.

I recommend, therefore, that you do two things with regard to satisfying your brochure needs:

1. Treat your basic brochure as you do your business plan. Regard the early versions, especially the first one, as penciled-in versions, reproduced in minimum quantities, with full expectation of revision, as experience dictates.

2. When you create a new activity as a new income center, develop a new brochure for it. However, while you do need a separate brochure for each separate income center, the various brochures can and probably should have a unifying theme of some sort. You are not trying to conceal the fact of several activities from your clients; far from it, it is in your interests to point them out. You do, however, want to enable your clients to understand and focus on each activity separately, and so you must pursue sales for each activity as though it were a separate venture.

One Brochure or Many?

You may have seen large brochures, with dividers, each marking a separate section of the brochure in which is discussed a separate activity. That may appeal to you. You can create a large, multi-section brochure, as an alternative to several small brochures. That may appear to be an advantage, presenting a more grandiose picture of your company. It may also offer some advantage in that clients may be more inclined to keep it for future reference. However, I see two immediate disadvantages, other than what I think to be the psychological disadvantage we have discussed of casting some doubts on your image as a specialist:

- One disadvantage is cost. One large brochure is almost certain to cost far more than several small brochures. Aside from the printing and the difficulty of printing small quantities economically, there is the problem of having so many pages that it is necessary to bind the brochure, adding further to cost.
- Another disadvantage is that you may have to revise the brochure periodically in only one section, but that means reprinting and rebinding the whole thing.

You thus lose all flexibility, such as would be afforded by having separate, "stand-alone" brochures for your various major activities. The loss of that flexibility, as described by those two considerations, would discourage me from creating a multi-section large brochure.

THE USE OF BOILERPLATE

"Boilerplate" is an interesting word in publications. Its origin is not clear, although it always reminds me of the circular plates used in printing newspapers in the letterpress days. They were fitted around a cylinder that resembled a boiler in size and shape.

In any case, regardless of its origin, boilerplate is copy that can be used over and over, such as a proprietary notice. The front matter of a book I wrote as a guide to consulting contracts carries a disclaimer explaining that the contents of the book are not intended to constitute specific legal counsel. I wrote a disclaimer and submitted it with my manuscript, but the publisher advised me that they had a standard (boilerplate) disclaimer that they printed in every book they published that dealt with legal matters of any kind, and they preferred to use their own boilerplate.

Today, with computers and word processors on virtually every desk, you have as perhaps your most useful writing tool your boilerplate files. If you do not have such files, you should have or should be developing them. They will save you a great deal of labor in the future.

In an earlier time, before the PC, "cut and paste" was a literal description of the methods we used to minimize the labor of revisions and corrections. Cut and paste became a leading tool of publications work a few decades ago, when printing began to move steadily from the older letterpress methods to the lithographic offset methods. Printing plates could be made by photographing the original copy, referred to as "camera-ready" and "mechanicals." You could change a paragraph, a page, or a few words—or even a comma—by cutting out some portion of the original and pasting fresh copy in its place. It was a laborious, messy task, but it was better than resetting the entire page.

We often inserted boilerplate statements, as appropriate, pasting them into the right places. Boilerplate, however, is not immutable; it can change and usually does, in time, for many reasons. They may be minor or major changes. Whichever they are, they do not detract from the usefulness of the boilerplate. Quite the reverse, the boilerplate is as useful as ever or even more so, as long as it is kept up to date with suitable changes, as needed.

Boilerplate copy can also take on another meaning and sometimes an even greater usefulness. Rather than being relatively unchanging or susceptible to change, it can be basically boilerplate, but adapted—changed—for each new use.

For example, if you have several brochures, you will want a unifying element that identifies you in each brochure. That may be a stylized title or standard blurb that will appear on the cover of each brochure, although the contents of each brochure will be quite different in each case. Or you may wish to make the same offer of some free report or mini-seminar in each brochure. However, when you are revising a brochure, you will want to keep much of the original, since we rarely are so far off with our brochures that we have to discard them and start over.

That is where the computer represents a remarkable labor-saving capability. "Cut and paste" has a different meaning today, as used in composing materials with a PC, and it is, of course, infinitely easier to use a computer and a word processor to change the copy and print out a fresh page as a new mechanical. You do well to build boilerplate files—

referred to by many as "swipe files," since they are files from which you may "swipe" copy for various uses.

A VERY SPECIAL SPECIALTY BROCHURE

The subject will come up again, as we discuss a very special specialty brochure that merits its own chapter. It has to do with qualifying yourself as a bidder for contracts. Let's talk about that next.

3

THE CAPABILITY BROCHURE

The capability brochure is a very special kind of brochure as a marketing aid, especially for those consultants who are in the early stages of getting established in their quests for clients and contracts.

THE CAPABILITY BROCHURE DEFINED

The capability brochure, also called "capability statement," is a special type brochure—if it is a brochure at all. It varies quite a lot from one kind of situation to another, and is often in a format that does not resemble that which most of us think of when we hear that word "brochure." As a result, the words "brochure" and "statement" are used rather loosely here. Whatever name it is known by, the capability brochure is a most basic marketing tool as a door opener.

The capability brochure is not designed, nor normally used, to help make sales directly. Its general purposes are to establish its author as a qualified prospective supplier or contractor for some described types of services in general, and often in particular for some given project. Capability brochures are a necessity in various situations and used to satisfy certain specific needs of marketing or pre-marketing conditions:

- A capability statement is often required in a specific case to respond to specific requirements stipulated by clients as a necessary preliminary to a contract competition. The client stipulates that only on the basis of the capability statements received will applicants (i.e., you) be judged suitably qualified for the project and permitted to compete for contract award.
- Capability statements are used generally to persuade respondents (e.g., contracting officers, purchasing agents, and other prospective clients and their agents) to include you in their lists of approved bidders, inviting you to submit your bids or proposals for future contracts to be let.
- Capability statements are used by many marketers as a general marketing tool (e.g., a "leave behind"), especially when you are competing in a market that generally calls for bids and proposals, to make yourself known to prospective clients.

HOW IT DIFFERS FROM THE GENERAL BROCHURE

An immediate question might arise in your mind asking how the capability brochure is different than the general brochure. Doesn't that latter brochure also describe my capabilities?

In fact, there is some common ground between your general brochure and the capability brochure you might need. The chief difference is focus and detail: The general brochure is just that—general—while the capability brochure is much more focused on your technical capabilities and resources you can bring to bear in a client's interest. Even that degree of focus and concentration on resources varies from one capability brochure to another, as you will see. In fact, it is helpful to view the capability brochure as sort of a generalized proposal, for it does bear some resemblance to a proposal.

Take that brochure of Michael R. Barnard Productions (Figure 1-9), for example. It is a general brochure. If it were a capability brochure, it might include much of what it presently has, especially the client and project examples. It would, however, probably present those examples in far greater technical detail. It would illustrate the specific technical and artistic capabilities and the resources of Michael R. Barnard Productions, including Michael's personal qualifications, those of others who would be available to serve clients' needs, and the physical facilities of the company. In the general brochure, you may be merely descriptive in claiming capabilities, resources, talents, and other virtuous and worthy attributes, but a capability statement must do more than merely list and aver capabilities: it must document and, to some extent, *prove* them.

WHAT IS PROOF?

The rules for proving something in a criminal case, for the board of a scientific academy, or for other formal requirements, can be rather rigorous. In other applications, such as in marketing, proof is whatever the client or other party will *accept* as proof. That is the kind of proof required here, and achieving that, in the practical case, involves a series of "do and don't" rules. A bit later in this chapter, we will get into a somewhat detailed discussion on the subject of credibility, but note for now that the major "do" factors are specificity, factual detail, and quantification, and the major "don't" factors are generalizations and hyperbole of all sorts.

WHY A CLIENT WANTS A CAPABILITY STATEMENT

Many organizations (e.g., federal agencies) normally accept anyone's request to be invited to compete for contracts. Sometimes, however, a client has a special requirement, and wishes to be sure that invitations to compete for the contract—usually to submit a proposal or a bid and set of specifications—are issued only to those who appear to be qualified to do the job, whatever it is. In those cases, the agency is likely to specifically require a capability brochure to be submitted for review and approval (i.e, as an application for inclusion on bidders lists). Even those suppliers who have a Standard Form 129, Application for Bidders List, on file and whose names are included on bidders lists, may be required to further qualify themselves to be invited to compete for a specific project when the contract is to be a large and unusual or especially important one.

The major purpose of this requirement is to screen out the inappropriate contenders. Any invitation to submit a bid or proposal for a contract, is almost certain to attract at least some responses from contenders who are totally unsuited and unqualified to do the work; this is so frequent an occurrence, that it cannot be called a phenomenon. It is especially the case when the economy is in a valley and a great many contractors are "hungry." It is almost incredible how many consultants will pursue and bid on contracts for work that is totally foreign to them, probably in desperation, under the theory that they will worry through, somehow, if they win, and that it is better to have any contract than no contract.

Clients do not look forward to winnowing 50 or more proposals—and it is not unusual to get as many as 200 responses in many situations—to find a relative handful of suitable contenders. That is not to mention all the difficulties of and time required to explain to the losers why their quotations, bids, or proposals could not be considered seriously. There is also the hazard of an unqualified competitor actually winning the contract and then being unable to perform. Such disasters have happened. Requiring prequalification via a capability statement is not a foolproof safeguard (there probably is no such thing), but it gives the client some degree of control. That minimizes that unnecessary burden of coping with a large number of unacceptable proposals, and also reduces the possibility of making a major blunder in choosing an awardee.

THE MOST SPECIALIZED (CUSTOMIZED) CAPABILITY STATEMENT

One kind of capability statement is so special that it is almost as customized as a proposal would be. It would include much boilerplate information necessarily, but would be written to respond to a specific request and situation.

Suppose, for example, that a client with a sizable insurance brokerage decides that his system and procedures are outmoded and inefficient, although they work, and should be computerized. The client knows that simply installing computers will not be enough, and he wishes to engage a consultant for a long-term project to redesign and reorganize his office systems and procedures, as well as to computerize operations. The client plans to invite proposals from all interested parties, but he knows what will happen if he invites everyone to participate: He is likely to get an unmanageably large number of proposals and be faced with the additional problem of prescreening to weed out those that are clearly unsuitable. He is also keenly aware of how much damage to his business could result from installing a bad system, and he wishes most ardently to reduce that possibility. The client therefore issues an invitation for capability statements, explaining the project for which consultants must qualify. He may even include a list of information items that he requires be included in the capability statement. (The client may have retained a consultant to write the invitation to submit capability statements, and that consultant may be the one who will evaluate the statements and make decisions as to which reflect a suitable capability.) This is usually a custom capability statement, written especially for this single occasion, although it may very well use boilerplate materials for some of its sections, verbatim or revised to adapt the materials to the specific application. (With proper organization of boilerplate files in your system, it should be quite easy to compose custom capability statements as needed.)

The Client Provides a Hint or Two

The client in this scenario probably suggests a few items that seem to be relevant—perhaps experience in or knowledge of insurance brokerage and relevant office needs, and perhaps a capability for designing a system of information automation—but usually he will merely describe in general terms what the problems and goals of the project are and leave it to you to tell him how and why you are qualified to do the job. It is then your task to write a capability statement that will convince the client that it is in his or her interest to read a proposal or bid from you. (It will almost certainly be a proposal, for a custom project.)

What you will write in response to the request will be almost a proposal, in this case, since it will be a customized statement or brochure, designed to qualify as a competitor for a single project. You believe that you can handle that project well enough, and you decide to put together a capability statement and qualify yourself as a potential contractor.

Your Response Must Be Based on a Strategy

Your capability statement ought to be based on a strategy of some sort, just as a proposal is. Its content will depend on the nature of what the project will require, of course, as described and as you can infer the ultimate system envisioned by the client. Your statement will depend on how you can present what you specialize in and how you pursue a project as qualifying you to satisfy the stated need. You will have to decide what are logically the major qualifications to handle such a project: Design experience? Insurance experience? Computer experience? Office management? Past projects? Client references?

You probably must have some preliminary notion as to the shape of the required end-system to determine what are the necessary qualifying resources of experience and technical capabilities. You will not, of course, be designing the system at this point, not even outlining it, but it may be necessary to offer ideas to illustrate your experience and resources as being qualifying. That will depend, at least partly, on how specific the request for a capability statement was.

THE MORE GENERALIZED CAPABILITY BROCHURE

The federal government and most state and local governments have forms for prospective suppliers to fill out as applications to have their names placed on bidders lists and thus to be invited to bid or propose on suitable projects. Getting your name on a bidders list does not ensure that you will be invited to bid on all suitable projects, or even on any future project. In some cases, there are so many names on the lists—many hundreds of names, in some cases—that the names are rotated so that perhaps fifty of those listed are invited, fifty more on the next procurement, and so on. Those listed are thus invited to bid on only a fraction of the procurements. In other cases, the purchasing agent or contracting official does not have a clear idea of how to select those best qualified for a given procurement, and thus omits some who would have been likely to bid. Most significant and relevant, however, is that not all organizations who contract for services maintain bidders lists. They may not be even aware of your existence, much less your suitability as a supplier of the services they need. It is a good marketing practice to mail capability brochures to such purchasing offices, with a request that it be kept on file as a prospective bidder for relevant contracts.

Here again, you may find it wise to have more than one capability brochure, according to the subspecialties you wish to pursue. You might, for example, want to sell your services as a designer of systems, a trainer of staffs, and a solver of certain defined kinds of problems. You would probably do well to have a separate capability brochure for each of these, especially if the purchasing executives tend to file brochures by types of services offered.

THE "LEAVE BEHIND" CAPABILITY BROCHURE

According to your marketing strategies and practices, you may want a generalized capability brochure that details all your resources for a wide variety of services, or you may want several separate brochures, as just suggested. You may want both a completely generalized version and several specialized ones as standard capability brochures. If you offer a rather wide variety of services, you probably need more than one "standard" capability statement. For example, I might conceivably have need for one brochure for general consulting, another for seminars, and another for ghost writing or newsletter editing and production. These would be brochures to mail out and "leave behind" in visits. Even if you use such diverse capability brochures as these, you would not need them in large quantities, unless you plan a mass mailing campaign.

THE PHYSICAL CONSIDERATIONS

Cosmetic aspects of capability brochures are of minor importance, although the product should be clean, businesslike, and professional in appearance. In fact, the highly cosmetic brochure—colors, graphics, and expensive papers or card stock—would be a disadvantage here, suggesting mass-produced "junk mail" literature, not to be taken seriously. Businesslike simplicity (e.g., ragged right, rather than justified right margin) is far more effective in this application. The typical capability statement is typed (laser printed today) on your letterhead, and if it is more than a page or two, it is bound in an ordinary binder such as all stationers offer. The binder is of a size to accommodate a small number of 8½- x 11-inch pages, and offers a see-through window for your title page. (See Figure 3-1.) Its physical appearance signals that it is a custom-

```
                    Capabilities of

               HRH Communications, Inc.
```

Figure 3-1.   Commercial Binder

prepared statement and not a mass-printed brochure, an effect you want. This brings up an important point.

Perceptions of the Client Still Count Most

Remember always, in marketing, that there is only one truth: That is the client's truth. What the client decides to buy, as well as from whom, depends on what the client perceives as the facts. We present what we believe to be the facts, but for marketing purposes, they are facts only if and when we persuade the client to agree that they are facts. Again and again in any discussion of sales presentations—and that definitely includes capability brochures—the same consideration will surface: how to control what the reader of the presentation perceives. He who controls and shapes that perception best wins the competition.

It Is Always a Problem in Persuasion

Writing a capability statement follows the principles of selling and advertising. The application and articulation of those principles are somewhat different here because the entire situation is different, but the principles of sales persuasion are not different. People who review capability statements react very much as anyone else reacts to persuasive strategies and tactics, and that is perhaps the first lesson of writing and presentation. Unfortunately, it appears too often to be one that some individuals appear to have trouble in grasping: Organizations do not make decisions and buy; *people* make decisions and buy, the people who work for and represent the organization. They respond to the same kinds of appeals, and are "turned off" by the same kinds of gaffes that all other people are. They are also individuals, and what motivates one does not motivate another. This too must be considered in writing presentations.

THE DEADLY SINS OF BROCHURE WRITING

In most activities, it soon becomes apparent that there are certain common shortcomings—even mistakes made by individuals—that appear to be endemic in the field. You find the same things happening over and over, the same problems recurring regularly. So it is with brochure and other presentation writing. Here are some of the common failings that are responsible for as many as two of every three presentations written to be rejected swiftly, even after a cursory reading:

- One symptom seen far too often is a reluctance to be absolutely specific, for fear that commitment is unwise. Again and again, consultants deliberately employ somewhat evasive tactics, it may be sometimes an almost instinctive act, and so perhaps not entirely conscious. The theory is, evidently, that commitment is hazardous for more than one reason:
  1. The client may not agree with what you propose, so it seems wise to be somewhat elusive and not too specific.
  2. It is sometimes difficult to forecast what you can and cannot do, so it can be hazardous to make promises that are too specific. Suppose you cannot make good on those promises? Such fears too often drive writers of brochures and even of proposals to be deliberately vague.
- Somewhat akin to the foregoing idea of being evasive in their commitments is the tendency of some proposers to be "polypharmacal," after the fashion of some early-day physicians, those of the day when the pharmacists actually compounded prescriptions, instead of soaking labels off already-compounded and -packaged preparations. Many physicians of that day wrote prescriptions with multiple ingredients. Their rationale was that with so many things in the prescription, *something* ought to work and help the patient recover. So in writing sales presentations, some consultants promise just about everything, with hope that the customer, confronted with a cornucopia of glowing promises, will like something well enough to reward the consultant with the contract.
- Another problem that plagues some consultants is an overdose of modesty. Perhaps it isn't really modesty itself but the fear that if the presentation praises the writer too highly it will appear to be in bad taste and prove offensive. Many of us are afraid to toot our own horns, even when we are justified in doing so.
- Even more common and disastrous, however, is the tendency to go the other way and lather the presentation heavily with exaggerated claims and hyperbole, without the slightest shred of evidence that any of this is justified. In fact, some proposers seem to have gotten that old TV western gunslinger's idea backwards. He warned off those who would challenge him by explaining how deadly he was with his guns and

said calmly, "No brag; just fact." Some consultants appear to be offering no facts; just brag. That is as deadly as any of the several other chronic mistakes some consultants make.

THE BASIC MUSTS OF CAPABILITY BROCHURES

The "deadly sins" just enumerated are focused on what not to do. There ought to be a corresponding set of things to do, and these ought to turn out to be somewhat the inverse of the things not to do. There are, in fact, do's as well as don'ts, and they are really what the rest of this chapter is all about. Let's enumerate them briefly here before we discuss them:

- Do study the client's requirement thoroughly before you begin to write, and be sure that you understand exactly what he or she wants. Nothing appeals more to any client than clear evidence that you do understand his or her need clearly and are responding directly to it.
- Do exercise the greatest care that you address what the client says he or she wants, not what you happen to think he or she ought to have. (There are exceptions to this, but this is a general truth. The strategic time for such disagreement will come later, in writing a proposal, although even then you will have to exercise great diplomacy.)
- Do cast off any ideas about modesty and confess your real abilities and assets, but through presenting facts, not bragging.) The best way to do that is through quantifying and identifying specific examples, while scrupulously avoiding superlatives and other hyperbole.

A recent issue of a business magazine carried a short story about a man named Howard Rohrlick. He was a seller of audiovisual equipment—a salesman on a company's payroll—a few years ago. One thing about slide projectors that customers found annoying was the abrupt changes of light level at every slide change, for which there was a cure but one that was too expensive for most people. The problem was annoying but didn't justify extensive investment to overcome it.

Rohrlick believes in one of the most sound principles of selling ever enunciated: The most effective salesperson is a consultant, not selling things to people, but solving problems for them. He therefore set about solving this problem and eventually did so, thereby launching a new venture, the nature of which is not relevant to the point to be made here.

What is relevant is that idea of selling by helping the customer solve problems. For that is what selling is all about: In most cases, customers face problems, sometimes consciously, sometimes unconsciously, during the routine of their endless struggles with each day's requirements. Customers buy benefits, as Madison Avenue reminds us regularly, with every purchase, but among the most appealing benefits are solutions to their problems: Most customers can be induced to buy whatever appears to be the best way to solve the problem of the moment. Ergo, solving customers' problems means making sales, and problem solving is inherent in the idea of consulting, the reason for the consultant's existence.

In short, you sell your services by demonstrating how your services will solve the client's problems most satisfyingly. That "most satisfyingly" may mean most rapidly, inexpensively, reliably, conveniently, or any of other possible "mosts," depending on the circumstances and nature of what you do, but it is the "most" that is the final persuader when the client finally makes a choice.

This is true whether you are helping a client solve the problem of hunger by inviting him or her to select his or her own steak from the refrigerated window, offering a better chip to an electronics manufacturer to solve a technological problem of some sort, or offering to write a training program for a client. Really successful salespeople—those thinking of themselves as consultants—are not shown the door or dodged and evaded by their customers; they are welcomed because they approach every sale with a "what problem can I help you solve today?" attitude. Being a consultant whenever you are attempting to persuade someone to what you believe or want the other to do is simply a way of saying, "Let's talk about you and your needs or problems." Do this, and the other party will regard you as a brilliant conversationalist, as well as a most reasonable, likable, and convincing talker. No one will find it easy to resist you, either in face-to-face conversation or in reading what you have written, if you talk about him or her. One's self is always a fascinating subject.

THE ISSUE OF CREDIBILITY

One of the most important elements of any presentation is credibility. Few things are either credible or incredible inherently. They are usually made credible or incredible by the manner of their presentation, and often by the authority or reputation of the presenter or source. There is also the factor of what the reader wishes to believe, and there is the role that logic and reason play: Few of us are so naive in this era that we will believe everything on pure authority, even when it emanates from "high sources" or other origins usually deemed trustworthy. As Bertrand Russell once pointed out in one of his philosophical essays, there are everyday truths and Sunday truths: Many of us tend toward a kind of double standard when it comes to what we will and will not believe or try to persuade ourselves to believe.

AVOID GENERALYSIS

In some years in technical publications, I found the problem of generalization prevalent among technical writers: many would only generalize in their writing and could not or would not go to the trouble to provide the details. After a while, it became obvious to me that it was necessary to distinguish between a manuscript on such technical matters as installation and maintenance of equipment that reported what ought to happen and a manuscript that explained to the reader how to make something happen. That, in fact, was and still is the essence of what was and is wrong with a great many technical manuals that have been and are being published. A manual might, for example, explain that a certain measurement in a given piece of equipment ought to be 85 volts, but fail to tell the reader what to do if the measurement were other than 85 volts, and what higher or lower readings might signify.

The same shortcoming was and is often to be found in theory manuals and elsewhere. The authors too often make blanket statements—pronouncements from on high—without backup explanations, asking the reader to accept the author's presumed authority.

This proved to be so common a failing among writers that I came to regard it as a virtual writing disease, which I was ultimately to call "generalysis," a coinage of my own. The pervasiveness of generalysis, deplorable though it is in such areas as technical manuals, is even more evident in some other areas, notably that of written marketing and sales materials. Generalysis is an obstacle to the effectiveness of technical manuals, but it is a fatal disease when it infects proposals, brochures, sales letters, and other such presentations. Arguments and explanations that really say, "Just take my word for it," are simply not at all persuasive, with only rare exceptions. Even the President of the United States cannot avoid the necessity to explain himself to the public eventually if he wants to be believed, as more than a few of our recent Presidents have come to learn.

Ultimately, I found in writing such materials that the amount and level of detail offered alone has a profound effect upon credibility: customers are persuaded far more by presentations that furnish a great deal of detail, and especially fine detail, than they are by those presentations that offer smug generalizations and glib promises, along with all the "Madison Avenue" hyperbole that necessarily goes hand-in-hand with this approach to persuasion. Anyone can generalize about almost anything, and the ability to do so proves nothing. On the other hand, it takes know-how to plan and explain plans in detail, and the detail tends to prove or is, at least, usually accepted as strong evidence that the writer is truly authoritative and has "done his (or her) homework." Ergo, a detailed presentation is almost without exception far more credible and persuasive than is one that only generalizes. The latter offers the promise, but not the proof.

SPECIFICITY AS A FACTOR

The moviemakers of Hollywood outdid the phrase-makers of Madison Avenue for years with such characterizations of their celluloid products as *stupendous, breathtaking, awe-inspiring, colossal,* and *magnificent,* each followed by at least one exclamation mark. They piled exaggeration upon hyperbole until they almost (but not quite) blushed themselves at their wild adjectival excesses. They were entirely oblivious to the fact that far from impressing anyone, such self-congratulation had become a source of great amusement for many people.

Despite a public that is orders of magnitude more sophisticated today than we were in those relatively early days, and despite a great deal more reserve and good sense in advertising, a glance through print advertisements in current magazines still reveals the following kinds of words and claims (direct quotes):

- Great hotels
- Fresh new styling
- Boldest, most ingenious
- Most advanced drivetrain
- One of the largest banks

- Handsome second income
- Big . . . Knowledgeable . . .
- Convenient
- Superb engineering
- A growing corporation
- *The* vodka
- Revolutionary, multilevel plan

These terms are supposed to be sales arguments, and, of course, they are not arguments nor are they really appeals. They are claims, hyperbole, self-appraisals, adjectives of exaggeration. Whatever they are, they are not credible, nor do they contribute to credibility. Quite the contrary, they only stress the weaknesses of the sales appeals when they are used. They sound very much like someone pounding on an empty barrel: they have a pronounced hollow ring.

Now aside from the fact that one major key to achieving persuasion is to tell the reader things the reader will welcome hearing, there is the matter of achieving an atmosphere of reporting, rather than claiming, and that is one of the keys to achieving credibility.

Once, some years ago, it was my lot to present a sales proposal to a federal government contracting officer to negotiate a contract the federal agency wished to enter into with us. I handed a copy of my cost proposal—which is normally a separate document when offering a proposal to a federal agency—to the contracting officer, and we sat down facing each other across a table. He glanced through my proposal and then:

"One hundred fifty percent overhead? Why such a nice, round number, Mr. Holtz? Why didn't you make it 149.7 percent? I would not have questioned that, but 150? Let's make that 125 percent, okay?"

Of course, that last was not really a question. It was an edict. I could only nod my head and hope that my face was not as red as it felt. He was right, but he was also wrong: That 150 percent was a bogus figure, but it represented a reduction of our true overhead, not a boost in it. (We thought our true overhead unacceptably high, but wanted the contract, even at reduced profit.) However, it did not appear expedient to argue the point. It would have opened a can of worms I didn't care to open.

It was, of course, foolish of us to have done that. We knew that our real overhead was excessive and we arbitrarily reduced it to be competitive enough to win. Under the circumstances, it would not have been dishonest to have made the number an odd one, as the contracting officer pointed out, and avoid the confession of a contrived number with, in this case, the appearance of being dishonest. Any reasonable person, detecting that the number was contrived, would have felt entirely justified in inferring that we had inflated our true overhead to the 150 percent quoted, rather than cut it from a higher figure, as we actually had.

Honesty itself is not the issue here: the *appearance* of honesty is the issue. More explicitly, the issue is the appearance of dishonesty, in the case cited. That is, the critical factor is what the client *perceives*.

When writers for one company in which I was employed reported in the company's brochures and proposals that Soandso Technical Corporation was the leader in its industry, the reader yawned and perhaps smiled indulgently. The claim is easy to make because it's an opinion, not a demonstrated fact. There are so many different bases on which to claim being the biggest, that there are probably at least a half-dozen "biggest" companies in every industry. I thought it had more meaning to simply state, in those proposals I wrote for the company, that we had forty-two offices in eighteen states and employed 4,400 people. Let the reader judge for himself or herself where we stood in relative size ranking, if, indeed, being biggest added to our image and chances for success in winning the contract.

The significant thing is this: my statement was accepted without question as a factual report. It is unlikely that it would even occur to anyone reading that statement to question it. It had the appearance of veracity because obviously the numbers were not rounded off; there were no superlatives or loud claims, and no effort to either praise or appraise ourselves. We simply *reported* the significant numbers, without emotion or apparent bias. It is just that, the appearance of reporting quietly and dispassionately, that carries with it a persuasive aura of authenticity. If a customer receives brochures, proposals, or other sales literature from a dozen suppliers, the customer is not going to start making inquiries to determine whether you are being absolutely honest or bending the facts a bit; that would be entirely impractical. Instead, the customer is simply going to judge what you say on its own merits. If it appears to be reasonable and honest, the customer will accept it as such. Likewise if it appears to be wildly inflated, the customer will assume that it is, and won't be greatly surprised by it, either. So common is the tendency to blow things up until they are far bigger than life, that the customer will probably examine your brochure or your resume in expectation of finding the typical breast-beating professions of greatness and will be pleasantly surprised if yours is refreshingly different. But there is another consideration than the readily apparent exaggeration of superlatives: specificity.

WHAT A CAPABILITY STATEMENT IS NOT

It is often more revealing to explain what something is not than what it is. In this case, we have the problem that most of us functioning as independent consultants are self-employed, one-person enterprises. We may call our ventures by a business name, and we may even be incorporated, but we still have trouble thinking of ourselves as other than individuals. Consequently, a great many independent consultants use resumes, rather than brochures. Even if they prepare and have printed some information in a brochure format, it often still reads much more like an individual resume than a company description. Figure 3-2 is an example of such a resume paraded as a capability statement. It is difficult to distinguish between this and a typical resume sent in quest of a salaried job.

Figure 3-3 is somewhat of an improvement, despite having overtones of a resume. It is still lacking in specific descriptions of services offered, or other evidence of capabilities.

Compare these with Figure 3-4, which is also the statement of an independent consultant, but is presented as the statement of a company. That is not merely because a company name is used, instead of an individual's name.

Many successful companies use the name of the founder as the name of the company: Elisha T. Otis (Otis elevators), Milton Hershey (Hershey chocolate), Gail Borden (Borden's milk), and Alfred Fuller (Fuller Brush Company), for example. However, it may be that using a fictitious name will be a help to you in thinking in terms of your business, rather than of yourself.

References to prior employment on someone's payroll is not appropriate, but it should be presented as a resume-type recital of dates, names, and places. It should be a narrative type of reference, as in Wilkens' description (Figure 3-4). Note that the statement is about TWI—Technical Writing, Inc., not the owner. In fact, his name does not appear until well after the introduction to the company.

CAPABILITIES

MARGARET KELLER   Home Phone: 404-555-1200
1020 Southern View Avenue
Swinburne, GA 30303

HIGHLIGHTS OF QUALIFICATIONS

- Writing, editing, and indexing
- Instructional design and scriptwriting
- Multimedia applications
- Communication and interpersonal skills
- 25 years experience in planning art and drama for adult education
- 15 years experience in educational research, course development, and classroom instruction
- Self-motivated, creative professional; can work independently or as member of a team
- Capability in the following:

WordPerfect 5.1	Word for Windows	AmiPro 3.0 for Windows
Wordstar	Microsoft Write	KEdit
Personal Editor	Microsoft Excel	Arts & Letters

Proficient in the following:
  IBM BookMaster and BookManager
  IPF (Information Presentation Facility) for online help
  XEDIT

TECHNICAL WRITING, EDITING, AND INDEXING EXPERIENCE

Wrote documentation for IBM products:
  Installation and operations guides
  Setup procedures
  Programming reference manuals
  Online help for applications
  Scripts for multimedia tutorials.
  Procedures manuals and courses for VAX/VMS applications
  Instructional designs and scripts for multimedia tutorials
  Audio scripts for IBM Marketing Education.
Developed and taught Indexing Skills Workshop for IBM ID Education.
Freelance work as a copy-writer, proofreader, and indexer

Figure 3-2.   Resume-type Capabilities Statement, First Page

OTHER WRITING EXPERIENCE

Grant-writing experience for theatre companies
Article for *Career Women*: "Finessing the Stress Interview"
Currently developing product reviews for several software publishers

COURSE DEVELOPMENT & TRAINING

Developed and taught computer courses (DOS, WordPerfect)
Trained customers in use of computer software and equipment
Developed and taught technical writing, editing and indexing courses
Produced instructional designs and scripts for interactive multimedia tutorials
Developed and taught courses on new VAX/VMS applications
Used knowledge gained through theatre experience to enhance both classroom and multimedia courses

EMPLOYMENT HISTORY

7/92 - Present   Freelance technical writer, editor, and indexer.

10/80 - 6/92   Project management, technical coordination,
                     contract management, course development, &
                     training IBM CORPORATION

1978 - 1980   Account representative, Bell Telephone

EDUCATION AND TRAINING

B.S. in Business Administration - Penn State

PROFESSIONAL AFFILIATIONS

Society for Technical Communication
American Society of Indexers
American Society for Development and Training

Figure 3-2 *continued.*   Resume-type Capabilities Statement, Second Page

Even so, the statement has some hyperbole in it, and is not quite as objective in tone as I would advocate for a document of this type. It should offer a great deal more detail about how TWI goes about doing things, and should describe some past projects, and physical and staffing resources.

Name: Walter Burkhart
Company: SoftServices
1000 E. Broadway, Suite 208
Philadelphia, PA 10999
Voice phone: 215/555-7071
Fax: 215/555-7072

SERVICES AVAILABLE

◆ Software-needs analysis and design
◆ Project Management
◆ Technical Writing.

I offer clients the development of custom database applications, the building of vertical market applications, and related technical writing. I also provide training in computer uses, via seminars, workshops, formal classes, and on the job training.

I undertake both short and long term consulting contracts that utilize my design and management skills for the purpsoes described.

EXPERIENCE AND PAST PROJECTS

◆ Developed a vertical market application for the apparel industry
◆ Developed and published an application for the mail order industry
◆ Written documentation for several major commercial packages
◆ Developed a database management system for a city government

Figure 3-3. Another Approach to a Capabilities Statement

The client wants to know how well you are equipped in all respects: relevant experience, physical facilities suitable for the requirements, proper equipment, and qualified staff. The contracting officials of government agencies will sometimes wish to visit and inspect your premises to verify your suitability to handle the work, if you are unknown to them. (They have good reason to do this. They have had their horror stories, such as bidders who have worked out of hotel rooms and used coin telephones as their resources.) The stronger your capability statement is, the less reason a client has to challenge your suitability as a

TECHNICAL WRITING INC. (TWI)
Services based on a solid engineering knowledge
111 Chase Circle
Franklintown, Illinois 60633
312-555-5000

A STATEMENT OF TWI CAPABILITIES

Services and Products

TWI addresses the needs of today's technology-based businesses by applying both engineering expertise and marketing experience to satisfy a wide range of technical writing, marketing, and advertising needs.

Specifically, TWI's capabilities include, but are not limited to the following capabilities, services, and products of our complete technical writing service:

- User Manuals for Operation, Training, and Maintenance
- Videotaped Presentations for Promotion or Education
- Newsletter Writing
- Multimedia Product Presentations on Computer Disk
- Overhead Presentations
- Direct Response Packages
- Advertising Copy and Layouts
- Press Releases
- Complete Press Kits
- Logo Development
- Publication Production Services

Background of the Firm

Technical Writing Services was founded by John J. Wilkens in 1978. In the course of managing three electronics manufacturing companies, Mr. Wilkens became increasingly conscious of the gulf between technical ability and marketing expertise that is a major problem in many high-tech organizations. Even the advertising agencies generally hired to help such companies with their marketing are typically staffed by individuals with graphic design experience, but lacking the technical know-how necessary to understand and market today's technical products and services.

Figure 3-4.   A More Professional Capabilities Statement, First Page

On the other hand, engineering personnel, while having in-depth knowledge of the company's products, are often too close to the product, producing documentation with little grasp of the typical user's need for detailed information and "hand holding."

Recognizing the need for a company with marketing capability and technical competence, John Wilkens created TWI, as an independent venture, using specialized freelance consultants as necessary.

TWI is engineering-based, with many years of experience in product marketing and business management. This enables us to get "up-to-speed" with any product or process very quickly, and guarantees the achievement of an optimal balance of technical information and clarity of communication. This then translates into high-quality documentation and effective promotional material produced efficiently and at reasonable rates.

Staffing Resources

Now in its 16th year of business, TWI has completed a number of projects which have capitalized on the combined engineering background and marketing experience of its staff. John Wilkens is the principal service provider of TWI. He is a member of the Institute of Electrical and Electronic Engineers. He founded TWI after more than 22 years experience in the management of high-tech manufacturing companies, including hands-on experience in manufacturing, product design, and marketing. His educational background includes a BSEE and MBA.

Mr. Wilkens personally leads and directs all projects, staffing them as necessary with carefully selected consultants and other specialists, as needed.

Physical Resources

TWI is equipped with the most up to date computer and related equipment, including the latest computer software programs. A list of all equipment and software available for TWI clients is included here as Appendix A.

Figure 3-4 *continued.*   A More Professional Capabilities Statement, Second Page

potential contractor. Listing references for the client to call is also reassuring of your legitimacy as a viable business service, even if the client does not call any of your references. Testimonial letters are also a great help in demonstrating capability.

THE SIZE OF A CAPABILITY STATEMENT

The size of a capability statement is not of any particular significance. In many cases, a statement of four or five pages has been ample to qualify as a competitor for quite large contracts. Remember, this is not a bid or proposal, but an application to be permitted to bid or propose. In fact, the typical client does not want to pore over a lengthy brochure, but appreciates a terse statement that furnishes all the information requested.

PART II

LETTERS AND NEWSLETTERS

4

GENERAL BUSINESS CORRESPONDENCE: INTRODUCTORY NOTES

To communicate in writing, you must know certain rules and principles of our language—spelling, punctuation, grammar, rhetoric, organization, and other guides to correct usage. But there is more, if you are to write *effectively:* You must know *what* you wish to say, as well as how to say it (i.e., to have planned ahead), and that is often the more difficult part of writing.

A STATEMENT OF INTENT

An explanation of intent is in order here because this book is not designed to be a how-to-write course per se, nor even a coverage of business writing in general. Rather, it is to be a guide to the preparation of letters, brochures, and related business instruments of greatest importance and most direct application to the success of your consulting practice. That will mean emphasis on those items that bear on winning clients and assignments. A major focus will be on models that may be adapted to your needs, rather than on training you in writing generally. Still, it is important that you have some understanding of broad objectives and principles of writing (i.e., what is necessary to write effectively and achieve your objectives); that is what writing effectively means. Hence, it is necessary to beg you to submit to reading a few brief lectures on the art of communicating in writing. We will then get on to specific examples and models that you can put to direct use.

A PRINCIPAL CAUSE OF "BAD" WRITING

Over some years as editor and manager of writing staffs in both technical and non-technical subjects and for a wide mix of media, I encountered my share of good and bad writing. One especially illuminating experience I had, as an editor, was that with a writer who delivered into my hands at RCA in New Jersey an account that purported to describe and explain the internal telephone system of the Thule, Greenland Ballistic Missile Early Warning System (BMEWS) installation of the United States Air Force.

The writer was a graduate of military training and service, as were a great many, probably most, technical writers of that day. He was an obviously bright and well trained young man, or else, he could not have been in this program at all. Certainly, he did not lack for basic intelligence and technical knowledge of the relevant subjects.

In reading his draft, I found it most difficult to understand the telephone system, especially the priority protocols, as he had described and explained the system in his manuscript. In despair and by necessity, I resorted to studying and analyzing the engineering schematic drawings, applying my own technical knowledge to the analysis, as I would if I were writing the manual myself. Technically, the system seemed to me to be straightforward enough, presenting no special difficulties of presentation. Yet the manuscript seemed to suggest to me that the writer really did not know the subject. Somewhat mystified therefore, I asked the author to confer with me.

"Duane," I said, "do you understand how the priority system works in routing calls in this system?" Duane assured me that he understood the system quite well.

I was not satisfied, so I probed his understanding further. Although I could see that Duane *believed* he understood the system, his manuscript suggested strongly to me that he did not, and nothing he said to me relieved my doubts. The simple fact was that I had been unable to understand the system from his manuscript, as I should have been. I had to analyze the engineering drawings for myself to understand it. (Of course, we could not expect the readers of the manual to do so.) Moreover, it was not any technical inaccuracy in Duane's manuscript that was responsible. What he had written was accurate enough, but there was an insufficiency of information. That is usually evidence of a conscious or even unconscious effort to brush swiftly by whatever areas the writer knows little or nothing about. I had learned by this time that this is usually due to a quite common fault: we humans appear to have an ability to persuade ourselves of things that are not so. As writers, we sometimes persuade ourselves that we understand something when we have at best only the most rudimentary understanding.

This is a writer's shortcoming that is usually apparent to an experienced editor who comes upon such a problem. Probably most editors assign the lack of necessary detail to laziness, however, whereas I have found it to be most often due to lack of knowledge, inadequate research and reflection. We have a reluctance, probably an unconscious one, to admit to ourselves that we are not yet prepared and ready, that we need to do some more research and thinking. We therefore often brush aside the details as unimportant to the overall purpose. It's an act of self-deceit, but not an uncommon one. I was convinced that such was the case here.

"Duane," I said, finally, "I am going to ask you to indulge me. Forget this manuscript, I will hold it here. Spend the next day or two studying these drawings, and then try again to explain the system from scratch."

A few days later, Duane turned in a much improved manuscript that I had no trouble understanding, editing, and processing for management's review. Duane had confirmed that what was wrong with his manuscript was his own lack of preparation: He really had not understood the system well enough, although he had been able to convince himself that he did and so brushed hurriedly past important technical details, probably persuading himself that they were unimportant and not necessary to describe.

This is not an uncommon problem. We are probably all guilty of it, at times, I certainly have been. However, as a professional writer, I have made this into a positive factor in writing. When I edit and review my own rough drafts, I am alert for such unconscious laziness (i.e., for lack of necessary detail). It dictates to me the need to do more research or more thinking and planning. Once you are aware that such a problem occurs often, even among professional writers, you can be alert for it. When you find yourself fuzzy on the details of the subject about which you are writing, it is probably time to turn back to research and planning before going further.

HOW IMPORTANT ARE RESEARCH AND DETAIL?

For many writers, research is the single most important element of their work. In many cases, what the writer reveals in the product is as little as one tenth the information uncovered by research. In fact, the art of researching is the major skill of many writers, even great writers, and is often the key to the writer's success. Even for the workaday individual writing letters and brochures, research is a must. It is necessary to know all the background, and in some detail, as a preliminary to deciding what your immediate objective is. Even more important to you as a somewhat reluctant (I presume) writer, the more information in detail you have at your disposal, the easier it is to set objectives, organize your presentation, and write it. For any writer, the piece, be it article, letter, book, or report, begins to almost write itself when you have gathered enough information and thus mastered the subject.

That is the substance of the matter: mastery of the subject. When you have achieved that, writing suddenly loses most of its terrors, and the words all but leap from your fingertips, almost unbidden, as you perfect your knowledge of the subject. (It may well be that the fear of writing lies largely in the reluctance to do the research.)

This means that if you wish to write an effective sales brochure, you need to understand marketing and selling in at least those respects that apply to the writing of a sales brochure. That would include understanding motivation: what wins a prospect's attention, stirs up interest, and provokes desire. It would also include some knowledge of layout that furthers that aim, however, for even having decided on a motivational strategy, it is necessary to implement it effectively—to "shout it," rather than whisper it, so that your message is heard clearly enough. We will thus not neglect these aspects of the job before us, as we go on.

BUSINESS CORRESPONDENCE:
WHAT DOES THE TERM MEAN?

Business writing today is varied in many ways. Once, the term referred mostly to letters exchanged among people in business and between business people and their customers or prospective customers. In a long ago era, business correspondence was rather stiff-necked and almost unbearably formal. The current month was referred to as the "instant" (often abbreviated to "inst," as in "In response to yours of the 12th inst"), and the general tone was one of ultra-polite self-deprecation a la the Chinese custom of super humility, with some business people signing their letters, "Your obedient servant."

Fortunately, that era has passed into a well-deserved obscurity, despite the reluctance of a few graybeards and their disciples to relinquish their grasp on obfuscating formality. The trend today is to state the case as clearly and as briefly as possible, while exercising reasonable tact and diplomacy. Moreover, no longer do those terms refer entirely to letters exchanged between businesses and their customers, but includes a large number of other types of written documentation and presentations. Still, even that element of business writing that does consist primarily of correspondence has evolved and become increasingly diverse in modern times, so that it makes sense to treat it as a separate section of this book. In fact, so extensive is the range of just this field of business writing that many complete books, sets of audio tapes, and computer software programs on the market deal with nothing but business letters.

Thus the very term *business correspondence* refers to letters, almost by definition. However, the basic term *letter* has itself acquired a somewhat flexible meaning in today's business world, stretched somewhat in many applications. For example, while a formal proposal is often quite a ponderous document—those for major programs, have often run to thousands of pages—an informal proposal is often referred to as a *letter proposal* because essentially that is what it is, a letter. It consists of only a few pages in which a proposal is offered. Similarly, a simple and informal contract is often called a *Letter of Agreement* or *Letter of Understanding* because it is such a simple, often single-page, document. (In the urgent atmosphere of the fifties, the Department of Defense often authorized work on very large contracts with a "Letter of Intent" or "Letter Contract," so that the beginning of urgent work would not have to wait for a formal contract to be drawn up.) Hence, such closely related presentations are covered in this second part, treated under the general heading of business correspondence. To give you a little idea in advance of the diversity of such presentations, in this part we will offer ideas, information, and models falling into the following categories:

- Answering inquiries
- Offering services
- Explaining services
- Presenting credentials
- Responding to complaints
- Adjusting errors of billing or other slipups
- Explaining delays
- Making inquiries of various kinds
- Reporting results to clients
- Requesting payment
- Miscellaneous other matters, essentially routine.

Even with such segregation of correspondence, there is a great diversity in the correspondence. The diversity is not only in the general classes, purposes, and functions of correspondence: It is also introduced by the great variety of the business enterprises that have evolved over the years. So it is not a simple proposition, despite our focus here on the needs of the independent consultant: Many independent consultants engage in diverse business activities in addition to basic consulting services, and there will be no effort in these pages to offer a model for each and every possible need—it would be an entirely impracticable goal—but principles and exemplifying models will be offered to point the way, with guidance to help you adapt these principles and models to meet your own special needs.

WRITING IS SIMPLER THAN YOU THINK

One problem in writing a book of this kind is that too many who teach writing make it appear to be a far more complex and difficult art than it is. The truth is that by following just a few simple rules, anyone with a grade school education—and that includes all or nearly all of us—can write effectively. No, you won't produce great literature, but the idea is not to write poetry, but to express ideas and convey information with clarity. Consider the following few basics of writing letters or anything else that are, in fact, basic to all writing.

Planning

Yes, even a simple letter must be planned, if it is to do what you want it to do. A long letter, such as some we will discuss later, may even require a written outline, but all letters (and all writing) require that you know where you want to go if you are to have any realistic hope of getting there. (More on this will be said later; it is that important.)

Simplicity

Even the expert writer has trouble when he or she gets into complex writing structures, and some of our most successful writers—Ernest Hemingway, for example—deliberately chose to use the simplest writing styles they could. (Hemingway, in fact, related how he learned to do so early in his career when he worked for a newspaper editor who impressed on him the need for simplicity of style. Those lessons stayed with him the rest of his life.)

The following are the measures that help you keep your writing style simple and easy to understand:

- Have a specific objective or goal for the letter or whatever it is you are writing. Never begin until you know with certainty just what you want to achieve, such as answer a question, explain something, provide a report, defend yourself, sell an idea, or give an accounting.

- Express one idea per sentence. You should have some specific purpose or idea to convey for each sentence, and that sentence should not go beyond that idea. Save the next idea for the next sentence. Use simple sentence structure: a noun or pronoun (subject of the sentence), a verb, and, when necessary, an objective. Then stop and go on to the next sentence.

- Stick to the point. Do not introduce any information or ideas that are not relevant to the point you want to make or to the objective of whatever it is you are writing.

- Use words that are familiar to most people and used in everyday conversation. (Never mind whether they are "long" or "short" words.) Use "undertaker" when you mean undertaker, for example; almost everyone knows what an undertaker is, but not everyone knows what "mortician," means. As Samuel Clemens is reported to have remarked, he never wasted space and energy writing "metropolis" when he meant "city."

- Use active and direct voice. Not "Company policy dictates that a 5 percent service charge must be made on all accounts over 30 days old," but, "We make a 5 percent service charge on all accounts more than 30 days old." Not "Customers are advised that in event of difficulty the unit should be sent to one of our authorized service dealers for repair," but "If unit malfunctions, bring or send it to any of our authorized service dealers for repair."

- Keep paragraphs short. Like sentences, paragraphs should have only one central idea, the one that was introduced in the first sentence. When you have finished with that idea, start a new paragraph. But only if you have a new idea to discuss.

Other Considerations

You should keep a good dictionary at hand and verify all spellings, if you are not absolutely sure of their correctness. Of course, if you are using a word processor, it is wise to have a spell checker review your draft before you print it. (I am quite a good speller, but my own spell checker turns up enough spelling errors—and typos—to make using it indispensable to me.)

Edit your own copy. This is especially important, for it is the "secret" of good writing. No professional writer ever lets his copy go without at least one cycle of self-editing and review, with rewriting as necessary. Almost all writers overwrite, but don't worry about it in writing first drafts because they intend to edit and revise later. Major functions of editing are reducing redundancy, simplifying language, and smoothing the flow of thought. Editing and rewriting are necessary to achieve that. So read what you have drafted, change all the $5 words to 50-cent ones, eliminate all the extraneous stuff that really has nothing to do with what you are trying to say, and rewrite it into a simple and straightforward, hopefully brief, message. Be sure that you don't run on. When you have delivered your message, stop. (That is one of the basic rules of selling and writing anything. Even a letter is an effort to sell something, if only an idea.)

Decide in Advance Precisely What You Want to Say— The Point of Your Letter

If there are three rules for writing well, this could easily be all three of them, for this identifies the most common problem: Far too many people write letters (and other things) without knowing exactly what they want to say. They simply doodle verbally, in fact, as though they were engaged in idle conversation over tea, in the hope that eventually they will stumble across the right thoughts and words. It rarely works, and even when it does the result is that much of it is rambling and pointless and most certainly not at all businesslike. (Have you ever gotten a letter that left you mumbling to yourself, "What are they trying to tell me?) In short, if you don't know clearly and in advance what you want to say, how can you ever be sure that you have said it?

Remember to Sell

In all things generally, but in all business writing especially, you must always sell. That means writing persuasively, no matter what the subject of the letter. Even a response to an inquiry can benefit or hurt your organization by presenting a favorable or unfavorable view of it. (Do not use those cold and stilted form letters of government agencies and many corporations that create that adverse image so many of us have of government agencies and major corporations.)

Do not be any more formal than circumstances and good taste dictate. Obviously you must address strangers and those you know only slightly by such titles as Mister, Madam, Colonel, and so forth. In the real business world, executives often address business letters to "Dear Bill" and sign them "Harry," when they happen to be friends or business associates of long standing. However, before leaving this introduction and going on to present a few specific examples, let us have a brief look at planning, which is principally a system of outlining your material, once you have set your goal, although the importance of that preliminary step ought not to be minimized either.

THE PLANNING PROCESS

The planning process for any piece of writing, however long or short and formal or informal, involves the same steps, although the method for doing them may vary considerably from one case to another. For a lengthy document, it may be wise or even necessary to develop a formal "book plan," a written plan detailing all the many steps preliminary to drafting the item. For a simple writing job, such as a brief letter, all the planning may be in your mind, with nothing formal on paper, but that is a difference in degree, not in kind. Many journalists and other professional writers use a "lead" as the planning document for a short article (I confess to being one who does so), and we may write and rewrite that lead many times before going on, as our way of planning and outlining, but we don't proceed, usually, until we are sure that we have that lead—plan—right.

I don't know that the "lead" method works for everyone. As one writer expressed it to me once, for him it was "thinking on paper." I happen to agree with that. I find that scratching out a lead "on paper" (actually on a computer screen now) helps me think things out. As I "see" what is wrong with my first attempt, I begin editing and revising my rough-draft lead until it seems right to me: It defines and sets the goal, as it should; the reader should get a firm clue from your first sentence or first paragraph of what you are about to tell him or her. But let's look at the three major stages:

1. Setting a goal or objective: What is it you want to do with this letter or other writing? Provide information? Placate an unhappy client? Report progress? Sell an idea? Ask for the order? Ask for payment? Request an interview? Explain the problem? Reassure the client?
2. Choosing a strategy: How do you plan to achieve this goal or objective? Logical argument? Promise of something? Offer to trade? Reinforce your guarantee?
3. Outlining: What information will you present and how?

Goal-Setting

Earlier, I offered a list of types of letters, essentially routine. In fact, these designators or definitions specify or imply an objective for each of those types of letters. Before you can even begin to formulate a letter, you need to know just what you want the letter to do. If you want to placate a dissatisfied and complaining client, that requires a much different letter than the one you will send to a client who wants to be assured that you understand their problem and can solve it satisfactorily, or the client who wants to know what progress you have made on his or her problem and when you will have the project concluded. Sometimes the distinctions are rather subtle, but it is necessary to make those distinctions and be sure you know what you are talking about before you commit yourself in writing. It is damaging to your image and reputation to have a client or prospect write you to straighten out your misunderstanding of the client's need or other want. It is thus usually well worth your time to do all the investigation and cerebration necessary to ensure that you are addressing the right problem before you write that letter.

Choosing a Strategy

The first element in devising a strategy is getting a good understanding of what the other party, your intended reader, wants. If you are responding to a complaint from a client, a defensive letter will not do. The client wants to be soothed, reassured that you know that you "done him wrong" and will make things right. That may be to apologize, make a price adjustment, explain why you went astray, offer some extra effort, do something over, or otherwise. It is important that you are *responsive*, that you demonstrate an understanding of the other's expressed want and offer a satisfying response to it, whatever that may be. Nothing very mysterious about the strategy in that case. For example, let us suppose that a client writes to complain that you are taking too long to complete a project for which you contracted. You would like to tell the client that the fault is his for not giving you complete information to begin with or not giving you total cooperation, but this is a client you do not wish to antagonize because he can offer you large and important contracts. You are thus willing to "eat" a few extra hours to keep the client's good will. What is the best strategy for a response?

It is never a good strategy to tell the client, "It's your own fault," even when it is, if you want to keep that client. It is better to invent a polite fiction, such as, "I regret the delay. Once well into the project, we uncovered a few factors we did not know about at the beginning, and rather than ignoring them, we acted in your best interests by extending our schedule a bit to cover these contingencies at no extra cost to you." It is difficult for a client to complain too loudly in the face of this kind of explanation.

On the other hand, if you are sending out a letter that is an initiative going out to strangers, you need to be clear as to what presumed want of the reader you are appealing. That should be made clear up front, as close to the opening message as possible, as in these examples:

- "If the cost of excessive inventory is a problem you would like to solve, we have a service that ought to be of interest to you."
- "We have recently helped four clients reduce the time for running their payroll by nearly one-half. Here is how we did it."
- "Last month we helped eleven clients find the skilled personnel they wanted in record time. We do that every month."
- "We have a new and different approach to physical plant security, and would like to demonstrate it at no cost to you."
- "Most warehouses are less than totally efficient in both storage and shipping. We have some radically new ideas that work and save you money. We would like to tell you about them here and then show them to you."

Successful strategies are based on the same factors on which selling is based: To sell a prospect something, you offer them whatever it is they want (or what you infer the other wants) and a convincing argument (persuasion) that you can deliver that. We will talk about this at greater length when discussing sales documents per se, but it is appropriate to every writing situation. People will believe what they want to believe much more readily than they will accept what they don't want to believe. Here are a few general rules concerning strategies:

- Some people like the idea of innovation. They like and welcome change. There are others who fear new ideas and methods. They fear risk and possible failure, and prefer to stick with what they believe to be "tried and true." The success of any strategy depends on your selecting the right one for the people you are dealing with—on understanding your readers. If they are a mixed bag, a general population and unknown to you, take the middle road, and when you offer anything new and different, explain how carefully thought out and risk-free it really is, while still refreshingly new and novel.
- The success of any strategy depends in part on how much confidence the other party has in you, your competence, intelligence, understanding of their needs, and personal honesty and integrity. Work at establishing these in whatever ways are available, such as presenting both

cons and pros, demonstrating your understanding of the others' concerns, and minimizing, if not entirely avoiding, the use of hyperbole.

Outlining Your Material

A formal outline of what you want to write is always a good idea, even for a short piece, and is all but mandatory for longer ones. Perhaps you can do the outlining for a really short piece (e.g., a letter) in your head, if writing comes easily to you. Otherwise, it's a good idea to get the practice of outlining, even for the short piece. (The alternative is likely to be several rough drafts that have to be totally discarded before you get one that you can revise, rewrite, and polish into final shape.) Outlining will thus serve more than one useful purpose:

- You can determine how complete and adequate your knowledge of the subject is by your ability to include details (or your lack of ability to do so).
- You can spot any deficiencies and determine what additional information you need, if any, to make your research complete.
- You can perceive the best order in which to arrange your topics to reach your desired objective.
- You can examine alternative presentation strategies and select one that seems most suitable for you.

To be useful, an outline must include detail. If you were writing a technical manual, you might be handed a rough outline by the client that included such items as the following:

I. Maintenance
    A. Preventive
    B. Corrective
    C. Overhaul and repair

That isn't much help. It may be the client's way of telling you what is to be covered, but you can't plan a manual at that level. You need to get into far more detailed levels, at least the following:

I. Maintenance
   A. Preventive
      1. Lubrication
         a. Schedules and frequency
         b. Points to lubricate
         c. Lubricants to use
   B. Inspection
      1. Schedules and frequency
      2. Points to inspect
      3. What to inspect for
   Etc.

GRAMMAR AND OTHER MECHANICS OF USAGE

I said earlier that this is not to be a general course in writing, but that does not relieve me totally of the responsibility to mention such important subjects as grammar and the other principles and rules for using the English language effectively.

First of all, as you know, no language in everyday usage is static, perhaps least of all English. Spellings of many words have changed, but that is not all that has changed. Most of us today favor the school of "open punctuation," which means a more sparing use of commas and other marks of punctuation than was once the custom. Splitting an infinitive was once a cardinal sin, but is accepted today if meaning or fluency is compromised in order to avoid splitting the infinitive. For many kinds of writing, non-sentences or sentence fragments are now acceptable, as a stylistic preference.

What it all means is that the so-called "rules" that were instilled in most of us as students are not hard and fast, but are *principles* reflecting the opinions of those deemed well qualified to recommend principles of usage. Samuel Clemens, writing as Mark Twain, objected violently to editors tampering with his punctuation. He insisted that no editor could possibly know as well as he just what meaning or shade of meaning he intended and so must not disturb his punctuation at all.

The most important principles of usage are those ensuring clear communication of intended meaning. Any writing that fails to deliver to the reader the message that the sender intended is poor writing, even if it faithfully follows all the dictates of the most honored texts on usage.

Thus I recommend to you the texts listed at the end of this chapter as excellent guides, among many others.

RECOMMENDED REFERENCES

Bates, Jefferson D, Writing with Precision: How to Write So That You Cannot Be Misunderstood, Acropolis Books, 1978
Strunk, William, The Elements of Style, Macmillan, 1972
Zinsser, William, On Writing Well: An Informal Guide to Writing Nonfiction, Harper Perennial, 1990

$$\text{—— } 5 \text{ ——}$$

GENERAL CLIENT CORRESPONDENCE

There are so many occasions and reasons for correspondence that there is little hope of exemplifying or illustrating all of them but we can predict and discuss the most common ones.

THE SPECIAL NATURE OF GENERAL CORRESPONDENCE WITH CLIENTS

There is no shortage of books on letter writing in general and in business especially. Most cover the gamut of needs and applications, with models for all. The coverage in this chapter, and in this entire book, is addressed to a more narrow range, that of subjects directly or closely related to the successful operation of your practice.

Inevitably, therefore, all documents concerned directly with winning clients and sales get first priority, and those only indirectly connected with winning sales get a lower order of priority. That does not mean that correspondence with clients is unimportant. It does mean, however, that attention in these pages is focused on whatever it takes to make your practice more successful. Priority is given to correspondence with clients and prospective clients, primarily, and with any individual or organization who may be influential in sending you clients or otherwise affecting your success in winning clients and contracts.

This chapter offers ideas and models for general business correspondence and exchanges among individuals and organizations in situations that affect sales and client relationships primarily. They cover situations that are common to most businesses and organizations offering professional services, situations that you are likely to encounter and which are likely to affect you and your practice significantly in one way or another in terms of your professional success. These ideas and models may extend and apply not only to corporations and other business organizations, but also to others with whom you may do business (e.g., nonprofit organizations such as associations and government agencies).

Among the broad class of situations or needs and relevant correspondence, are these in the following short list of examples:

- Responding to inquiries
- Making inquiries
- Confirming appointments
- Requesting bids/quotations
- Reporting progress/results
- Responding to complaints
- Explaining delays
- Transmitting responses to bids/quotations
- Requesting payment
- Making informal agreements

RESPONDING TO INQUIRIES FROM PROSPECTIVE CLIENTS

As you make yourself more and more visible as a consultant, you will receive a number of inquiries to which you must respond. In many cases, you may be able to respond with a form letter, a capability statement, and/or one or more brochures. In other cases, you will have to compose a letter to make a proper response, although you may be able to base the letter on one of the models you will find here.

There are many situations that affect the way you must respond to inquiries. Some of the situations create or reflect problems that must be investigated and solved before you can respond as you would wish. In some cases, circumstances affect or even dictate how you must respond. For example, some inquiries may be from prospective clients, with potential contracts in the balance, while others will be from individuals and organizations who can or will do little more than waste your time. Much of the mail you will receive each morning, as your name becomes more and more widely known and is added to a countless number of mailing lists that are rented to marketers everywhere, is what many refer to as "junk mail." That is, it is advertising, seeking to sell you something. Some of it is rather cleverly disguised to make it appear to be personal mail, offering you great business opportunities. Soon enough, you will begin to recognize these offers for what they are, but at first you may not. You must therefore regard every letter from a strange source with a reasonable degree of skepticism and not dissipate your time and energies in responses to such items. You will not want to ignore inquiries that may lead to new clients and substantial contracts. Therefore, read them carefully, and be alert for possible worthy offers or true business possibilities. Not everything that looks like junk mail is junk mail.

One note of caution: Do not be too hasty in judging. There are many successful business proprietors who are of the "self-made" school: They may have begun life with few advantages, had little formal education, and therefore write in a manner that is not the most cogent or fluent expression. Despite this, they may choose to write their own letters of inquiry. Not too long ago, for example, I made an inquiry of the proprietor of a dealership where I had purchased an automobile. It happens to be a dealership owned by a man who owns several other successful automobile dealerships, and whose business assets run to many millions of dollars, a most successful businessman. I got a scrawled, handwritten note in response from the gentleman, an entrepreneur well known in the entire metropolitan area as a frequent advertiser on TV, among other reasons. He could easily have had someone on the staff of one of his several dealerships compose a letter for him or send me a brochure or two, but he chose to respond to me personally. Many highly successful, distinguished, individuals are equally unassuming. It would, of course, be a mistake to underestimate their importance as prospective clients.

Aside from that, each situation or set of circumstances will affect how you must respond. However, there are some general rules that are appropriate for guidance in responding to inquiries of any sort, including suggested guidelines for coping with typical inquiries. The following are a few injunctions that I recommend to all as sensible guidelines.

Be Sure You Understand the Inquiry

Take the time to read carefully and understand the inquiry completely. If it is a telephone inquiry and exchange, be at pains to ask the right questions. If it is an illegible or incoherent scrawled message from someone who took the inquiry by telephone, call the inquirer and find out what the inquiry is before attempting to compose an answer. Be absolutely sure you know precisely what the inquirer wants. So often, one gets a hasty response to an inquiry that is totally and irritatingly irrelevant. Few things create a worse impression than a response that indicates complete failure to understand the inquiry, suggesting the letter of inquiry was not read. Another is getting a fancy, colored brochure extolling the company or its products, when you asked for a simple quotation or why your request has not been followed up. Unfortunately, the response you get often has no discernible connection with the matter about which you wrote, and leaves you scratching your head in bewilderment. (Despite all the efforts to overcome this kind of problem, letters arriving from bureaucracies, such as government taxing agencies, often give us vexing exercises in trying to determine just what the letters say. You may be familiar with this situation as a rather common one.)

Be Sure You Understand the Problem

If a problem is involved—and be sure to determine if there is a problem to be solved (e.g., permitting something to slip between the cracks, getting the wrong report, not getting what was ordered, items missing, your program not working correctly, or other such all-too-typical business problems) it is essential that you understand the problem exactly and precisely. You won't be able to respond intelligently if you do not have a clear picture of what the original message was all about, although you may have to spend a little time studying the original message. Otherwise, you may then risk complicating the problem, instead of solving it, and quite possibly then be faced with the new and additional problem of trying to placate an indignant and outraged client.

Be Sure You Understand What the Client Wants You to Do

It is not always apparent immediately what a client wants or expects you to do as a direct result of the call or letter. It is easy enough to assume something and to make the wrong assumption. First of all, there is often a difference between what the client wants as an end result and what the client wants as an immediate action. A client with a malfunctioning product may want the product repaired or replaced, but not necessarily expect you to do the repair or make the replacement: The client may want you to intercede with the manufacturer to provide the repair or replacement. (My own computer guru has done that for me on more than one occasion.) The client may simply want your expert opinion and recommendation. (I sometimes call my computer guru for that, too, often to assure myself that my decision was a correct one.) It is easy to misunderstand the client's wishes and intentions, which can lead to trouble. I once worked for a chief engineer who managed to avoid this problem by repeating what another said to him and asking verification (i.e., "Let's see, you want me to okay a change from a 12-second response to a 15-second response? Do I have that right?"). It did not prevent problems, but it did minimize misunderstandings.

Be clear in your own mind, therefore, as to whether what the client wants is the same thing the client expects or asks you to do. One successful consultant I knew, Sam G., alienated his most important client because familiarity bred contempt. Sam had worked with the client for so long that he fell into the practice of not listening carefully to what his client asked him to do. Often, he decided that he understood the client's needs better than the client did. He thus began to tell the client what he thought the client really needed and should have, regardless of what the client requested. Asked for a quotation or bid for some need the client had specified, Sam would actually provide a bid or quotation for something quite different, advising the client that this was what the client really needed. Eventually, he lost that key account as a result, wounding his business quite severely.

Give a Direct and Honest, but Tactful, Answer

Do not temporize or evade the issue in some other manner. If you cannot give a final or definitive answer for some reason, state so clearly and frankly, but tactfully, with reasons for your inability to do exactly what the inquirer wants. (For example, if you need more information, ask for it or suggest whatever is necessary as a preliminary to supplying whatever the inquirer asked for.) If you must say no, say no nicely and in a thoughtful and friendly way. Amazingly often, simple logical responses to inquiries appear somehow to be hostile and antagonistic, even when the writer does not intend to give that impression. Being too businesslike may come across to the other party as being curt or impatient. People who write to ask for your expert opinion are probably groping somewhat uncertainly, and surely do not want to be made to feel like fools. Remember that while many people have the hide of a rhinoceros and are not easily offended, many others are quite sensitive and will perceive insult even where none was intended unless you are quite careful and tactful in expressing yourself.

Be Brief (but Not Brusque)

Come to the point as quickly as possible and don't stray unnecessarily, but be sure that your memo or fax has a pleasant tone. The other person's time is probably as valuable as yours is, and he or she also does not wish to waste it. They also don't want to feel "brushed off," as they might if your response appears to be brusque. Businesslike brevity is itself a display of courtesy, as wasting another's time is strongly suggestive of discourtesy, but you can always sign a message "Cordially" or "Warmest regards," to indicate friendliness. Be careful not to *appear* impatient or hurried. Most of all, never do anything to make the client feel unimportant. Quite the contrary, do everything you can to achieve the opposite effect. Every client *is* important, and you should never hesitate to make that obvious to them.

Answer Promptly

Unfortunately, many businesses today take weeks to respond to inquiries with even a brief letter, resulting in many sales and much good will lost. I have known executives of companies with whom I have dealt admit to me quite frankly that they do not take letters as seriously as they do telephone calls. Their philosophy is that if the matter were really important, the other party would have called or faxed a message, and so they feel quite justified in taking a month or more to respond to a letter.

Their rationale is nonsense, of course, and is much more likely an excuse than a reason. There are many reasons for writing, instead of calling, such as establishing a record. In any case, any message from a client or prospective client is important and merits immediate acknowledgment, if not immediate resolution. I make it a practice to respond within 24 hours maximum to all orders and inquiries, with a simple acknowledgment on the rare occasions when I cannot offer a more substantive response immediately. I mail most things first class, even when they are substantial packages, and I use air mail for all overseas correspondence. I find clients suitably grateful at getting such prompt reaction. Often, in fact, they are not only pleased but agreeably surprised because they have become somewhat accustomed to responses being at a snail's pace.

The message is simple enough: Feel and show suitable appreciation of the client and his or her patronage. Many books of the past few years have stressed this message, but some have not been listening, and they have vanished from the marketplace as a result.

I am myself quite annoyed by suppliers who do not respond promptly to my orders or requests for information, and am thus prejudiced against doing business with them again. Even if a sale or possible sale is not at stake, common courtesy and, especially, public relations considerations should dictate a prompt and courteous response. If you get and value word-of-mouth sales promotion, do not neglect the benefits of a reputation for prompt response.

Aside from that, there is this practical consideration: I find that any delay in answering always increases the possibility that the inquiry will never get answered at all. It is likely to become lost among the many "things to do" that never get done, resulting almost certainly in ill will and/or lost sales. I recently ceased, sadly and regretfully, doing business with a software developer principally because they failed to respond to my repeated inquiries regarding delays in shipment, and I canceled an order today, having lost patience. I would have waited patiently for the late shipments had they answered my letters or returned my telephone calls promptly, but their failure to respond at all caused me to lose faith in the firm and to cancel my orders outstanding with them. If, for some reason, you cannot make a satisfactory response immediately (e.g., you must investigate something before you can respond), a brief note explaining that the matter is not being neglected, but it will take a few days to respond fully, will usually placate the other party. *Any* response, if it is prompt, is better than a great response that is delayed at length. You may even use a form letter for this. Many entrepreneurs use a simple post card to assure a client that the order has been received and is being processed as promptly as possible.

Prepare the Groundwork for Follow-Up

Make notes to plan the sales follow-up if the inquiry appears to be a sales lead, as so many are, laying the groundwork in your letter for that follow-up. Inquirers are generally good prospects and inquiries thus become virtual invitations to pursue sales. But follow-up must be prompt and direct, and the principles of selling dictate that you should prepare the prospect to expect follow-up where that is an appropriate action. Do, however, respond specifically to the inquiry first.

There are a few general observations following. They apply to all letter writing, and not especially to responses to inquiries, but it is as well to point these things out here and now.

Use a Friendly (but Not Familiar) Tone

Use the less formal and friendlier "I," instead of "we," unless the situation mandates the use of the plural pronoun. The use of "we" when you mean "I" is outdated (by about a century, in fact) and more impersonal than it has to be or ought to be. Be informal generally, although not excessively familiar.

Use Proper Salutations

Proper salutations today are generally Dear Mr., Mrs., Ms., etc., rather than the more archaic Sir or Madam. Use them whenever possible. Try to avoid using the salutations of yesteryear; they suggest that you are sending the other a cold and impersonal form letter. However, you may use first names when you know the other party well enough, or they address you by first name. (I get many inquiries from strangers who address me by first name because they have read my books, columns, or messages on electronic bulletin boards, and they feel that they may be that informal because I write in an informal style. In such cases, I respond similarly.)

Many problems arise in finding the right salutation. Sometimes a writer uses only initials, such as B. K. Jones, so that you have no way of knowing whether the inquiry is from a man or a woman. Often enough women write and give no clue as to whether they are Miss, Mrs., or prefer to be addressed as "Ms."

One way to solve this is to address the letter to Dear B. K. Jones or Dear Lilian Smith. That is perfectly proper, although it has become a commonplace today to use the form Dear Ms. Smith, when you know the other party is a woman, and is also quite acceptable. (Still, it is not always easy to tell gender with names such as "Tony," "Terry," and "Bobby.")

In many cases protocol or standard practices of courtesy in our society dictates that the individual you are addressing is entitled to be addressed by his or her title. Retired military officers, for example, usually are addressed by their rank at the time of retirement—major, colonel, general. Officers on duty or retired are addressed by the higher or more general of their ranks when it is a compound noun: Both second and first lieutenants are addressed as Lieutenant, both lieutenant colonels and full colonels as Colonel, all ranks of general as General, etc.

Government has its own protocol generally, with respect to correspondence and forms of address. By now probably everyone knows that the President is always addressed as Mr. President, even by intimate friends, and the proper complimentary close is Sincerely, as it is with other government officials, elected and appointed. In most cases—cabinet members, under secretaries, assistant secretaries, heads of other agencies, special assistants to the president, senators, representatives, judges, ambassadors, and most other government dignitaries—the proper address is The Honorable (full name), followed by the title if the individual has another title, such as Secretary of State, Special Assistant to the President, Speaker of the House, Committee Chairman, or other. Foreign ambassadors are addressed as His or Her Excellency, followed by the ambassador's full name. Then, that protocol observed and courtesy accorded, the direct address may be made to Dear Senator Willoughby, Dear Madam Secretary, or whatever is appropriate.

There are occasions when you must address a company and do not know of any individual in the company. "To whom it may concern" is somewhat outdated and smacks too much of a preprinted form letter. It is far better, usually, to address the letter to whatever functional title you think most appropriate, such as Dear Marketing Manager. Someone at the other end will see to it that it gets into the right hands, undoubtedly.

Complimentary Closes

The same philosophy applies generally to complimentary closings: they should be friendly and informal, without becoming overly familiar, but should be suitable for the occasion. One friendly closing that can be used in a great many cases is "Cordially," but you may also use such closings as "Thank you, With best wishes, Warmest regards, In sincerest appreciation" or another such friendly and informal closing if it fits the situation and relationship. Still in widespread use are several slightly more formal closings: Sincerely, Yours truly, Very truly yours, or others of a similar nature, all perfectly proper. ("Sincerely" is generally considered proper in writing to government dignitaries and for other formal or semiformal uses.) For many cases, where you are well acquainted with the addressee, you may sign off with Regards, As always, or some other informal close.

Form Letters

With today's facilities, computers (desktop, laptop, and main-frame) and word processors it is easy to turn out form letters that appear to be custom-written. Still, it is easy enough to make mistakes that signal the reader that the letter is a form sent to all. I recently got a thank you letter from an author who had asked me to write a few paragraphs he could use in his book. His letter thanked me for "contributing to or helping me with my book." Had he eliminated the phrase "contributing to or," I would not have known that this was a form letter, but his phrasing was a dead giveaway that he was thanking two classes of helpers. I have also been addressed in letters as "Dear Mr. Reports" by people who had rented a mailing list that had picked me up from my advertisement for "Herman Holtz Reports." That kind of thing results from people sending out letters en masse using "mail merge" software to turn out form letters addressed individually to respondents today. (The system prints each letter individually, but pulls the name, address, and proper salutation from a list of names and addresses in a database management program.) It is even easier to do with random correspondence: You have the form letter in your computer files, and you need type in only the proper name, address, and salutation.

Frequently, you can handle inquiries with such a simple form letter, individually addressed, and in some cases enclosing a brochure or other material.

In the 1990s, "Correspondence" refers primarily to conventional mail, but also to many other kinds of communication. There is the increasingly omnipresent fax, of course, but there is also e-mail, transmitted by computers to other computers and then available to recipients as characters painted on a screen or as a message printed out in paper. The sample "letters" in the following sections apply equally to all of these types of communication. It is only the mode of transmission that varies.

I am not going to attempt here to cover all ten classes of correspondence referred to earlier, but only to a random sampling. Some of these will be covered in much greater depth in Chapter 6.

A FEW MODELS OF RESPONSES TO INQUIRIES

Figures 5-1 through 5-4 are a few models of letters responding to inquiries of various kinds. Note the use of "I" and "my," as well as "we" and "our." Grammarians and others deemed to be authoritative are divided in their opinions of usage, with respect to personal pronouns. Many credit de Montaigne (Michel Eyquem) with inspiring a change from the traditional "we" to the more modern "I" in writing, as deduced from his own writings, but it was Mark Twain (Samuel Clemens) who put it more pungently as, "Only editors, royalty, and people with tapeworm ought to say 'we' when they mean 'I.'" You may feel more comfortable using the "we" and "our" euphemisms, despite being a one-person venture, especially if you use a trade name (e.g., Success Associates, Inc.), rather than trading under your personal name. You are free to use either set of pronouns, of course.

Dear Mr. Prospective Client:

I am most pleased to send you my brochure and capability statement, as you requested, to explain my services and areas of special experience. I believe that you will find these of interest vis-a-vis your own needs for direct marketing support.

I would be quite happy to meet with you or your staff, at your convenience, to discuss your needs specifically, answer any questions you have, and explore the ways in which I can help you. Please feel free to call me at any time for additional information of any sort.

Cordially,

Figure 5-1.   Sample Letter Describing Consulting Services

Dear Mrs. Prospective Subscriber:

We are pleased to enclose a sample copy of our newsletter, per your request. I hope that you will find it appropriate to your needs and expectations.

Also enclosed are forms for subscribing. We look forward to adding your name to our list of subscribers.

Cordially,

Figure 5-2. Sample Letter to a Prospective Newsletter Subscriber

Dear Senator Willoughby:

I regret that the demand for our Report No. G-764-AT-34 was so great that we have completely exhausted our stock, so I am unable to comply immediately with your request for three copies of this report. The size of this report is such that duplicating three copies by office copier would be impractical. However, the report is currently being reprinted, as a result of the unexpected great demand, and additional copies should be available in a few days.

I will, of course, send you three copies by special messenger as soon as the copies arrive here.

I hope that this will satisfy your need. In the meanwhile, if you wish you are welcome to visit and examine our file copy.

Sincerely,

Figure 5-3. Sample Response to a Request for Information

Such correspondence need not be embellished with flowery phrases, as was once the custom. They should, of course, be courteous, but in most cases, they can be brief and to the point—businesslike. In many cases, an enclosure of some sort—a brochure, flyer, or sample of some kind—may be in order. That helps expedite answering and keeps your letter brief, thus easing your writing task itself.

Dear Dr. Carter:

Thank you for your interest and letter. We are pleased to have been able, as part of our service, to recommend an item of equipment that appears to be suitable to your need.

Unfortunately, we are not in a position to furnish more details of the equipment than have appeared in the brochure we sent you originally, describing the Excalibur office copier. However, we have forwarded your request to the marketing department of the manufacturer, Excalibur Office Equipment, Inc., and you should be hearing directly from them in response to your inquiry.

Please let us know if you have any difficulties in getting the information you need.

Sincerely.

Figure 5-4.   Sample Follow-Up Letter

Bear in mind, always, the difference between responding to inquiries as a purely routine administrative need and responding to inquiries that hold the promise of business for you. The latter are at least potential sales or leads to sales, and your responses should be written with that prospect in mind (i.e., with the expectation of following up in some manner, probably a telephone call attempting to set up a meeting with the prospective client, after the client has had time to read the materials you enclosed). In those cases, use your response to establish a basis for follow-up. At the least, in such cases, you will make follow-up mailings to the prospect. (More on this later, in discussing sales correspondence.)

MAKING INQUIRIES

It is often necessary, in the course of business, to make your own inquiries, as well as to respond to inquiries by others. In fact, an inquiry made of you may lead you to find it necessary to make a counter-inquiry. This correspondence, like that above, may sometime have a direct or indirect linkage to sales prospects. Figures 5-5 and 5-6 are two samples of such letters of inquiry you might wish to make.

Dear Colonel Potter:

Acme Marketing Professionals, Inc. specializes in supporting companies such as your own through guidance, counseling, and related custom services in direct response marketing via all media. Having read descriptions of several contract awards made by your company to our competitors, I believe that we are in a position to be of service to you in satisfying your needs for marketing support.

I am enclosing a brochure explaining our services in general. However, my major reason for writing is to inquire into your contemplated need for support services in the future and procedures for applying to have our name added to your regular bidders list.

Thank you for your help in this.

Cordially,

Figure 5-5. Sample Inquiry Offering Support Services

Dear Mr. Delacorte:

Please forgive the delay in responding to your request for information on rights to translate our manual on direct marketing into French and German for resale on the Continent. I was out of the country when your request arrived, and returned only yesterday.

To respond to your request, I must ask for some clarification:

1. Will you do the translations yourself, or will they be subcontracted to a third party?

2. Can you furnish some estimate of sales and describe your distribution network?

3. What would be the initial print run for each edition?

4. In what countries would you distribute the manual?

Cordially,

Figure 5-6. Sample Request for Additional Information

CONFIRMING APPOINTMENTS

It is always a good idea to confirm appointments, whether you are the vendor or the client, but especially when you are the vendor. I am always grateful to clients who send me written confirmations, whether by surface mail or by fax. They act as reminders to me, on the one hand, where I might easily forget them, so that I am both prepared to meet with the client and able to do so punctually. Properly, it ought to be my obligation, as the vendor, to send off the confirmation, but I find that my clients often do this before I can. This requires only the briefest of communications, a mere documentation of the agreed-upon appointment with the usual compliments and thanks, as shown in Figure 5-7; Figures 5-8 and 5-9 offer more detailed and specific confirmations.

REPORTING PROGRESS/RESULTS

On ongoing projects, especially those of extended terms, the client usually expects a series of progress reports. In some cases, the most informal verbal reports are satisfactory, but even where the client will accept those, your own interests are much better served by filing written reports. (Many consulting contracts require such reports quite specifically.) Such reports, now a matter of record, may be essential to your own defense should contract disputes arise. For that reason, even if you make verbal reports to the client, it is wise to follow these up with a written report.

Written reports may be quite formal and even in a format dictated by the client, but letter reports are most often quite acceptable. They are most effective in all respects when they are highly specific, rather than general.

Dear Dr. Randolph:

This will confirm our appointment of Monday, January 9 for the presentation of your seminar on Databased Marketing in our Conference Room. We look forward to a rewarding session.

Cordially,

Figure 5-7. Brief Confirmation

Dear Ms. Radcliff:

This will confirm our telephone conversation and agreement of yesterday concerning the two-day workshop you have agreed to conduct for our staff on 25–26 March. The terms include payment to you of a fee of $750 plus expenses for travel, meals, and lodging. (A copy of our travel regulations is enclosed.)

The workshop will be conducted at the Footsore Rest Motel in Daly City, Missouri. The sessions will run from 9:00 a.m. to 4:00 p.m. each day, with two coffee breaks and an hour for lunch.

If you have handout materials you wish duplicated please send us a master set not less than three weeks before the session is to be held. Please advise, also, whether you require an overhead projector, blackboard, or other presentation devices.

I have enclosed literature describing our organization, as I promised.

Please sign and return one copy of this letter to confirm your agreement with its terms, and retain the copy I have signed for your own files.

Cordially,

Figure 5-8.   Detailed Confirmation of a Speaking Engagement

Try to identify any and all specific problems or obstacles encountered and explain how they were overcome or your plans to overcome them. Quantify as much as possible. Try to present progress in terms of actual percentages or whatever means you can use to offer a quantified estimate. Figure 5-10 is an example of a semi-formal report offered in the form of a letter.

RESPONDING TO COMPLAINTS AND EXPLAINING DELAYS

Complaints are inevitable in business. Sometimes you are at fault, and sometimes you are not. Some clients are quite reasonable and some are not. Getting along with clients demands that you appear at all times to

Dear Dr. Wharton:

Thank you for the confidence you have expressed in retaining me to aid you in designing an organizational development plan. I am returning a signed copy of the Letter of Agreement and will be in your offices at 8:30 a.m. on Monday the 22nd of this month, for the kickoff meeting and initial discussion session.

As we discussed in our earlier conversation at the Training '86 Conference, I will bring along those resource materials I have from earlier projects.

I look forward to working with you on this interesting project and making a contribution to the Forward Corporation.

Sincerely,

Figure 5-9. Sample Confirmation of a Consulting Engagement

be a reasonable person, even when the client is not reasonable. It demands that you always take the position that the client is right. Soft words *do* turn away anger and do placate most disgruntled clients, if not all.

The exceptions are a special case that we shall address after we address that which serves in most cases, a courteous and apologetic explanation. You need not go to the extreme of abasing yourself, but do consider that he who pays the bill—the client—is entitled to a courteous accounting, even if he or she has been brusque.

There are a few basic ideas that should be applied to all or nearly all responses to complaints, and they follow below:

- Thank the writer for bringing the problem to your attention, stating your regret (i.e., apologizing) that the complaint was made necessary.
- Explain why (if you know) the problem occurred, and what you plan to do about it. If you do not know, state that you are investigating the matter, and will report back as soon as you have uncovered all the facts. Then, in your follow-up letter, explain what you plan to do to adjust the matter, if an adjustment is necessary, and/or what you plan to do to prevent a recurrence.
- If you do not have enough information, explain that and ask the writer to furnish the additional information required.

Mr. Honorable P. Worthy
President
Traditional Mercantile Corporation
Small Corners, OH 55445   Ref: First monthly report
                                           on Contr. 87-B-74A

Dear Mr. Worthy:

   This is the first of six monthly progress reports on our research into changes in rural markets for Traditional Mercantile Corporation products.

   For the record, to place this informal report into proper perspective, your company, Traditional Mercantile Corporation, has suffered a steady decline in rural markets over the past 35 years. Prior to that time and for over 40 years, Traditional Mercantile Corporation had enjoyed a steadily growing catalog/mail-order business in rural markets throughout the United States, selling general consumer merchandise.

   The contract between us (cited above by reference) provides that we, Motivational Research Associates, Inc. (MRAI), will (1) conduct research into the base causes of the continuing decline in orders and (2) will report on these causes, with recommendations to your corporation of measures to reverse this trend and restore the business volume and growth pattern your company enjoyed before the decline began.

   We have agreed to provide six monthly progress reports to keep you posted on our research/investigation and such related considerations as problems encountered and plans for coming months. Not later than 90 days after the final (sixth) month of the contract we are to provide you with a formal final report with the complete project history, data collected, conclusions drawn, and specific recommendations for reversing the sales and marketing trend you are now experiencing.

   In this first month we have investigated typical rural markets, each in a different area of the United States. The investigations were conducted in the following six rural counties, after determining that this would give us a good demographic cross-section of the United States:

Figure 5-10.   Sample Progress Report in Letter Form

Greenwillow, Maine
Seawater, New Jersey
Coastline, Georgia
Cattlecountry, Texas
Hillanddale, Montana
Balmybreezes, California

Our main effort in each of these counties was to determine what changes of the past four decades would have affected these counties as markets for general consumer merchandise.

We found, as we suspected we would, that many changes have taken place in all rural areas of the United States since World War II. The following are the most significant ones, we believe, as far as the objectives of this project are concerned:

1. Virtually everyone in the United States, but especially rural dwellers, has become far more mobile today, with few families lacking an automobile and a very large percentage of families having two and even three automobiles in the family.

2. The same thing may be said for telephones, radios, and television receivers. Except for those few living in the most remote areas, everyone has such conveniences today and uses them freely.

3. Equally popular and nearly universal has been the proliferation in credit cards of many kinds and in their use. Millions of families who never could or would have bought on credit before now enjoy and exercise almost unlimited credit.

4. These factors have contributed to an apparently still-growing trend of local merchants taking orders by telephone, "charging" orders, and delivering purchases to customers who have ordered by telephone.

5. This ability to buy even before one has the cash available, coupled with the eagerness of local merchants to deliver immediately, appears to have brought about some hitherto uncharacteristic impatience on the part of rural consumers. They appear less willing to wait many days for delivery and now seek faster (usually local) sources to satisfy their wants and needs.

Figure 5-10 *continued.*

6. This latter problem has been made even more serious by the decline in mail services.

(Points 4, 5, and 6 made here are based on premises which we propose to investigate in future months.)

This appears to add up to a general decline of rural dwellers' dependence on the traditional catalog sales method of doing business in rural areas. However, this is only the initial data collected, and it is much too soon to draw any conclusions. In fact, although we suspected that we would find some of these trends to be the case, the scope and intensity of these changes appears to be far greater than we suspected originally. We think it wise to change our original plans somewhat and expand this investigation into a great many more areas of the United States, especially those areas where post-war growth has been the greatest and thus presumably should offer you great increases in your sales volume.

We, therefore, plan to conduct a similar study in 24 other counties throughout the United States, about two-thirds of them rural, but the remainder urban, so that the latter will act as something of a control—a reference—for the other portion of the research data so gathered.

If there are questions regarding any of this we will be pleased to discuss and/or otherwise respond to your request for more information.

Very truly yours,

Figure 5-10 *continued.*

- It is important that you respond promptly, even if it means that you will have to respond a second time, after you have done whatever you have to do. Simply responding promptly and courteously, with an apology, is often itself enough to pacify the other party. (Sometimes the other party merely wishes you to be made aware of the complaint and does not expect any direct action.)

- There are occasions when you cannot do what the writer wishes. However, if you have to reject the complaint as unjustified, do so diplomatically and without counterattacking.

Illustrations are offered in Figures 5-11 and 5-12.

Dear Mr. Colodny:

I sincerely regret our failure to ship all the necessary training manuals with the new program design delivered to you last week. Unfortunately, I did not know that our printer did not ship these manuals to you on schedule, as he was instructed to do.

I spoke with him this morning, and he assured me that the full shipment will be on its way to you tomorrow morning. Please let me know immediately if you do not have these by the end of the week.

Thank you for bringing this to our attention and please accept our apologies for this oversight on our part.

Sincerely,

Figure 5-11. Sample Apology for Delayed Materials

Dear Mrs. Gulden:

Thank you for writing to let us know about your problem in connection with the software we developed for your inventory management. That problem somehow escaped us when we tested and debugged the program.

We are checking the program out, giving it our highest priority, and should have the matter completely straightened out in a few days.

I will personally deliver and install the amended program immediately when we finish work on it.

Please accept our apologies for any inconvenience this causes you.

Very truly yours,

Figure 5-12. Sample Apology for Problem in Product Developed for a Client

THE DIFFICULT-TO-SATISFY CLIENT

It is true that some clients are almost impossible to deal with. They bargain hard to get the best price they can, and complain constantly about the cost. They demand far more than they are entitled to get and complain that they didn't get enough. They come back with endless complaints and demands for adjustment when the job is complete. Sometimes their attitudes are due to simple ignorance and their strained efforts to conceal their ignorance and appear to be knowledgeable and sophisticated. Sometimes they are truly the mean people they appear to be.

You should not have to deal with such people. At best, they will give you a sour stomach. At worst, they will provoke a heart attack. Surely, your business won't perish for losing such clients. The best thing—probably the only thing—to do is to get rid of such clients, or at least offer to. Oddly enough, most of the time spent politely telling such clients to get lost is the best way of keeping them! Somehow, difficult clients who discover that you can be pushed only so far and are quite willing to live without their patronage do a 180-degree turnaround and seem to suddenly gain respect for you. Often, they beg you to continue serving them and promise to give you no more problems.

Figure 5-13 is a letter addressed to such a client, probably in more courteous terms than you would like to use (and, I admit, more courteous terms than I have used in a few cases), but expressing the general idea.

REQUESTING PAYMENT

Collection letters are normally part of a progressive system. The need to send out letters prompting or soliciting payment is a common one. In many ways collection letters are the most difficult to write, for it is necessary to find and strike a proper balance between extremes in being courteous and being businesslike. Going to an extreme in one direction may suggest to the other party that you don't really mean business, while an extreme in the other direction is likely to become offensive and unnecessarily cost you the patronage of the other party.

There are some extreme cases when you no longer wish the patronage of the other party except on a cash basis, if at all. However, you can't know that in the beginning. The unpaid obligation may be simply an

Dear Miss Impossible:

I apologize for any difficulties you encountered in using our recommended training methods and the lecture guide we prepared for you. We used techniques that we have used for many other clients who found them satisfactory, and included all the variations and modifications you told us you wanted.

I must confess that I am now at a loss for any further changes that might conceivably satisfy you. It seems to me futile to proceed further in our efforts.

I am willing to make some kind of accommodation in the price, in view of your dissatisfaction, and I will furnish you with a list of other consultants who do this kind of work. Perhaps one of them may be able to better satisfy you than we have been.

I apologize for any inconvenience we have caused you, and trust that you will find this a satisfactory settlement.

Very truly yours,

Figure 5-13. Sample Conciliatory Letter to a Dissatisfied Client

oversight requiring a gentle reminder, or it may be that the respondent is simply a little late in making the payment, but will make it without excessive lateness, once reminded. Too sharp a tone in the first reminder may prove highly offensive and anger the other party, causing you to lose his or her patronage, and no one wants to lose anyone's business.

For this reason collection letters are ordinarily of many kinds, usually making up a system of letters that begin with gentle and even subtle reminders and only gradually become less forgiving and more insistent on payment. The hope underlying such a system is that the first letter or two will bring payment so that further correspondence will not be needed and the respondent will not be offended or angered. On the other hand, the assumption in escalating the severity of the tone in the demands for payment reflects a growing conviction that the other party needs to be dealt with firmly if payment is to be elicited. If continued efforts bring no results, the assumption then becomes that the party does not intend to pay, and is probably not worth having as a patron, at least not as an account to which credit must be extended. At this point, but only at this point, the main objective is to induce the payment without very much concern (if any) for continued patronage by the respondent.

Dear Mr. Latepayer:

Just a friendly reminder that this account is past due. Your prompt remittance would be greatly appreciated. Thank you for attending to this.

Cordially,

Figure 5-14. Friendly Reminder of Late Payment

Dear Mr. Latepayer:

You have probably overlooked it, but your payment of $_____ is past due. If there is any question regarding your account please call.

Thank you in advance for your prompt attention to this and for your valued patronage.

Regards,

Figure 5-15. Gentle Reminder of Late Payment

Dear Mr. Latepayer:

We note a balance of $35,516 remaining on your account, which has now become overdue.

May we expect your attention to this within the next few days?

Thank you for your continued patronage and for your help in clearing this small matter up quickly.

Sincerely,

Figure 5-16. Request for Payment

Dear Mr. Latepayer:

There still remains a substantial balance owing us for recent work, as shown in the attached copies of the original invoices. We would deeply appreciate your timely remittance of payment for these invoices, as agreed upon by you in opening your account with us.

Thank you for your cooperation.

Very truly yours,

Figure 5-17.   Request for Payment, with Invoices Enclosed

Collection letters are usually form letters for those who bill numerous accounts regularly. You will probably not have a great many individual accounts to address. Still, with word processing computers in even the smallest offices, it is possible to automate the process so that every letter is individually typed and addressed, without requiring you to compose each one individually.

It is entirely feasible to develop your own system of collection letters by using the models in Figures 5-14 through 5-21 to design your own standard letters and recording them on disks in your own system. (More suggestions about this will be offered later.) Notice the progression of the models, from gentle reminders to stern insistence.

Dear Mr. Latepayer:

Perhaps it has escaped your attention that there is still an outstanding balance of $6,210 owing for your new software, which we developed and installed in your system recently.

We thank you for your patronage of our establishment, but we must ask you to help us by making a prompt remittance to clear up this now overdue account.

Thank you for your understanding and cooperation.

Sincerely,

Figure 5-18.   Request for Prompt Payment of Overdue Account

Dear Mr. Latepayer:

Our records do not indicate receipt of the July installment on your account. Our computer shows an amount currently owing of $1,760. It is necessary to remit that amount immediately to bring your account up-to-date and in good standing.

I look forward to receiving your remittance promptly. (If you have remitted your payment in the meanwhile, please disregard this notice.)

Sincerely,

Figure 5-19.   Request for Immediate Payment

Dear Mr. Latepayer:

You have failed to respond to our previous correspondence, and your account is now seriously delinquent, with $2,873 in over-due installments. This can have serious consequences for you and your credit rating. We have tried to be patient, but we must insist that you attend to this matter now so that we shall not have to demand payment in full of the entire account or take other action.

Sincerely,

Figure 5-20.   Demand for Immediate Payment in Full

Dear Mr. Latepayer:

Your account is now unacceptably in arrears, and I must advise you that this is our Final Notice. Unless a minimum payment of $1,234 is received from you within 10 days we shall be forced to turn this entire account over for collection.

I sincerely hope that you will remit payment so that we will not find it necessary to do that.

Very truly yours,

Figure 5-21.   Final Notice of Late Payment

6

MARKETING AND SALES CORRESPONDENCE

You don't buy coal; you buy heat.
—Anonymous

Good counselors lack no clients.
—Shakespeare, *Measure for Measure*

CONSULTING IS THE HEART OF MARKETING

Nominally, the chief objective of your consulting practice is to serve the needs of your clients. However, for you to achieve this objective, you must recognize the realities of business, the *purpose* of business, as observed by Peter Drucker, noted business consultant, author, and acknowledged sage: He has stated that the purpose of business is to "create a customer." If that is so, marketing must be the raison d'être of the independent consulting practice.

Even without Drucker's sage observation, it should be evident that no function of any business can be of more direct importance to success than the winning of clients. Without clients, the practice cannot exist; with enough clients, the practice can tolerate some weaknesses and deficiencies elsewhere. (In fact, a great many successful enterprises survive because their marketing success enables them to tolerate many faults of organization and operation.) Thus the importance of this chapter, focusing on correspondence dealing directly with marketing and sales, as much of your correspondence and literature inevitably will.

Probably in no other society in the world is as much emphasis laid on marketing and selling as in our own American society. Our business literature is more than replete with books, periodicals, and other matter dealing with the two subjects. Technically, and in formal studies, clear distinctions are drawn between marketing and sales, with sales, pursuing the actual order as the final act of marketing. However, the general goal of both is to gain clients and make sales. They are treated synonymously in general discussions and references, and I shall so treat the subject here, using the terms interchangeably as is so commonly done in the business world.

Ironically, in all that literature of how to sell most effectively, the point so often made is that the successful salesperson is a consultant in fact, if not in title, especially during the selling effort itself. I soon learned the most effective approach to selling, not a new discovery, of course, but one well-known to others, was that of probing to find a pressing problem besetting my prospect that my services could solve. For example, I called on an executive in the training and publications department of OSHA, the Occupational Safety and Health Administration of the U.S. Department of Labor. Seeking information on his duties, responsibilities, projects, and/or programs, I soon learned that he was currently struggling to assemble a training curriculum based on manuals recently created for the department by a contractor. He was having great difficulty in drafting a curriculum based on those manuals, and was most interested in getting any help possible. We discussed this for a few minutes, I volunteered a few general ideas about how to solve the problem, and aroused his interest. He agreed to accept a brief letter proposal from me, which I submitted a few days later. He reviewed my proposal, checked on the references I supplied, and awarded me a contract.

By that logic of selling, you, as a consultant, ought to be a "natural" in the art of selling. Everyone has problems and is seeking solutions. Busy people are usually delighted to have someone else, an expert (you), handle the problem, if you satisfy them that you are, indeed, the expert who can solve the problem at an acceptable cost. Proposals, whether informal letter proposals or formal proposals, should always address a problem and offer a solution. Proposals are in general powerful marketing tools, and they are "naturals" for marketing consulting services.

THE NATURE OF MARKETING

One of the oldest cliches that offers a how-to-succeed formula in epi-grammatic form is "Find a need and fill it." If that is a sound formula for founding a successful business, it is an equally sound formula for how-to-sell advice. That is really not too surprising a coincidence, since it meshes perfectly with Drucker's observation about the purpose of any business. The admonition to "find a need" is the purpose of probing to identify the problems of prospective clients and focusing on those prob-lems for which you can offer solutions.

You must bear in mind that all prospective clients have problems, and probably have problems that are the kind you can solve with your services. The probing you do or should do in the preliminary stages is an effort to uncover problems of which the prospect is already conscious.

It happens that prospective clients do not always "feel" their wants. In marketing, it is often necessary to help clients gain that recog-nition by "educating" them or, at least, reminding them, so that they become conscious of their need to have some pressing problem solved. (Note, for example, how insurance companies "remind" us of the haz-ards of being caught without enough insurance to protect us against disasters of all kinds.) Later, in discussing proposals, we will delve a bit more deeply into this, but the concept applies equally in developing the general sales letter.

SALES LETTERS

There are many kinds of sales letters possible, even within the con-straints of those appropriate to an independent consulting practice. Sales letters used as the lead piece in a direct-mail package are most often in pursuit of orders as a direct result. In consulting, sales rarely come that way. Sales, at least to new clients, normally require at least two steps: Getting a sales lead and following it up with a presentation of some sort. (In many cases, it will take several more steps to win the client and the assignment.) Let's therefore look first at sales letters appropriate to the initial step. (With today's computers and mail-merge capabilities, it is no longer necessary to address mass-mailings as "Dear friend" or "Dear Madam"; you can have your computer address and send out each letter on your letterhead addressed to the individual on your mailing list.)

Sales Letters Making Bids or Quotations

You will probably have occasion to submit written bids and quotations. These are not quite the same thing, especially not in the formal procurement environments, such as those of government agencies. There, quotations are requested as a matter of information only, with no certainty of purchase or obligation by either party, although usually the agency will subsequently issue a purchase order in response to one of the quotations, presumably the lowest. Bids are requested as formal requests, with contract award to the lowest bidder normally following. Government agencies normally use preprinted forms and follow prescribed procedures; private-sector organizations are less formal and may request quotations or bids via simple correspondence.

Ordinarily, you do not send out bids or quotations without having had a request to do so. It may be a formal written request, such as government agencies and large corporations send out to lists of known suppliers. However, while you may get formal letters requesting your quotation or bid, you may also act on your own initiative in sending out

---

Dear Mr. Mandela:

Forthright Computer Services Co., Inc. is pleased to supply the following quotation, as you requested in our conversation at the Office Expo trade exhibit last week:

For a two-day session to train fourteen of your staff in using our new inventory management software, STOCKIT, our fee will be $1,750. That fee will include two copies of the program, complete with instruction manuals and templates.

Thank you for inviting our quotation. It is a privilege to respond to your request, and we will be honored to handle this requirement for you.

Enclosed is a brochure presenting the specifications of the software and describing its features.

Cordially,

Figure 6-1. Sample Letter Quoting Fee for Training Services

Dear Henry:

I've gone over your specifications for the new sales training system you wish to have developed and installed, and I am sure that we can do a great job with this. As you know, sales training is what we are all about.

Fortunately, we are in a position to start almost immediately on this project if we can get an early response to our bid. Here is the complete schedule of items and costs:

1. Development of the three training modules $26,450

2. Delivery of the first program to demonstrate the system 1,200

3. Training your instructor 3,765

   Total: $31,415

I am enclosing a detailed description and outline of the program as we see it in the present perspective.

I look forward to doing this job for you, and I thank you for giving us the opportunity to submit our offer.

Regards,

Figure 6-2.   Sample Letter Listing Fees for All Services Offered

such quotations or bids as a follow-up to a conversation or discussion with a prospective client. Figures 6-1 through 6-4 are some examples of such letters.

LETTER PROPOSALS

Unlike sales letters, letter proposals are not normally sent out in bulk and unsolicited; at least they do not normally arrive unexpectedly. Normally the respondent expects the proposal, having requested it or agreed to receive and consider it.

A letter proposal is different from a formal proposal only in that it is informal and as it's name suggests it is a letter. It is only a few pages

Dear Mrs. Mulligan:

HRH Communications, Inc. is pleased to respond to your invitation to bid for the presentation of three seminars on proposal writing to federal government agencies.

The enclosed brochure describes our program as presented to former clients. In preparing this seminar for presentation to your own staffs in the three offices you identified, we will make modifications such as will make the coverage more nearly customized to your own industry and needs.

The cost for each seminar is $1,150. That includes handout materials. Travel and per diem expenses will be billed at our actual costs as additional items.

We look forward to serving your needs and thank you for the opportunity to submit our bid.

Sincerely,

Figure 6-3.   Basic Response to an Invitation to Bid

long, on a letterhead, and in letter style, rather than as a bound document. What this means is that the proposal is a special, one-of-a-kind letter, addressing a specific problem or need of the respondent, and making some specific offer to satisfy the need or solve the problem.

When Proposals are Needed

Proposals in general are used in many kinds of sales or marketing situations, calling for more formalized and extended efforts than a single call or sales situation. They may result from the clients' specific requests for proposals, but they can and should often result from the seller's (your) own initiative, usually following an initial meeting and discussion.

The size of the proposal is usually in some proportion to the size and/or complexity of the project to be undertaken. Obviously, the client who is going to make a large investment will want to study the pros and cons of each proposal submitted. Hence it follows that a letter proposal will be used, normally, for relatively small and/or uncomplicated projects.

Dear Mr. Wister:

The Four-Star Printing Company takes pleasure in responding to your invitation to bid for the design and writing of your Annual Report, as specified in your request. As you requested, our bid includes the following principal phases of work and the functions:

1. Initial research, based on your previous annual reports, and notes supplied by your staff, and interviews.

2. Preliminary design, with mock-up, for your review.

3. Final design development, per your comments.

4. Preparation of draft, with photography and other illustrations, as necessary.

5. Preparation of printing specifications, printer's dummy, and running sheets, ready for the printer.

We estimate a final product of approximately 96 pages, with 18 color photographs, and anticipate 60 days as the necessary time for all. On that basis we submit our quotation of $23,675.

Enclosed are samples of our work for other clients and testimonials many have been gracious enough to supply.

Thank you for giving us the opportunity to offer our bid.

Sincerely,

Figure 6-4. Detailed Response to an Invitation to Bid

Why Clients Want Proposals

Each party has his or her own reasons for wanting the recommendations to be on paper, as a written proposal, rather than verbally or as a simple bid or quotation. To evoke a flat price bid or quotation requires that the client knows precisely what he or she wants and is able to specify the requirement in detail. Frequently the client cannot do that or even when the client can do so he or she may prefer to benefit from the consultants' experience and ask for recommendations. With the set of recommendations and costs on paper, the client can study and evaluate the recommendations. (This is particularly true when the client asks several suppliers to submit proposals to be evaluated competitively.)

Why You Should Want to Write a Proposal

If you have a good marketing instinct you have your own good reason for preferring to supply a written proposal: A proposal, formal or informal, large or small, is a sales presentation. It enables you, as the seller, to argue your case for what you offer, and to argue that case almost at leisure: It overcomes that disadvantage of face-to-face selling of the impatient or overly busy client. In a proposal you have the time to think out all your sales arguments and the opportunity to make your *complete* written presentation without interruption. There is also the advantage that the client may read and reread your presentation, studying it carefully, instead of relying on memory.

This means that you should welcome every opportunity to submit a proposal, even to the point of making a distinct effort to do so whenever you do not close the sale in a face-to-face (usually initial) meeting with the client. The smart marketer takes the initiative in situations where it normally requires two or more presentations and negotiations to consummate a sale, and advises the client that he or she will follow up promptly with a written proposal. (No sales contact should ever be permitted to end without either an order or a definite next step planned and projected. For certain kinds of sales activity the proposal is the logical and best planned next step.) Still, you do not want to appear to be forcing a proposal on the prospect or begging for its acceptance.

Persuading the Prospect to Want the Proposal

Thus in all exchanges with clients and prospective clients, it is wise to bear in mind at all times that you want them to be always conscious of their needs and problems. Accordingly, you must probe to discover of what the prospect is and is not already aware along these lines, relevant to the kinds of help you can provide. Perhaps you can win a contract spontaneously, as a result of direct discussion. However, consulting is not usually a "one call business," and it is quite likely the prospect will require some time and follow-up persuasion before reaching a decision. A simple letter proposal is an excellent way to make that follow-up. It is best if the prospect is eager to read your proposal, so it helps to suggest that you have several ideas of how to best solve the problem, but you would like some time to think things out and present your ideas for the prospect's consideration. You are quite willing, therefore, to write all this up and send it along in a few days as a letter.

Note that this is posed as an offer, without obligation by the prospect, rather than a request to receive a proposal. You may want to send a brief proposal even if the prospect does not reveal any great desire for it, but it is much more effective if you can help the prospect develop a desire to see your proposal. Therefore, once it becomes clear that a follow-up is going to be necessary to close this sale, start selling the proposal, instead of the service itself.

What Belongs in a Letter Proposal

Obviously, a letter proposal is going to present a sales argument. However, you have one of two basic sales problems: In some cases you have to sell against typical resistance to change; that is, you must persuade the client to try something new and different. In other cases, where the client is definitely going to buy the service and/or product from someone, you must sell against competition. (In practice, some sales situations are hybrids or combinations of both circumstances.)

The letter proposal is normally contained primarily in a few pages, three to six for most cases, which should make the entire presentation. However, in some cases a letter proposal may be accompanied by a brochure, catalog sheet, specification sheet, standard price list, prepared statement of your qualifications, reprints of articles you have written or have been written about you, and any other enclosures deemed appropriate. That would be the case where you propose a design which uses standard, off-the-shelf components, for example, or where you enclose printed materials or other boilerplate to support your sales argument.

The letter proposal is in the form and spirit of a letter, and the principles advocated for sales letters are equally appropriate here, with two basic differences: 1) The proposal is normally longer and more detailed than the mass-mailed form sales letter; and 2) the proposal is based on knowledge of the client's specific need or problem and so may focus sharply on that and ignore general and irrelevant considerations. Your proposal must make clear that your proposed service is custom designed for the client.

The fact that a letter proposal is relatively brief and informal does not alter the fact that it is a sales presentation and must include the same kind of information that a multi-volume, major proposal for a multimillion dollar project would contain. The only differences lie in amount of detail and format considerations.

Sometimes the client prescribes a format and requests information other than that listed below, although that is rarely the case with letter proposals and especially not when the client has not requested the proposal. You may be quite informal, but you must nevertheless cover certain key points, preferably in the order presented below. However, proposals are custom presentations for custom work, and so can never follow rigid rules, but should be in accordance with whatever were the original understandings and discussions that preceded and led to the proposal. Here are the components, in order, of a letter proposal:

1. Introduction: title, background of submittal, and brief description of the proposer (you).
2. The client's perceived need or problem defined. If the client has issued a formal statement of his or her need, restate it in your terms to demonstrate that you understand it.
3. The possible approaches with pros and cons of each: an analysis and discussion to demonstrate (sell) the validity of your argument.
4. The selected approach and rationale for it.
5. The specifics of what you will do and/or provide: what, when, and where.
6. Costs, with enough data to show their reasonableness.
7. Useful information about your own experience, qualifications, capabilities, references.
8. Terms.

Specific formats and content are up to you, but those that are apparent in the models that follow are suggested, insofar as they fit your own situation. The depth and scope of the analyses and arguments will be in accordance with the size of the project. It is probably wise to include a statement of terms with your cost quotation, especially if you require a retainer before starting work and want progress payments. It is sometimes difficult to get a client to agree to these things if you did not make them clear in the beginning.

Models for Letter Proposals

Figures 6-5 through 6-8 are a few models of letter proposals. In many cases, it is appropriate to include or append relevant brochures, but do not make the mistake of depending on the brochures to make the sale. A proposal, even a simple letter proposal, offers a *custom* design for a *custom* project. Brochures can elaborate and provide some detail, but the burden for selling the project is in the proposal itself. (These would be on your letterheads, of course.)

SALES LETTERS FOR DIRECT-MAIL AND SPECIAL OFFERS

Probably you have seen the typical direct-mail sales letter, that two- or three-page letter in blue ink, with inserts scrawled by hand in bold red ink, with exclamation marks and underlines, urging you almost pleadingly to pay attention and buy the item while the opportunity exists. It is quite a common formula for such letters.

That is a bit extreme for consulting. We don't have to be quite as circumspect or restrained in advertising as physicians must be, but neither can we afford to be blatant hucksters if we want to be taken seriously. If you are going to use direct mail in your marketing, you will have to be careful to remain dignified and not go a great deal beyond formal announcements of the services you offer, your qualifications, and an invitation to take advantage of their availability. That may include products, as well as services.

In many respects, these letters are not greatly different from letters seeking sales leads, nor even from capability statements, which were discussed in Chapter 3.

Figure 6-9 is one model that strikes something of a reasonable balance between loud huckstering and discreet announcement. Figure 6-10 is an invitation to a prospective client to request a free subscription, which includes a questionnaire. The information asked for in the questionnaire will be an aid to you in marketing to those who respond to this letter.

Figure 6-11 is quite different. It lists a catalog of services and offers a free consultation as an inducement to call and permit you to make a sales presentation in person.

Ref: Proposal for Development
of Office Automation Plan

Dear Mrs. Springer:

Following our original conversation regarding your need to automate your office functions and procedures, I did some extended research, as I promised I would. First, I reviewed your specific situation and requirements, which are basically to do that which will solve your cash flow problems.

After study I concluded that your problem stems largely from the lack of coordination among three major activities, all of which relate directly to the problem—each of which, in fact contributes directly to the problem—and to each other:

1. In re your accounting department, where the burden of work is in payroll and payables, there is a particular need to focus attention on financial controls, such as aging payable invoices to enhance cash flow, but yet ensuring that payments are made so as to take advantage of all discounts.

2. Your purchasing function needs to be streamlined, to relieve the bottlenecks in processing purchase orders and following up to ensure on-time deliveries. This is necessary to reduce and eliminate, if possible, all premium prices and other extraordinary costs in making purchases under emergency conditions that require accelerated deliveries.

3. Inventory management should be tightened up, to reduce the unnecessary immobilization of capital—money tied up in excessive, slow-moving inventory and inventory that thus becomes obsolete and loses even its original value.

Each of the affected departments and offices in your organization has one or more desktop computers and is using them effectively. However, each operates in isolation from the others, despite the fact that all the functions are interrelated, especially with regard to cash flow. This typifies the problem, and the solution lies in integrating these systems via a common database with common access and shared functions.

Figure 6-5.   Proposal Offering Consulting Services in Systems Analysis and Design

There are two ways to address this. One is to link all the desktop computers in a LAN (local area network) so that each is a terminal/work-station in a common system. That would require extensive work, including the purchase of at least one large hard disk system for storage of an enlarged and common database and a central printer to turn out reports for management. However, because not all your desktop computers are fully compatible with each other, certain technical problems must be solved. Moreover, such a system is not easily expandable to accommodate future growth.

The alternative is to create a LAN by installing a large system, consisting of a minicomputer, which would then utilize the various desktop computers as terminals. The technical problems are much simpler to solve in this configuration, with expansion to accommodate future growth less difficult, and for this reason I recommend this approach.

A second and also important consideration that impels me to recommend the second course of action is that the development of the database and other software can be done far more efficiently using a central minicomputer as the "host" computer in the system. Moreover, such models as the one illustrated in an enclosure of this proposal has all the flexibility necessary to minimize the compatibility problems inherent in linking different models together in one system.

These are the general considerations and preliminary conclusions drawn. I am sure that they are correct in principle, but more intensive research and study is necessary to translate these principles into specific details of a conversion plan, the logical next step.

The cost overall for the study and development of the plan is estimated at $28,700. The basis for this estimate is shown in the accompanying cost analysis. The result of the study will be a plan that lists equipment, procedures, software requirements, and training requirements in sufficient detail to enable you to solicit bids or quotations from suppliers, should you choose to pursue that course later.

Figure 6-5 *continued.*

I am enclosing several items:

■ A detailed cost analysis, with an explanation of our terms.

■ A brochure describing the minicomputer that is typical of those I believe to be most suitable.

■ Preliminary ("ballpark") cost estimates for services and equipment estimated to be necessary to implement the conversion of your office system.

■ References describing other, similar installations we have designed and listing individuals you may call to verify this.

I believe that you will find this by far the most practical solution to your basic problems. I am most pleased to have the opportunity to submit this proposal.

Please feel free to call on me at your convenience for answers to any questions you may have, additional information in general, and/or a complete, detailed presentation, where you and your staff may ask any questions you wish.

Very truly yours,

Figure 6-5 *continued.*

LETTERS OF TRANSMITTAL

It is customary, when submitting a formal proposal, quotation, bid, cost summary, or other such document, to submit them under a letter of transmittal. Some consultants are of the opinion that a transmittal letter is of minimal significance and is at best merely an obligatory courtesy and of little value otherwise. Their rationale is that the letter will not have anything to add to the document it covers in transmittal—at best, only iterates what is in that document—and so has little value. They therefore tend to use a strictly "vanilla" format and content, such as the example in Figure 6-12.

On the other hand, many consultants believe that the letter of transmittal is or can be of utmost importance, if handled properly (i.e., if used as a positive influence). One argument that appears to be a sensible one is that the executive to whom the letter is addressed may not him- or herself read the document, but will read only the letter. Thus the letter of transmittal offers an opportunity to sell directly to the executive, rather

Dear Mr. Hannigan:

As I promised when we discussed your problem at the recent Education & Training convention last weekend, I did some research immediately upon getting back to my office on Monday. I found that we did, indeed, handle a quite similar problem several years ago for the Williamson Electrical Parts Company. They, too, were suffering the drawbacks of an overly rapid expansion—a sharp drop in productivity, as a result of breaking in large numbers of new employees at the same time, contributed to in no small measure also by the tremendous burden this placed on their supervisors.

Williamson retained us to take over the training burden from their overworked supervisors, relieving the latter so they could concentrate on maintaining productivity with the older workers.

It worked out well, for Williamson was thus able to absorb the expansion much more rapidly and they got back to full productivity in about six months. (We worked closely with John Murphy, their Director of Administration, and I am sure that John would be quite willing to talk to you and confirm what I say here.)

What is needed, Mr. Hannigan, is a three-phase program. The first phase would be a formal Task Analysis, to do the basic research, establish the specific parameters of the problem, and draw up the specifications for the phase-two training program. The second phase would cover the actual development of the training program and administrative plans to conduct it. The third phase would be to implement the plans by actually conducting the training.

All of this would have to be done in close coordination with your staff, of course, and all plans would be subject to review and approval by whomever you appoint to oversee the program for your company.

The schedule of main events would be approximately as follows:

1. Task Analysis and training-design development: 30 days
2. Training program and materials development: 60 days
3. Training implementation: 90 days
          Total: 180 days

Figure 6-6. Proposal Offering Training Services

Costs are estimated as follow:

Task Analysis:	$11,500
Training development:	33,700
Training (our staff):	27,500
Total:	$72,700

Our normal terms are for approximately one-third in advance to act as a retainer, a second third upon approval of the draft materials, and the final third within 10 days of completion.

We are prepared to get under way with this important program on a week's notice, and I am prepared to quote the above schedules and costs as firm if we consummate an agreement within the next 30 days.

Of course, I welcome any questions you may have, and will be pleased to meet with you for discussion, to make a formal presentation to you, with or without your staff, and to enter into serious negotiations immediately.

Under the circumstances I think you will agree that there is nothing to be gained by waiting, and delay is likely to be, in fact, quite costly.

Thank you for the opportunity to offer this proposal. I will be most pleased to serve your fine company in this matter.

Most cordially,

Figure 6-6 *continued.*

than waiting for his or her staff to present findings. (This theory is borne out by my own experience.) Under this theory, the letter of transmittal permits you to make some positive sales arguments or at least make one or two major points and plant an impression even before your proposal or quotation is read and evaluated. Figures 6-13 and 6-14 are examples of this kind of letter of transmittal.

For an example of a highly successful sales letter of this type, see Figure 6-15. This is a letter I used a number of years ago to promote my seminars on marketing to the government and writing proposals. I mailed it in bulk to several thousand firms I thought to be likely prospects, firms

Dear Mr. Warrington:

Kensington Security Associates, Inc. is pleased to respond to your invitation to propose the study and design of the most suitable security system for your new warehouse addition. We have had the privilege of designing such systems to many area firms over the past 27 years, and we are grateful for the opportunity to offer you our design service. We believe we can provide you the most economical and yet most reliable—state of the art—system available today. It will save you considerable expense, while giving you great satisfaction and peace of mind.

Before preparing this proposal one of our most experienced representatives visited the location and studied your basic problem, as you described it and as it appeared to him, while considering most carefully the conditions under which the installation must function and the costs for various alternatives that would provide an equal degree of protection.

Overall Design Consideration

Inasmuch as the warehouse space is largely clear span and is to serve for the storage of both raw materials and packaged products of varying sizes, values, and bulk, we judged that you would have need for and should be interested in protection against both nocturnal break-ins and internal pilferage. We therefore believe that you will require a design that will provide both physical barriers to nocturnal forced entry from the outside and a reliable alarm system. However, you will need and we will also provide for an internal security zone within which you will store all products of a size and value that might make them subject to pilferage.

The locking and alarming devices we select and which we will propose as most suitable for your needs will be extremely durable, quite easy to install and maintain, and yet quite inexpensive, with a firm one-year guarantee. The specific types and models will depend on a more complete study and analysis.

Figure 6-7.   Proposal Offering Security System Design and Installation

The number of locking and fastening devices required depends, of course, on the number of means of access from the outside—doors and windows on all sides of the building—as shown in the contractor's blueprints and verified by our physical inspection. We found eleven doors, including those on the loading platform, and twenty-two windows. Each such door and window is to be protected by a secure lock suitable for the design and nature of the door or window. However, in the more penetrating and detailed inspection that would precede design work, we would also determine whether there are other possible means of surreptitious entrance, such as by cutting a hole in the roof.

Backing up the physical barriers—locks and fastening devices—will be an alarm system, the exact nature of which will be determined in our study. Possible candidates include but are not necessarily restricted to infrared and ultrasonic sensors, motion detectors, and strain gauges.

The internal security zone will be within a wire cage with locking doors, to provide you with control over access to those items stored within that area. That can be separately alarmed, as well.

The recommended design will include equipment, with complete analyses and rationales for each recommendation. However, options and alternatives will be offered in each case.

Schedule and Costs

The study and preparation of a design package will require 90 days from date of start, per the following schedule:

- Inspection, analysis, and preliminary plan: 20 days
- Draft of plan and review by client: 30 days
- Draft of final plan and specifications: 40 days

Cost of the study will be as follows:

- Consultant/designer, 120 hours @ $75: $ 9,000
- Travel and miscellaneous expense: 1,356
- Drafting and clerical support: 2,400
- Total: $12,756

Figure 6-7 *continued.*

Terms are one-third in advance, one-third on approval of draft design by client, and one-third on completion.

Please feel free to call for more information or to discuss alternatives, should you wish to consider other approaches than a complete formal analysis and design study.

Thank you for the opportunity to furnish this proposal. I look forward to being of service to you.

Sincerely,

Figure 6-7 *continued.*

that were either already in the government contracting business or appeared to me to be good candidates for that business.

This letter was the centerpiece of my direct mail package for marketing my seminar. A brochure accompanied it, adding information, listing former attendees of the seminar, presenting an outline of the promised presentation, and otherwise reinforcing the letter. However, the letter was capable of standing alone, as a sales letter ought to be, even if it is part of a larger package.

The text of the letter is self-explanatory, but there are a few features that need brief discussion. The first is the routing box in the upper right corner.

Inasmuch as I did not have the names or even the proper titles of the most logical addressee in each company, the box served to suggest an addressee. The envelope was addressed to "Marketing Director" or "Marketing Manager," but the box suggested another addressee and left room for still a third addressee. This was an appeal to whomever opened the envelope for help in getting the letter and brochure into the right hands in the company. (It is possible that there were no people with either of these titles, especially in the smaller companies where each executive wears several hats.) The device worked quite well, and was most helpful in directing the letter within the company.

The lengthy postscript gave me an opportunity to turn the letter into a virtual brochure on its own, while still appearing to be a rather informal letter, lending it greater credibility at first glance, than a brochure usually earns. In today's small office environment, it is possible to do quite a creditable job of composition. Were I doing this today, I would

Dear Dr. Walters:

Herman Holtz & Co. is pleased to offer our professional services to develop a curriculum for the training of occupational health technicians, per our conversation of last week at the Occupational Safety and Health Conference. Your need happens to correspond exactly with the type of work we do as developers of training systems and materials.

We are primarily in the business of writing verbal and visual presentations for training in a variety of environments and to suit a variety of needs. We are able to offer also the advantage of proximity to your own office, which will facilitate liaison and coordination of the project functions between us.

UNDERSTANDING OF THE REQUIREMENT

Your requirement, as we see it, calls for a review of the twenty-one internal engineering and development programs, and the development and printing of a document to provide an overview of these programs for fiscal years 1976 and 1977, for the edification of a diversified audience, including developers, contractors, users, and managers.

The audience is diverse in more than one respect: Developers, contractors, users, and managers may be expected to want and be able to understand a technical exposition of the programs being described, whereas it must be assumed that most, if not all who read the document, will be unable to follow or to appreciate technical information, but will require explanations in general layman's language.

We believe, therefore, that early in the effort, we will have to review the intended readership and their information needs most carefully with your own Project Manager, to ensure that the research is properly oriented and all relevant information is gathered.

Figure 6-8. Proposal Offering Training and Development of Supplementary Technical Documentation

We propose to utilize a conventional project-staffing method of organization: a dedicated Project Director who is expert in the type of product to be produced and in the functions involved in producing that product, Herman Holtz, who is himself expert in a number of the subjects which the content of the product will address. However, we believe that even that is of lesser importance than the first consideration of being a highly qualified expert in publications development and all the skills entering into that activity.

SCHEDULE AND SIZE OF EFFORT

ACTIVITY	NO. HOURS	WDAA*
Initial research effort	80	12
Submit first draft	120	27
Client review	—	37
Revise, submit second draft	60	57
Client review	—	67
Make final revisions, deliver five copies, with camera-ready text and art	80	90

TOTAL HOURS: 340

COSTS

340 hours @ $60/hour	$20,400
Photography: 75 color photos mounted and cropped	3,450
TOTAL.......................................	$23,850

*WDAA: Working Days After Award

Figure 6-8 *continued.*

Dear Mr. Marten:

How would you like to double or even further expand the scope of your marketing activity and become a national or an international business, without expanding or moving your physical facilities from your present location? It is possible to do so.

You can do that through the magic of direct mail. With direct mail, you can reach prospects and gain new customers throughout the world.

I am a direct marketing consultant, and I have helped many small business owners add the entire world to their marketing service area. My clients are doing business today in Europe, Asia, Africa, and elsewhere around the globe. They are businesses no bigger than you are, but their morning mail is packed with orders, and payment is enclosed because orders by direct mail are normally paid in advance.

I offer a variety of services and products to help you make this exciting addition to your business. First, the services: The procedure I recommend includes the following steps:

■ A preliminary meeting and discussion with you and your staff to suggest the best approach for you to take in entering the wonderful world of mail order.

■ A written proposal I will develop, presenting a customized plan designed expressly to suit your needs and make the most of opportunities I perceive for you.

■ A custom program and direct-mail campaign I will design and prepare for you.

■ My own hands-on guidance through your initial campaign.

■ Training of your staff to operate the program.

■ My availability to support you at any time in the future that you feel the need for my help.

Figure 6-9. Sample Sales Letter Promoting Direct-Mail Consulting Expertise

---

This, you should note, is a turnkey program. That means that after I design the program for you, I will install it, run it, make any changes necessary to ensure that it runs properly, and train your staff to take it over and run it (or help you find a qualified direct-mail manager, if you wish to hire someone to handle the job).

Even then, I am not gone, but will be always available, if and as needed.

I have, also, several products that would aid you in your expansion into direct-mail:

■ A monthly newsletter of tips and ideas to help you.

■ A videotape training program for you and your staff,

■ A computer program to guide you and automate much of the work.

These items are described and explained in the enclosed brochures.

The next step is to meet with you to explain the program in greater detail and answer your questions. I will call you in a few days, after you have had time to read this and think about it.

Cordially,

Figure 6-9 *continued.*

be using mail-merge capabilities, and the letterhead would be addressed by name at least to the company.

Note, especially, how you may bring in the biggest guns you have in re your credentials and qualifications, and yet appear to be modest and reluctant to brag a bit. In fact, this tactic actually draws special attention to those credentials, while you are being apologetic about expressing them, and lends them more weight.

Dear Dr. Berger:

Enclosed is a sample copy of our bimonthly periodical, which brings readers the latest information about the most modern medical electronics for hospitals, clinics, and private offices. There is no charge to qualified physicians and medical administrators for this new service, but certain considerations mandate that we ask you to supply us certain information, plus a specific request for a complimentary subscription.

Enclosed, therefore, is a brief questionnaire and application for a cost-free subscription. We look forward to adding your name to our list of subscribers.

Enclosed, also, is a brochure describing our consulting services for hospitals, clinics, and private offices.

Very truly yours,

Figure 6-10.   Letter Offering Complimentary Subscription to a Newsletter

Dear Mrs. Martineau:

HRH Communications, Inc. offers a complete service to support your marketing efforts and help you increase your success in winning contracts with the federal government. It is truly a custom service, with a wide array and diversity, so that you may choose those services you find most appropriate to your needs. You may thus have proposal writing support, including any or all of the following functions and services provided for you:

- Request for proposals (RFP) analysis and bid/no-bid recommendations
- Program design recommendations
- Program strategy
- Presentation strategy
- Proposal-team briefing
- Proposal writing
- Proposal management
- Proposal editing

Costing:
- Recommendations
- Cost strategy

Staff training:
- Seminars
- Workshops
- Formal classes

I take great pride in reporting that over the past four years we have provided these services to help our clients win 239 contracts of various sizes and types, totaling more than $27,345,000. I am sure we can help you too.

I will be pleased to visit at your convenience and explore your needs with you and describe the many ways we help our clients to greater success in the difficult business of developing successful bids and proposals. This initial consultation is entirely complimentary: It places you under no obligation.

I look forward to the opportunity to explain our services and answer your questions in person.

Sincerely,

Figure 6-11.   Sales Letter Offering Free Initial Consultation

Dear Mr. Honcho:

Enclosed is our formal proposal for designing and carrying out the Eagle One marketing campaign you have described to us as your need.

We have given this project much thought, and the enclosed proposal reflects out joint and carefully considered judgment as to the optimal approach.

We look forward to hearing from you. Please feel free to call on me personally if you have questions or need for amplification.

Sincerely,

Figure 6-12.   Basic Transmittal Letter Enclosing Detailed Proposal

Dear Ms. Smith:

Enclosed is our quotation for supplying the services you have described to us as your need to develop and carry out the training program you identify as Operation Maximize.

The costs cited reflect an extended and most careful cost study to ensure that all services you listed will be available, and yet not obligatory. That is, rather than provide you with an all-or-nothing total price, we have broken the price down into phases and functions so that you have the opportunity to opt for what you need and bypass what you feel you do not need.

We look forward to hearing from you. Please feel free to call on me personally if you have questions of any kind, need for amplification, or would like us to offer you an extended presentation.

Sincerely,

Figure 6-13.   Letter Transmitting a Quotation

Dear Mr. Contracting Officer:

It is our pleasure to submit herewith our proposal to develop a manual for the Condor Missile Tracking System in response to your RFP XTA37CON45MTSY.

You will find that our total price is $27,876 to make delivery as specified in the Request for Proposal.

This is an unusually low price, and we are well aware of that ordinarily such a low price would probably arouse the suspicion that we are either naive and inexperienced or desperate, traits that would make us undesirable contractors. Neither is the case here. We are well aware that we shall probably be about 20 percent under competitive prices.

There is a good reason for this. It is that we were the authors of the manual for the Eagle Missile Tracking System, a system from which the Condor design derived. Our computer files include not only the final Eagle System manual, but also the early drafts, the residue, and the source material. Thus some 75 percent of our early research is already accomplished, enabling us to pass on a considerable savings to your agency.

Please do not hesitate to call on us for further explanations or discussions relative to our proposal.

Cordially,

Figure 6-14.   Sample Transmittal Letter Pitching Low Price

HERMAN HOLTZ
P.O. Box 1731   Wheaton, MD 20915-1731
301 649-2499   Fax 301 649-5745
CompuServe 71640,563

```
 _____
|                          |        |
| Director of Marketing    |        |
|--------------------------|--------|
|                          |        |
| Proposal Manager         |        |
|--------------------------|--------|
|                          |        |
|                          |        |
|_____|_____|
```

Dear Director of Marketing:

To understand exactly what my seminar on proposal writing--*Proposalmanship*--is, it is necessary to understand first what it is NOT:

It is NOT a rehash of government handout brochures, nor a tedious recitation of the mechanics of government procurement. It is NOT how the government buys, but it *is* how to SELL to the government, which is not the same thing at all!

Thousands have found these seminars especially valuable for two main reasons: They are able to ask questions freely and get straight answers from an experienced, successful practitioner, not from a theorist quoting the official literature of the government. I do not teach what ought to work in theory, but what has been working for me, for the past 25 years.

These sessions are not teaching attendees how to "write proposals," but how to win contracts. The concentration is on pricing, technical, and presentation strategies that win.

It's strictly no-frills; it's all business. Only by concentrating intensively can I deliver in one day all those most essential insider tips, methods, and techniques that make the difference between the "almost" proposal and the WINNING proposal.

Attendees represent companies at all levels from new-hires and junior people sent to learn basics, to senior executives devoting a day to picking up a few priceless techniques which will make the difference in their next proposal. Even the successful, experienced proposal writers can gain useful new insights, learn some "new tricks."

I deliver the entire session personally. I answer all questions, withhold nothing, and reveal everything I know about winning, all that has worked for me all these years.

Sincerely,

Herman Holtz

P.S. Each attendee receives a personal copy of my exclusive proposalmanship seminar manual. This manual is not available separately.

Figure 6-15.   A Successful Sales Letter, First Page

MAYBE I'M JUST LUCKY . . . Or maybe I know something you should know--SUCH AS HOW TO:

- Appear to be a low bidder, even when you are not.

- Guarantee yourself a high technical score in proposal evaluation.

- Get special attention paid to your proposals

- Organize your letter of transmittal for greatest impact.

- Use the Freedom of Information Act to gain advantages.

- Handle the hard-to-price RFP to improve your chances of winning.

- Avoid the common faults that spell disaster for so many proposals,

- Develop winning strategies for your proposals.

- Write persuasively.

These are just a few of the things you will learn at my exclusive PROPOSALMANSHIP seminar. There is more, much more. Do these things work? You be the judge:

- One large defense contractor, pursuing a Job Corps Center contract, spurned my offer to help with their proposal. I wrote that proposal for another company, a much smaller one that had never done government work. They won the contract for the Fort Custer Job Corps Center, worth $25 million. (The first company never did succeed in winning any of the Job Corps work.)

- Two minority firms approached me to help them with a proposal to handle the software requirements for the EPA pesticides registration program. The one I helped won a 3-year, $12 million contract.

- One firm turned away from a requirement for engineering support of the Fort Belvoir Night Vision lab; they were sure the job was wired for the incumbent. I wrote the proposal, over a weekend, had them submit it. They won the $250,000 contract.

In none of these cases was there any marketing other than the proposal itself. No "contacts," no "influence," no secret meetings. Just superior proposals.

Maybe it's just luck, If so, it's luck that has worked consistently for many years. And if so, it's luck that has rubbed off on my clients and audiences, for they report their successes back to me, after attending my seminars.

It isn't luck, of course, but know-how, experience, techniques, knowledge, skill, and--probably most important--the strategies that grow out of all this.

Figure 6-15. A Successful Sales Letter, Second Page

I apologize for all this bragging. I wish it weren't necessary to toot my own horn quite this much, but you have a right to know what my credentials are--why I am so confident I can help you win more contracts. Besides, as Yogi Berra was reported to have said, it really isn't bragging if you can do it. And I can do it, as I have proved, over and over.

There's a lot of art in the process, of course. I can't teach art. No one can. But I do teach METHODS THAT WORK. I do teach methods for analyzing RFPs and work statements, for finding the critical factors, for developing the winning strategies.

I also address some of the most difficult problems proposal writers face:

- Organizing the ad hoc proposal team for effectiveness.

- Making the basic decisions, especially the make-or-buy decisions.

- Costs--understanding them, analyzing them, presenting them.

- Getting answers to questions without tipping off the competition.

- Leading, managing, and coordinating the proposal effort.

- Solving production problems, such as duplicating large drawings.

- Establishing and maintaining a unifying theme.

- Coping with wired procurements.

- Handling special problems, such as shortage of qualified staff, lack of specific experience, lack of track record generally.

Are these familiar problems? I'll bet they are. They are typical. Many companies face them. But there are answers to all of them, answers you will learn at this seminar. Probably the very ones you need most.

Figure 6-15.   A Successful Sales Letter, Third Page

7

MISCELLANEOUS MARKETING CORRESPONDENCE

Marketing is a complex set of activities, with greatly varying degrees of relevance to sales. The result is that there is need for a wide variety of correspondence, much of it bearing only indirectly on making sales.

COLD CALLS

Selling consulting services is normally not, of course, a one-call business. Few clients and contracts of any significant size are won in or via a single contact. Most sales require an initial contact and at least one follow-up. Even cold calls, although they are one of the most effective ways to win clients and contracts, often require one or more follow-up presentations to close sales.

Unfortunately, almost everyone hates to make cold calls in person, to approach complete strangers in their offices or other places of business and ask for permission to interrupt them in whatever they are doing

and permit you to make a sales presentation. The probability (and inci-
dence) of rejection is quite high, of course, and rejection is never easy to
endure, no matter how diplomatically deployed. Even the most self-
confident and "positive thinking" individuals are reluctant to face situations that all but invite rejection whether the rejection is direct and blunt
or tactful and indirect, by evasion of some sort.

PROSPECTING BY MAIL

The resourceful use of correspondence can minimize and perhaps even
eliminate entirely any necessity to make cold calls in person. Recognize
that there are the two or more stages usually required, the prospecting to
develop sales leads, and the follow-up to close sales. The sales letter can
be a great help with this.

Cold Call Sales Letters

To use a sales letter to make the initial contact with a stranger, you must
normally use direct-response methods. That is basically relying on probability, mailing to a large list of prospects, although the list is selected to
increase the probability of success.

"Success" in direct response marketing is measured ultimately as
any business function is measured: by the profitability of the operation
or, in more modern business thinking, by the return on investment. On
the first and more immediate level of measuring success, however, there
is the question of the *rate* of response.

The rate that signals success varies enormously, according to certain practical factors. One-half of one percent might be a signal success,
in some cases (e.g., when you are seeking prospects for a $1,000,000
house or yacht) while two or three percent might be marginal in another
case. (In the end, it is that ROI—return on investment—that is the arbi-
ter.) Despite that, there is a definite correlation between the rate of response and the ultimate success of the marketing program. (Usually
referred to as a "campaign" by those in the direct response field.) Obviously, if no one responds, the program will fail, and the probability of
success increases directly with the percentage of response. Thus, in such
a program, increasing the rate of response is always a direct and immediate goal.

Were you to mail to a random list of people, even with a masterfully written letter, the return would be almost infinitesimal. It would be by pure chance that any on the list would be in a situation that would make them prospects for whatever service you offer. Obviously, then, you don't mail to random lists. You mail to lists that are qualified to at least some minimal extent.

Qualifying Your Prospects "Qualified" is a term in marketing that can have a variable meaning, according to circumstances. Making cold calls in person is a time-consuming process. If you were making cold calls and found someone who appeared to be interested enough to discuss what you offer, you would want to know how serious a prospect he or she is and, ergo, whether you can afford or be justified in spending a great deal of time and effort trying to close a sale. It is surprisingly easy to waste a great deal of time on false prospects, individuals who have the time and interest to chat with you, but could not contract with you because they lack the authority or money to do so. Thus, you must find, at some early time in the discussion, whether that party has serious intentions and authority or money. Doing that is called "qualifying" the prospect. In prospecting by mail, you cannot qualify each prospect in that manner, nor would you want to do so, but you can qualify them to the extent that you minimize wasting your postage and related costs by mailing to people who are not good prospects. And so the selection of mailing lists is important.

You have some idea who are the best potential clients. Perhaps you specialize in inventory management systems, and so you want mailing lists of companies and other organizations with large inventories to manage. If you want to restrict your service area geographically, you will limit your mailing lists along that parameter too. If you know that retailers are your best prospects, you will further limit your mailing lists. Thus, you can qualify your initial prospect lists to maximize the probabilities for success—for addressing those who are probably most likely to become interested in the services you offer.

At the most basic level and in its simplest form, the sales letter sent out in quantity describes the benefit to be derived and invites the reader to call or write for more information, along the lines shown in Figure 7-1. This is a low-key letter, which would appear on your normal business letterhead. It makes the general promise of direct benefits, after pointing to the two major hazards of inefficient inventory control, and then describes the cure offered for the problem.

Dear Inventory Manager:

Among the several common hazards in inventory management, perhaps the two most serious ones are miscalculation of rates of consumption and resultant stock level requirements, and underestimating lead time necessary in ordering. Only slightly lesser in degree is that hazard of over-stocking so that obsolescence of stock becomes a problem.

Fortunately, those problems are easily solved today with modern computer systems and software, such as our STOCKIT inventory management program, a program designed especially to cope with these common problems that can be so costly to your organization.

We shall be happy to provide more detailed information about this modern approach to inventory management. Please call or write for a free brochure that will provide you with an insight into the newest and most revolutionary approach to efficient inventory control.

Cordially,

Figure 7-1.   General Sales Letter

Note that stress is laid on the practical benefits in the application of the program, and not on technical features, cleverness of design, or other elements that may be highly praiseworthy, but are not of concern to the prospect.

On the other hand, if you were offering a seminar to train computer specialists in the customization and installation of your STOCKIT program, you would want to approach the matter quite differently, perhaps as in Figure 7-2, which talks more about the program's features and offers technical specifications.

In Figure 7-2, there is again the promise of benefit, although indirect, with the prediction that there will soon be a large demand for the system. The focus and the promise can be sharpened considerably, according to the specific market you are targeting. For example, if you are addressing the large management consulting firms, the appeal would be to their marketing executives to alert them to a market they ought to get ready to satisfy. On the other hand, if you are addressing the data proc-

Dear Data Systems Manager:

Our new inventory-management program, STOCKIT, offers revolutionary new approaches to maximizing profits and minimizing hazards for those businesses that require the maintenance and management of large and varied inventories.

Quite frankly, there is nothing like it offered elsewhere: We threw the rule book on inventory management out when we designed this new system, based on a relational database management approach that is updated continuously with information drawn from the client's other databases—shipping records, orders, sales, supplier's catalogs, and other inputs that should dictate what is to be ordered, when it ought to be ordered, and in what quantity it should be ordered. This is an opportunity to get in on this while it is new. We have no doubt that it will soon be in widespread use and popular demand.

It is obviously a complex program, since it does so much more than any other inventory management software. Installation involves a great deal more than transferring it to a hard disk and decompressing a few files. It requires custom installation in a turn-key mode.

It is for this reason that we offer special seminars to train computer specialists in the installation of this new software.

A brochure is enclosed, with detailed specifications of the product. A second enclosed brochure describes the training seminar and includes a reservation form for the next seminar session.

Seating is limited, so we advise you to reserve places for your staff as early as possible. Please feel free to call or write for more information if you have questions.

Cordially,

Figure 7-2.   Sales Letter Describing a Specific Technical Product

essing departments of large industrial firms, the promise is that they can improve the efficiency of their firms and enhance their own positions. Both might be exhorted that they "owe it to themselves to learn about this most modern approach to inventory management." Remember, you cannot be subtle or modest in advertising if you want your message to get across.

The principle always in this approach to prospecting is to decide:

- What is the most important benefit you can promise.
- How can you back that promise up so that it is credible.
- What is the next step you want the prospect to take.

Always suggest an action by the prospect. Many prospects will respond if you suggest a response, but will do absolutely nothing—let the entire thing die of neglect—if you do not suggest an action. That leads to a directly related matter: What can you do to increase the probability of a response by those who receive your sales letter and brochure? Yes, you can do something to increase response.

Further Maximizing Your Response   There is at least one way to increase the response rate of those cold-call sales letters you are mailing out. In principle, it is extremely simple: You offer the addressee some special inducement to respond. If you have been troubled to read much of the "junk mail" you have received, you will almost surely recognize the tactic.

Inviting the reader to call or write for more information is probably the minimal special inducement you can offer an addressee to become a respondent. That is because, first of all, it requires the addressee to exercise some initiative, which is a no-no in itself. Second, that is not really an inducement for anyone except the rare individual who immediately recognizes a need that your offer can satisfy. That individual may respond, but many others will not.

Thus, the first step or level in getting individuals to respond (thus indicating the probability of enough interest to make them "suspects," if not prospects) is to tell them *how* to respond or what to do (e.g., "Pick up the telephone and dial 555-1212 now, and ask for our Software Information Department").

The next level of persuasion is achieved by providing the recipient some convenient means to respond, such as a form on a postcard, addressed to you and with postage-paid indicia so the addressee does not need even a stamp. It should not be a blank card, however, for that, again, requires initiative to write something. It is best to have items preprinted, with check offs and perhaps a blank line for a write-in or, in some cases, nothing except "Send me full information."

At this point, you are still appealing to the individual who has some immediate interest in what you offer. That still is placing some reliance on the individual addressee, while not giving him or her a special inducement to respond. That is the next level of persuasion.

You may have gotten a letter at some time that urged you to write for your free gift. That was a special inducement to respond. If the gift bore no relation to what the author of the letter wanted to sell, the response had no great significance, however, and that is an error of which you must beware. To be useful, the response must suggest that the respondent is interested and the interest is relevant to what you offer.

If, for example, you offer respondents a free notebook with pages of reference data in it, many will respond and ask for the free gift, but the responses will be of not great significance because anyone might have an interest in and desire for a free notebook. If, however, you offer a special list of tips on managing inventory, it is likely that anyone sending for that list has an interest in inventory management and control, and is thus a prospect for you. That request is a further qualification and suggests that this may be a lead worth following up. You want to increase the response rate, but only in terms of respondents who appear to be suitable prospects for follow-up sales effort.

Figure 7-3 is an expansion of an earlier letter, Figure 7-2, making the special offer. Note that you should request the respondent to enclose his or her business card. That request has two purposes: It discourages idle curiosity seekers, who would waste your time and money, and—much more importantly—it identifies the requester and his or her organization, which you need if you are to follow up.

Letters Following up an Initial Contact

In the course of your daily activities, you will make many casual contacts that may have a potential for future business. You meet an individual at some event—a trade show, convention, on an airplane, or elsewhere—who appears to be a possible prospective client. In a chance business or social contact, you don't attempt a direct sell, but neither are you unaware of the business possibilities of the chance contact. You have tactfully probed the other's business activities in your conversation and

Dear Mr. Dealer:

Decisions about inventory in a retail environment can be among the most critical to one's success. The lack of sufficient inventory or of the right inventory can mean many lost sales, while the oversupply of items in inventory can force large losses due to obsolete items. The busy executive cannot afford to spend the time in complex calculations of best times to order, how much inventory to have in stock, and otherwise coping with the very difficult problems of managing a large, diverse, and dynamic inventory.

Fortunately, you do not have to continue to struggle alone with this problem. help is available. Our exclusive new inventory management program, STOCKIT, will help you avoid both hazards. The program tracks your sales record continuously, projecting future inventory needs, with daily updating. At the same time, the program keeps track of lead times for ordering various items, based on your prior orders and delivery schedules, and alerts you with suggestions of when and in what quantity to order each item.

To do this efficiently, the program must be installed and customized for you. We provide that service. We customize the program, install it, and train you in its use.

Additional details are included in the enclosed product description and brochure.

We will be pleased to answer any questions you may have. In fact, we invite you to call for a full demonstration of the system. There is no charge for this, of course.

We have prepared a special list of tips on inventory management and control, which we wish to send you. Simply mail back the enclosed form (it is postage-paid and preaddressed, so you don't even need a postage stamp) with your business card attached, and we will mail you the list of tips immediately.

Cordially,

Figure 7-3.   Sales Letter that Includes a Special Offer to Elicit Response

gained a little insight into his or her needs and problems. Obviously, you can't close a sale spontaneously here—that would be both an ethical and a strategic no-no—but neither can you afford not to make use of the potential. What should you do?

Consider follow-up a must, and the proper follow-up depends on what transpired in the initial meeting and discussion. In some cases, you may be justified in simply calling and suggesting a meeting. If you do not feel confident enough yet in the relationship for that, a formal, semi-formal, or even informal written follow-up is proper.

If the prospect revealed enough details of some specific need, it may even be that a proposal, probably an informal letter proposal, is in order. That is, you know enough of the prospect's need to offer a detailed program, as in the models of letter proposals already shown. At the other extreme of the possibilities, perhaps little has come to you at the meeting except the general nature of the other's business activities and that he or she may be an executive who has direct need for help you can provide and has the authority to contract directly with you. Another possibility may be that he or she might not be in a position to deal directly with you, but might be able to put you in touch with the "right" people in their organization. In that case, your follow-up would be of a more general nature, seeking to meet again and pursue your quest of business opportunity.

Of course, the meeting and discussion might very well fall somewhere between these extremes, and thus suggest various approaches for follow-up, from the most general correspondence to something just short of a letter proposal or quotation. In either case, the proper elements for this kind of correspondence are simple and logical enough:

- A pleasant greeting and a reference to the occasion of the meeting.
- A suggestion that you have mutual interests.
- A suggestion for a meeting or a presentation of some sort.

One thing is a must: You must propose something concrete as a next step. A vague ending (e.g., "Let's have lunch soon" or "When can we get together?") leads directly to a dead end. You have suggested nothing concrete, and the whole thing will most surely die there if you allow it to do so. You must be specific and direct, if you want something to come of the encounter, and it is best if you state the next move as something *you* will do. That puts *you* in control, to some extent at least.

The probability is always that nothing will happen if you are not in control. Successful marketing is never a passive process. Take note of that (i.e., what the writer proposes to do) in the models offered in Figures 7-4 through 7-6.

These examples illustrate the several possible situations and suggest ways to handle each situation, starting with the completely general one and progressing through to more well-structured ones. The content of the models will paint in the backgrounds. (Incidentally, note that it does not hurt to be a bit complimentary and show some recognition of the other's assets. As Andrew Carnegie pointed out in his writings many years ago, it is almost always possible to find something laudable to comment on about the other party, if you concentrate on the positive and not the negative.)

These letters would go, presumably, to executives of their organizations. In practice, not everyone you meet in this manner is an executive, at least not at the higher levels. That does not mean that the contact is

---

Dear Linda:

It was certainly a pleasure meeting you and discussing some of our mutual business problems. I found the accounts of your company and how you do business quite interesting. You show rare insight into some of our problems.

I am enclosing a brochure to provide you with a more complete portrait of what we do and what we offer others to help them solve some of their business problems.

I would be grateful for an opportunity to meet with you and your associates in an initial consultation to discuss your needs and problems. I believe I have some information and ideas your organization can put to good use. I will call you in a few days to discuss a meeting, but you can reach me at the number listed here, if you prefer.

There will be no obligation for this initial consultation, of course.

Cordially,

Figure 7-4. Simple Follow-up Letter

Dear Mr. Tremblejack:

It was a privilege to meet and chat with you at the Energy Trade Exhibit last week. I found your analysis of business problems most provocative, and I have been giving a lot of thought to some of your observations, especially those referring to the difficulties in inventory management.

It is, indeed, a sticky problem trying to balance the several factors for most efficient management of inventory. In fact, there are really four factors to consider:

1. Capital tied up in slow-moving inventory.
2. Problems in maintaining stock of long-lead items.
3. Seasonal fluctuations in sales of certain items.
4. Inventory shrinkage.

It is, of course, a most difficult balancing act. It seems to me to require, first of all, a fairly sophisticated spreadsheet analysis to develop one or more algorithms (depending on the size and complexity of your inventory) for your inventory management and control. That can be done only after collecting a great deal of historical data from your orders and invoice databases to provide the raw data to be analyzed.

This falls into our own area of specialization. The capability statement I enclose here will illustrate that. I am sure that we can help you solve the problem. Here is what I propose:

1. A meeting with your staff to set some ground rules defining your objective or requirement precisely.

2. A proposal to you.

3. Negotiation and agreement.

I will call you in a few days to discuss such a meeting.

Most cordially,

Figure 7-5. Detailed Follow-up Letter

Dear Mrs. Williams:

I have given a great deal of thought to your remarks made at last week's meeting of the Abracadabra Association. You pointed to some acute needs of all industry in general, if we are to cope successfully with the revolutionary changes now taking place in the economy.

Every industry is facing the need to increase marketing efficiency. The cost of acquiring a customer by old methods is prohibitive today. We must be more efficient and successful in our marketing—in finding prospects and converting them to customers.

That is, as I explained to you last week, the field in which we specialize. We not only support the marketing programs of our clients, but we troubleshoot their programs and redesign them for greater efficiency or design new programs from the ground up for them. (I am enclosing a sheet of testimonials attesting to that from a few of our clients. I hope you will indulge me by taking a few minutes to read them.)

I would be delighted to present you and your staff with a full demonstration and explanation of some of our programs and how we would develop them for you and your products. We will make this presentation at a time and place convenient for you. There is, of course, absolutely no obligation on your part for this.

I will call you to make arrangements.

Kindest regards,

Figure 7-6. General Follow-up Letter Enclosing Testimonials of Previous Consulting Services

not worthy of follow-up. It means only that the approach is a bit more indirect. The letters in Figures 7–4 through 7–6 are still valid approaches, in such cases, with a little modification, as shown in Figures 7-7 through 7-9. A great deal of tact is required here so that you do not appear to be simply using the individual or brushing by him or her as someone of inadequate importance.

Note that the models in Figures 7-7 through 7-9 ask the individual to pass the offer along or to pass on to the writer the names of the

Dear Linda:

It was certainly a pleasure meeting you and discussing some of our mutual business problems. I found the accounts of your company and how you do business quite interesting. You show rare insight into some of our problems.

I am enclosing a brochure to provide you with a more complete portrait of what we do and what we offer others to help them solve some of their business problems.

I have a general idea of your own duties and functions, but I am unclear as to whether it is you or others in your company I should be talking to. I would therefore be grateful for your guidance in this (i.e., in which of your associates I would be best advised to approach to investigate how I might best serve your organization). I think it would be in our mutual interest to meet with whomever you suggest to discuss the needs and problems of your company. I believe I have some information and ideas your organization can put to good use. I will call you in a few days to discuss this, but you can reach me at the number listed here, if you prefer.

There will be no obligation for this initial consultation, of course.

Cordially,

Figure 7-7. Simple Follow-up Letter (Compare with Figure 7-4)

relevant individuals. Ideally, you should make an effort to get the contact to introduce you to the right individuals. It is far more effective than introducing yourself, even when you are able to cite the original party as having referred you. However, it would be a tactical error, usually to make this request directly in the initial follow-up letter. It would appear to be brushing past the contact rather brusquely, using the contact cynically, and/or simply asking for too much too soon. The more effective way of persuading the contact to make those personal introductions is to wait until you have the follow-up discussion where the contact supplies the names of the parties involved. In fact, if possible, try to get the contact more directly involved in arranging the initial meeting, consulta-

Dear Mr. Tremblejack:

It was a privilege to meet and chat with you at the Energy Trade Exhibit last week. I found your analysis of business problems most provocative, and I have been giving a lot of thought to some of your observations, especially those referring to the difficulties in inventory management.

It is, indeed, a sticky problem trying to balance the several factors for most efficient management of inventory. In fact, there are really four factors to consider:

1. Capital tied up in slow-moving inventory.
2. Problems in maintaining stock of long-lead items.
3. Seasonal fluctuations in sales of certain items.
4. Inventory shrinkage.

It is, of course, a most difficult balancing act. It seems to me to require, first of all, a fairly sophisticated spreadsheet analysis to develop one or more algorithms (depending on the size and complexity of your inventory) for your inventory management and control. That can be done only after collecting a great deal of historical data from your orders and invoice databases to provide the raw data to be analyzed.

This falls into our own area of specialization. The capability statement I enclose here will illustrate that. I am sure that we can help you solve the problem. Here is what I propose:

1. A meeting with your staff to set some ground rules defining your objective or requirement precisely.
2. A proposal to you.
3. Negotiation and agreement.

I realize that inventory management may not be your responsibility, despite the fact that you have an excellent grasp of the problems surrounding it. However, because you do have such a great understanding of the problem, perhaps it would be a service to your organization if you brought my offer to the attention of the proper executive for that function by passing this offer on. Certainly, I would be grateful for your help.

I will call you in a few days to discuss such a meeting.

Most cordially,

Figure 7-8.   Detailed Follow-up Letter (Compare with Figure 7-5)

Dear Mrs. Williams:

I have given a great deal of thought to your remarks made at last week's meeting of the Abracadabra Association. You pointed to some acute needs of all industry in general, if we are to cope successfully with the revolutionary changes now taking place in the economy.

Every industry is facing the need to increase marketing efficiency. The cost of acquiring a customer by old methods is prohibitive today. We must be more efficient and successful in our marketing—in finding prospects and converting them to customers.

That is, as I explained to you last week, the field in which we specialize. We not only support the marketing programs of our clients, but we troubleshoot their programs and redesign them for greater efficiency or design new programs from the ground up for them. (I am enclosing a sheet of testimonials attesting to that from a few of our clients. I hope you will indulge me by taking a few minutes to read them.)

I would be delighted to present you, your staff, or anyone else in your organization with a full demonstration and explanation of some of our programs and how we would develop them for you and your products. We will make this presentation at a time and place convenient for you. There is, of course, absolutely no obligation on your part for this.

In the event that this would not be of direct interest to you in your own functions, perhaps you would do your organization the great service of making this offer known to your chief marketing executive.

I will call you to discuss this.

Kindest regards,

Figure 7-9. General Follow-up Letter Enclosing Testimonials (Compare with Figure 7-6)

tion, or presentation you seek, but do that later. This letter is only a preliminary, and should seek only to begin opening the doors.

SUBCONTRACTING

Few companies do everything. That is especially true of large and busy companies who undertake large contracts. Large contracts often require certain functions that the contractor is not equipped to do or doesn't want to do. A contract to "reverse engineer" a system of equipment, for example, might well require that the contractor write a large technical manual, as one of the products of the contract. The contractor may not have a technical writing staff or may have such a staff but be so overwhelmed with other commitments that he or she cannot handle yet another writing task. As a result, the contractor will go in quest of someone else to handle the manual writing job. That contractor thus becomes the *prime* contractor, seeking to let a subcontract. It is a quite common situation in the business world.

As far as you are concerned as a potential subcontractor, you will bid or propose to the prime contractor as you would in the case of any contract you might pursue from any prospective client. In practice, for this type of work or any other skilled, creative work, it is much more likely that you will have to submit a proposal than a bid. You might submit a letter proposal, as explained in Chapter 6, or you might submit a more formal proposal, as will be covered in Appendix B. However, before you go to that expense and commit your time, you must be invited to submit a proposal or at least know that the other party will be interested in subcontracting. That calls for a sales letter of some sort, addressed to those you consider to be likely prospects (e.g., those companies to whom contract awards have been announced).

Sales Letter Seeking Subcontract

Figures 7-10 through 7-12 offer models of letters you might send out to firms who, you have special reason to believe, have need for your services because you have learned of a contract they have been awarded, heard stories on the grapevine that suggest that this company needs such help, or you happen to know that they often subcontract for such services.

Dear Mr. Primo:

An important and large part of our business is the direct support of companies such as your own: We can ensure that you meet your client's needs completely, in a highly professional way, and with complete satisfaction to your client in providing training services in the use of database and spreadsheet programs.

The enclosed brochure describes our services and lists a few of our clients, whom you are free to call to verify the quality and dependability of our services.

We are prepared to submit a bid or proposal, at your request, offering a specific plan and program to meet whatever need you describe. If you prefer, we will be quite pleased to meet with you for a more formal presentation of what we can do for you.

I will call you in a few days, although you are certainly free to call me immediately.

Most cordially,

Figure 7-10.   General Letter Offering Subcontracting Services

A tip here: Don't be discouraged because the company happens to have its own staff specialists in whatever skills and services you offer. Quite the contrary, pay special attention to that company; it is likely to be one of the best prospects. Companies that have entire departments providing some kind of support service to their main activity obviously require quite a lot of that support, enough to maintain an entire department. It is a safe bet that the department is often overloaded and subcontracts the overload to independents, such as you. Again, that is a most common situation in the business world.

There is yet another special situation of which you should be aware, since it also offers opportunity to you as a prospective subcontractor. You may be able to appeal to another organization before they even bid or propose, with an offer to help them prepare their proposals by handling that part of the proposal that corresponds to what you do and that part of the project for which you will subcontract. That offers your prospect at least two advantages:

Dear Mr. Primo:

First, let me congratulate you on your success in winning the major software development contract of the Ouija Corporation. We followed that competition as closely as we could, and are pleased that one of our own local companies was successful.

We are documentation and training specialists, and an important and large part of our business is the direct support of such companies as your own. We ensure that our clients meet the documentation and training requirements of their contracts completely and in every detail, as prescribed by their clients and contracts. We assume full responsibility for those functions, under subcontract.

The enclosed brochure describes our services and lists a few of our clients, whom you are free to call to verify the quality and dependability of our services.

We took the trouble to study the original RFP quite thoroughly and are thus fully aware of what your client requires of you under the contract. We are well prepared to support you in carrying out this part of your contracted obligations, and are eager to do so.

We are prepared to submit a bid or proposal, at your request, offering a specific plan and program to meet the needs of the contract. However, we are also quite willing to meet with you first to discuss those requirements and what we can offer you to meet them.

Please feel free to call me to arrange a meeting and discussion. If you prefer, you may wait for my call, which I will make in a few days.

Most cordially,

Figure 7-11.   Detailed Letter Offering Specific Subcontracting Services

Dear Mr. Primo:

I would imagine that the announced RFP of the Ouija Corporation would interest you, since it appears to us to be the kind of work you specialize in doing. We sent for the RFP and studied it carefully, with a view to supporting a prime contractor such as yourself. We are thus quite familiar with what the Ouija Corporation wants, in this regard, and have identified the role we could and would like to fill.

We are documentation and training specialists, and an important and large part of our business is the direct support of such companies as your own. We ensure that our clients meet the documentation and training requirements of their contracts completely and in every detail, as prescribed by their clients and contracts. We assume full responsibility for those functions, under subcontract. We are well known to, and respected by, others in this and related fields.

Our purpose here is to offer our help in developing and writing the proposal you will need to win this award. We are prepared to carry our full share of the burden in writing this proposal, including participation in all relevant brainstorming sessions and meetings, and providing camera-ready final copy of our own portion of the proposal.

The enclosed brochure describes our services and lists a few of our clients, whom you are free to call to verify the quality and dependability of our services.

Please feel free to call me to arrange a meeting and discussion, as necessary preliminaries or, if you prefer, wait for my call to follow in a few days.

Most cordially,

Figure 7-12. Letter Offering Documentation and Training Services on a Subcontract Basis

1. Proposal writing is difficult and expensive at best. Those who write them are delighted to get help, especially from a prospective subcontractor for a part of the contract they know they will subcontract.

2. The proposer's chance for winning the award is at least partly dependent on the quality of all services, as perceived by the prospective client of the prime contractor. If you can offer impressive credentials and/or are a highly skilled proposal writer, your contribution will be an important one.

Another tip: If you work with a prospective prime contractor/client at your own expense to develop his proposal, be sure you have a firm, written contract that binds him to utilize your services and pay for them, in the event of award. Beware of being stalled with the assurance that you will be written into the contract because you are written into the proposal. That will not bind the other party to use and pay for your services. (Serious businesspeople write agreements or contracts, and it is hazardous to do business with others who are reluctant to put their commitments in writing. My own bitter experience testifies to this.)

Figure 7-10 is a general letter, based simply on a belief that the company is likely to be a good prospect, at least occasionally. Figure 7-11 is a letter based on more specific knowledge of the prospect's probable need. Finally, Figure 7-12 is a letter offering proposal support.

Letters Seeking Co-Bidder or Subcontractor

Among the many special situations that can arise in marketing is coming across an opportunity for a contract that you cannot or would prefer not to undertake alone. Actually, there are several sets of circumstances that would impel you to seek help, resulting in at least one of these two general situations:

1. You think you can win the contract, but it is either too big for you to do alone or it includes certain functions you don't feel comfortable in doing yourself and you don't want to handle a payroll.

2. You think you can win the contract, if you can get someone "strong" to bid with you, but not if you go it alone.

Thus, you need a co-bidder, someone to either handle one-half the load of work or to handle certain specialized chores you believe requires skills you don't have.

Co-bidding is a philosophical term, not a precise business term. It describes an intent, but it is not a practical approach to contracting, unless implemented in some special way. That is, in practice, you can't run a contract in escrow; clients need someone, a single entity, in charge and responsible for results. You simply cannot contract very well without having some single, identifiable entity as the contractor. Thus, "co-bidding" means, in practice, that one of you must be the prime contractor and the other the subcontractor, or must form a third, separate entity, to act as prime contractor.

That leaves you with several possible choices:

1. You can bid, or propose as the prime contractor, and ask the other(s) to be your subcontractor(s). (You can form a consortium of several independent consultants to become a "virtual corporation.")
2. You can form a separate company, in which all hold shares.
3. You can form a limited partnership, organized and applicable to only the single project.
4. You can form a corporation, each with shares, and each a subcontractor to the corporation, which will be the prime contractor.

You should, of course, draw up agreements if you form a consortium or partnership of any kind. If you set up a corporation and each subcontract to it, you should have formal contracts drawn between the corporation and each of you. Of course, someone must be empowered to sign contracts in behalf of the corporation, and that must be worked out between you in establishing the corporation.

Figures 7-13 through 7-15 are model letters broaching the idea of co-bidding to someone you know and to strangers. Each letter corresponds to a different situation that may be inferred easily from the content. Figure 7-13 is quite informal, and probably would not be written at all: It is likely that in such a case as that described, you would just pick up the telephone and call "Jerry." However, you might not be able to reach Jerry when you want to or you may feel a need to lay the whole thing out on paper.

Figure 7-14 is more formal because it will go out to one or more strangers.

Figure 7-15 offers still another approach. It is a straightforward and unabashed RFP—Request for Proposals—offered to anyone who wishes to respond with a proposal.

Dear Jerry:

I am in a favorable position for a sizable contract to design, develop, and manage a rather large direct-mail program: I think the contract is mine, if I want it enough to write a formal proposal for it. I have a problem with it, however: It is really a bit too big for me to handle alone, and I do not want to hire someone for a temporary job and start meeting a payroll, with all its problems.

What I do want to do is co-bid this job with someone whom I know can hold up his or her end, and with whom I am sure I can work amicably and with mutual trust. You are my favored candidate and first choice for this, if you are interested.

Of course, to do this, we have to set up some kind of working relationship: either some kind of limited partnership or an arrangement where I go after the contract and subcontract some part of the job to you.

That has to be worked out. Please give me a ring and let me know if you want to go into this with me. Then we can get together and work the details out.

All the best,

Figure 7-13.   Informal Letter Requesting Co-Bid Support

LETTERS OF AGREEMENT

Although many clients may wish to sign rather formal contracts with you, there are others who prefer to execute rather informal ones, especially for small projects. Many clients prefer to issue purchase orders or execute simple letter agreements for any but the large projects. In fact, some clients will be "turned off" by any insistence on formal contracts, inferring that as a sign of mistrust or lack of honorable intention.

A letter of agreement is just that, a letter, usually on the client's letterhead, stipulating the conditions: What you are to do, how much you will be paid, and any other pertinent factors. It is usually—although not always—executed in duplicate with spaces for two signatures, yours and the client's. The client sends the two copies to you, and you are to sign one and return it, keeping one copy as your own.

Dear Mr. Independent:

You were recommended to me as an excellent independent consultant in direct-mail who might be interested in subcontracting to me.

I happen to be in the fortunate position of being highly favored for a contract to design, develop, and manage a large direct-mail program for a major corporation. I shall need at least one and possibly two or three subcontractors. I wish to identify these in advance and be able to pledge that they will be active in supporting the program.

I am enclosing a specification of the work to be done, and I identify therein all the areas I intend to handle personally, as well as those I wish to subcontract.

If you are interested in subcontracting, please do these things for me:

1. Identify those tasks/functions that you would feel comfortable undertaking and would agree to contract and be responsible for.
2. Provide a firm price for each of those functions you check off.

If you indicate an interest in this, please include with your response information in re your professional credentials, with permission for me to use this in my proposal.

If you wish to offer a different working relationship than that of prime contractor and subcontractor, please indicate this, with your suggestions of a more suitable working relationship.

A response is required by 5:00 p.m. October 17, 1995.

Sincerely,

Figure 7-14.   Formal Letter Seeking Co-Bidders

Dear Mr. Candidate Subcontractor:

HRH Communications, Inc. will award a subcontract for the work described in the enclosed Statement of Work for Project XX-Y75WW, for which we are the prime contractor. Your proposal is invited.

We will require a full explanation of your approach to this requirement, a clear specification of the deliverable items you pledge to produce, proposed schedule for carrying out the project, staffing, and your credentials. The latter are to include a description of your relevant resources and experience.

A firm fixed-price contract will be awarded, and we require such a cost proposal.

Award will be based on our evaluation of these items, and may be made without further negotiation.

Please address all questions to the undersigned.

Sincerely,

Figure 7-15. Request for Proposals to Co-Bid on a Consulting Engagement

The letter of agreement *is* a contract, as binding as any multi-page contract bound in blue covers, and bearing notary and corporate seals. The difference lies in the degree of detail incorporated in the agreement. It is a matter of how much effort is deemed necessary to agree on terms for a small project.

Your client may or may not have such a form of his or her own, depending on whether the client does a great deal of contracting or contracts only rarely. Thus, the client may look to you to furnish a form, although the client may prefer to retype your form on his or her own letterhead. I have found it useful to keep such a form in my briefcase to explain my usual terms quickly. It often saves discussions and the necessity to defend those terms.

The typical formal contract includes clauses that are truly not necessary because they are automatically included by common law or statute. What any contract requires to be binding are these:

- An offer.
- An acceptance.
- A consideration.
- Legal competence of the parties.
- Legal activity offered and agreed to.

If the client offers you a consideration for doing something that is a lawful activity, and you accept it, and if both of you are legally competent to enter into the agreement (of legal age and in possession of your faculties), you have a contract. It need be in writing only in certain, special cases to be a binding contract, but it is risky, of course, to rely on memory and allegations of what was agreed to. It is wise to always have something in writing. (There are many other factors, but these are the general principals and truths in re contract law.)

The letter may be a pure letter or it may be an abbreviated contract form executed on an ordinary letterhead. A model for each format is provided in Figures 7-16 and 7-17.

LETTERS REQUESTING BID SETS AND INCLUSIONS ON BIDDERS LISTS

If you wish to bid and propose competitively, you should be taking advantage of every opportunity to have your name added to the appropriate bidders lists of all organizations who award contracts more or less regularly. Those who do so, whether they are companies, corporations, government agencies, or other non-profit organizations, usually maintain lists of bidders: suppliers of various products and services the organization has need for, at least occasionally.

Many such organizations have a standard form, constituting an application for inclusion on the bidders list. The federal government, for example, has a Standard Form 129, which anyone may request, fill out, and file with the contracting office of each agency. Federal procurement is almost entirely decentralized, and so there are no master bidders lists. You must file a copy of your application individually with each federal agency you believe to be a suitable market candidate.

State and local governments tend strongly to centralize purchasing in a single purchasing and supply agency, so you need usually to file only one form—they tend to call it a "registration form," rather than a

Dear Contractor:

Speedy Response Systems wishes to engage your services to design a marketing database for our marketing department and train our personnel in building the database. You will be given free access to our records, computer systems, and personnel for the duration of this work.

The work will commence on August 1, 1995 and be completed by November 1, 1995. You agree to furnish progress reports every 30 days and be available for discussions of these, as required. You will furnish a complete set of system specifications and an operations manual. You will also conduct a training seminar of not less than one full day's duration for our personnel before turning the system over.

You will be paid $125 per hour, for a maximum of 120 hours, including all functions described.

This agreement may be canceled by either party on 30 day's notice, with settlement on the basis of hours worked.

Client	Signature
Contractor	Signature

Figure 7-16.   Sample Agreement in Letter Form

bidders list application—with state, county, city, town, and township governments.

Getting your name on a bidders list is not enough to ensure that you will see all the bid and proposal requests that interest you. For more than one reason, not relevant of themselves here, your name on a bidders list will bring you only a fraction of the bids, at best. It is necessary to take all measures to become aware of all bid and proposal requests and ask the issuing organization for a copy.

Figures 7-18 through 7-20 are several model letters relevant to this, which explain themselves by their content.

It is necessary, if you wish to be kept on an active bidders list, to write when you receive a bid set and choose not to bid, and a model letter (Figure 7-20) is enclosed to cover that situation also.

AGREEMENT

Client: _____

Contractor: _____

Services to be provided or relevant specifications/proposal:

_____

_____

Reports/presentations: _____

Beginning date: _____ Target completion date: _____

Fees: $_____ per _____ Total est. _____

Advance retainer: $_____ Balance: _____

_____   _____
Client   Signature

_____   _____
Contractor   Signature

Figure 7-17. Sample Agreement in Contract Form

Dear Purchasing Agent:

　　HRH Communications, Inc. is in the training business, furnishing both the development and delivery of training systems of all kinds. We wish to be placed on your bidders list to receive bids and proposals in the future.

　　If there is an application or registration form of some kind to be filled out and filed, please send us a copy, along with any special instructions you may have.

　　I have enclosed a descriptive brochure for your information and future reference.

Sincerely,

Figure 7-18. Letter Requesting Application for Placement on Bidders' List

---

Dear Contracting Officer:

This is a request for a copy of your Invitation to Bid, Bid Set Number ARR56HYT95, for the development of a personnel manual.

Our firm, Documentation, Inc., has written many such manuals, and we expect to submit our bid for the requirement in question.

Sincerely,

Figure 7-19.   Letter Requesting "Invitation to Bid" Form

Dear Contracting Official:

We are in receipt of RFP 768AXXFY97, inviting us to propose the development of an audiovisual Job Safety program.

We regret that the pressures of current projects underway will prevent us from responding to this request. However, we do wish to be kept on the bidders list and to continue receiving requests.

Sincerely,

Figure 7-20.   Letter Asking to Be Retained on Bidders' List

LETTER REQUESTING PROCUREMENT INFORMATION

Many organizations that contract regularly publish their own literature, in fact, quite often extensive literature, explaining their procurement systems and policies. In many cases, the literature made available to prospective suppliers is quite voluminous.

That can be most helpful in pursuing contracts and even in general market research, to determine which are the most suitable targets for what you do. It requires only a simple letter to request a copy of such material, as in Figure 7-21.

Dear Purchasing Manager:

Dunbar & Associates are management consultants specializing in accounting systems and tax matters. We are currently expanding our services, and believe that we can be an asset to you as an external resource.

We would be grateful to you for any material you can make available to us explaining your usual needs and procurement methods and policies.

It is our intention to be responsive to your future needs.

Sincerely,

Figure 7-21.   Sample Letter Requesting Information on Procurement Needs

8

SPECIAL PROMOTIONAL LETTERS

The power of the pen has long been legendary in its ability to strike great blows and bring the winds of change. In our modest roles as independent consultants, we do not seek revolutionary upheaval, but we can put the pen to good use in bringing about events to serve our needs.

THE PRESS RELEASE: WORKHORSE OF PUBLIC RELATIONS/PUBLICITY

The typical business relies on conventional advertising, salespeople, and the other classic methods as the mainstays of its marketing programs. Other, more novel means of winning new customers are usually relegated to subordinate roles if they are used at all. For most independent consultants, these conventional and classic means may serve to sell some of the spin-off products of consulting—seminars, tapes, newsletters, software programs, and other items—but for marketing your consulting services per se, these methods rarely work well. Some consultants do resort to cold calls to win at least some of their clients, especially in the early days of launching a fledgling practice. Most shrink from the stress of the inevitable rejections that are inherent in cold-call selling, and seek less unpleasant means and measures of winning new clients and consulting contracts, such as those we have discussed in the preceding chapter.

By its nature, marketing consulting services normally requires a relatively subtle and dignified approach, much as lawyers, physicians, and most other professionals employ. Building a professional practice is usually dependent in great part on building and maintaining a prestigious image, one of great dignity and professionalism. It depends in large part on evoking word-of-mouth recommendations and referrals. That, in turn, derives in large part on making yourself highly visible as having a prestigious image of great competence, integrity, and dependability. This, in turn, is partly the result of having pleased earlier clients so that they unhesitatingly recommend you to their friends and acquaintances. That is the passive marketing activity. It is a marketing benefit that develops rather slowly, and is a practical approach to building your practice only if you are content and able to wait patiently for growth to occur spontaneously and most gradually. It also depends on the kind of consulting service you offer; there are some kinds of consulting services that your satisfied clients will not wish to help you promote: If you are a marketing consultant, for example, there is the problem that satisfied clients are not likely to want to recommend your services to their competitors. In fact, the more effective you are at marketing and at helping your clients to greater success in the marketplace, the less likely it is that any client will recommend you to anyone who might be in competition with them.

If you cannot afford to wait for growth to proceed slowly, you must take positive steps to build your image and become well known much more rapidly in that community of those most likely to need your help and thus become clients. However, we know that conventional commercial advertising does not work well for consultants normally. That means you need to develop and exploit an effective promotional public relations (PR) campaign (i.e., one of image projection and promotion).

The principal media for such promotions are the written and the spoken words. Here, we are concerned with the written word as presented via very special classes of letters, chiefly press releases and newsletters as two of the most prominent examples. In fact, the press release is a primary public relations tool, reflecting a number one goal of public relations activity: gaining publicity.

Publicity—editorial coverage as contrasted with advertising coverage—has the immediate advantage of being much more credible than paid advertising, for rather obvious reasons. It is also more visible, since many people simply hurry by print advertisements, whereas they will read news stories. It is for both these reasons that PR is preferable to advertising, although there are exceptions. There are ways to use commercial advertising beneficially.

The kind of commercial advertising that is an exception is the advertising of an event or activity that helps build the image you want. While offering your consulting services via paid advertisements will probably pay limited dividends directly in making sales and winning new clients, advertising a seminar, newsletter, or participation in a symposium or convention helps greatly to build your image as a prominent, busy professional. In this kind of usage, commercial advertising can be almost as effective as the best publicity.

Press Releases, News Releases, and Product Releases

The word *release,* with or without the adjective, *press* or *news,* refers to a communication, has as its major objective, persuading editors to publish the information offered in the release. That is information that publicizes you and what you offer. In fact, that kind of release is also referred to often as a *publicity release,* for that is its true purpose. The *product release* has the same objective, but is focused on getting publicity to introduce a product, usually a new one, to the world, often with photos offered the editors, if it is a product where a drawing or photograph adds materially to its appeal.

For format standards, there are only a few principles, rooted at least in part on the principles of journalistic practice. In fact, I would regard these as rules, despite the fact that all are violated frequently, usually in all innocence by individuals who simply do not know better. Here are a few of those "rules," in order of importance (I refer to *my* judgment of importance, that is), and not necessarily in the progression of steps you would usually follow to create a release. Figure 8-1 is offered as a first example, a release written on a letterhead, which is rather typical of releases issued by those who do so only occasionally. Check it as you read the following items to see examples of those items in that figure.

HRH COMMUNICATIONS,. INC.
P.O. Box 1731   Wheaton, MD 20915
Fax: (301) 649-5745   Voice: (301) 649-2499Z

6/28/96
For Immediate Release

Contact:
H. Holtz
301-649-2499

HOW TO SELL TO THE $200 BILLION GOVERNMENT MARKET

Information Now Available in Audiocassettes

Business people have long had difficulty getting information and guidance in selling to the U.S. Government, despite the literature on the subject, published by the government but poorly distributed.

Now, for the first time, a complete information and instruction package on selling to government agencies is available in a convenient audiocassette. The set includes four 1-hour cassettes and a 65-page directory of government purchasing offices, with a summary of the Federal Acquisition Regulations (FAR).

The package was developed over the past year by a team of government-marketing experts, who interviewed dozens of government purchasing officials and reviewed over 12,000 pages of official documents.

The program is available from HRH Communications, Inc. at $98.50 (discounted for quantity purchases).

(END)

Figure 8-1.   A Typical News Release

1. Copy is—should be—always double- or triple-spaced. That is to provide the editor with enough white space on the copy to make necessary editorial marks and changes in preparing it for publication. Editors will want to mark your copy up with their own changes and format ideas before submitting it to their typesetters.
2. Copy should be on one side of the paper only.

3. The word *NEWS* or *RELEASE,* with or without one of those adjectives I mentioned earlier, should appear prominently at or near the head of the page to identify it clearly.

4. The name of the issuing entity appears somewhere on the page, preferably also at or near the top. (Many people type releases on their normal letterheads, with the word "NEWS" or "RELEASE" at the top.)

5. The bottom of the page indicates whether there is more copy. Each page thus says "more" or "end" (or "###" or "30," which also indicate "end") on the last page.

6. The top of the page furnishes a "contact" for the editor to call if he or she has questions or wants to follow-up the release. Preferably, this should be a person's name, along with a title and telephone number.

Every one of these rules is violated regularly. That does not mean that the offending release will not be "picked up"—published—by some editors, but it does mean that if acceptability of the release is marginal, even slight defects may cause it to be banished to the waste basket without hesitation. The fact is that even under the best of circumstances (i.e., without the handicaps of less than optimal formatting and questionable newsworthiness) by far the majority of releases never make it beyond the editor's desktop for reasons other than clumsiness in format, such as a lack of newsworthiness, awkward writing, or of less interest and importance than other material available for the edition under preparation. Editors may rewrite poorly drawn releases, if the content is attractive enough, but the need to rewrite the release further reduces its chances for success in finding print. Bear in mind that editors of periodicals receive large numbers of releases every day. They are the competition you face, for the editors cannot use all the releases and must choose those of greatest interest. I listed those items I thought most important, in re format of the release. Much more important than format itself, however, is newsworthiness of content. Editors will never pass up a good story, and especially not on a "slow day," a day in which they have less than an abundance of usable material to publish.

Newsworthiness

"News" is or has become, at least, a most general, catchall term. There is such a thing as "hard news," which term usually refers to happenings of only hours ago and of interest to the public at large, such as a recent sensational murder, economic upheaval, war, national disaster, or other event that sells newspapers. That is time-sensitive information. When more than a few hours have elapsed since the information became public, it is not worthy of being called news, in the strictest sense. Yet, in another sense, anything that has happened but is not yet common knowledge is news—to someone. It is news to me when I learn that a magazine I read will suspend publication next month, for example, or that John Executive is leaving his position as Vice President of ABC Corporation to assume a new position as President of XYZ Corporation—if those corporations are either so big that such a change merits a story in the daily newspaper or they are of an industry in which I happen to be interested. The quality of newsworthiness depends not only on the information itself, but on the match of the information to the readers and their interests: What is important news in one periodical may be a "by the way" item or not worthy of mention at all in another periodical.

In fact, the term *news* can be and is stretched even further than that. The daily newspaper carries a great deal of material that is not, strictly speaking, news in even the most extended sense. They are *features* or *feature stories*. They include an enormous variety of information.

Newspapers carry many kinds of news. The *Washington Post* is probably a typical example. It's "Metro" section carries news of interest to those in Washington and its suburbs. The business section covers business news, of course, and includes information for investors. There are sections on travel, food, and health, among other subjects.

I don't read all of these, of course, probably nobody does. I read that which interests me, for whatever reason. What is in the food, health, or travel sections is usually of no interest to me. Those who read those sections may spend no time at all reading business news or even the front page. Of course, there are people who will read combinations of sections I do and do not read.

Editors understand, of course, that releases are sent to them in quests for publicity—free advertising, in fact—but there must be a *quid pro quo*—an exchange of useful copy for the publicity. Newsworthy copy is anything deemed to be of enough interest to be worthy of publication by the editors—of interest to their readers.

"Newsworthiness" is, therefore, relative to the interests of the readers. What is newsworthy for the readers of *Popular Mechanics* is probably also of interest to readers of *Mechanix Illustrated* but may not be to readers of *Money* magazine and probably not to readers of *Family Circle*.

Editors weigh this as a first consideration in reviewing a news release. The job of an editor is to present their readers with what they want to know. Readers of a magazine on antiques are not interested in tips on tuning up the newer automobile engines.

You therefore begin by deciding who you want to reach, what publications they read, and what will fit the publications' and the readers' interests. If you address those readers and their interests accurately, you will be in step with the editors. They are also guided by what they believe their readers want to read.

Consider Figure 8-2, a release of the National Association of Temporary Services, the members of which are companies supplying temporary workers in a wide variety of skills and professions. Note that this is a special form the association uses for their releases. The form is pre-printed, and releases are typed on that form. My name is on distribution for the releases of this organization because I requested information from that association some time ago in conducting research for a book I was writing. I will probably continue to get their releases for several years to come before my name is purged from the list. However, I did cite the organization and use some of the material in that book, so we both accomplished our purposes.

Release Dates

Note, in Figure 8-1, the words "For Immediate Release." That is not obligatory. If there is no statement regarding a release date, the editor will assume that the information is for immediate release. On the other hand, the release of Figure 8-2 provides a release date (i.e., the release is *embargoed* until 8:30 a.m., EDT, October 1, 1995). A release is usually embargoed to forestall premature release (e.g., the release reports the contents of a speech not yet delivered, the contents of an announcement yet to be made, or other such event yet to come). The word *embargo* may or may not itself be used, but the release date should be supplied if it is not to be immediate.

Headlines

The use of headlines in releases is arbitrary. Some advocate against it, some for it, and I am for it. I think it helps to capture the editor's interest

PRESS RELEASE

NATIONAL ASSOCIATION OF TEMPORARY SERVICES
119 SOUTH SAINT ASAPH ST., ALEXANDRIA, VA. 22314

TELEPHONE: 703/549-6287   **FOR RELEASE:**
CONTACT: Bruce Steinberg, Media Relations .
                [home 703/799-8918]   February 3, 1994

TEMPORARY HELP ASSOCIATION SAYS EMPLOYER MANDATES
COULD WEAKEN "JOBS BRIDGE"

(Washington, DC, February 3, 1994) -- The National Association of Temporary Services (NATS), which represents the nation's temporary help employers, testified today before the House Ways and Means Committee on the employer mandate and related provisions of the President's Health Security Act (H.R. 3600).

Edward A. Lenz, NATS senior vice president, legal and government affairs, said that the temporary help industry supports the principle of universal coverage, but has serious concerns that the cost of mandates could weaken the ability of the temporary help industry to act as a "jobs bridge" to regular, full-time employment.

According to Lenz, the temporary help industry has recently "assumed a new and vital role -- by helping to ease the burden on individuals during the current restructuring of the American work force. Temporary work offers displaced workers a critical safety net of income, benefits, and skills training and often provides a bridge back to regular, full-time employment."

In addition, the Association is concerned that the mandates, as currently structured, would "also impose enormous administrative burdens" due to annual temporary employee turnover in the range of 400 to 600 percent. If employer mandates are adopted, Lenz urged Congress to create a mechanism that relates premium payments to hours worked, such as a simple payroll tax.

The temporary help industry, in the third quarter of 1993, employed approximately 1.68 million people on a daily basis, or approximately 1.5% of the total work force.

Figure 8-2.   An Association Release

and help him or her grasp the essence of the story immediately. The argument made against the use of headlines in releases is that editors prefer to write their own headlines. That may be true, but it is irrelevant because the editor is free to change the original headline and very likely will do so. Why deny yourself one of the key opportunities to make your "sales argument" (capture attention and arouse interest) immediately?

Cautions

It's easy enough to make mistakes that will nullify all your work, and even to make some that will make it difficult for you to ever get your releases accepted in the future. Be careful, check your facts and figures for accuracy and proofread your copy thoroughly. If you make a mistake that causes an editor to commit some faux pas and be embarrassed, you will probably kill your chances of ever again having that editor consider your releases seriously. It is therefore especially important to be careful about accuracy in general and such other details as have been mentioned here; your relationships with editors is at stake, and that is an important factor in conducting PR successfully. So is your image, not only as a consultant but also as a business executive and professional person. Offering your releases in meticulously correct form lends the editor some assurance that you are a reliable professional, just as making too many mistakes of format may stamp you in the editor's mind as a bungling tyro.

One of the common mistakes has to do with where to send releases. It is a mistake, generally, to address a release to a large publication or other medium without specifying an individual destination. (An exception to this would be in the case of a small newsletter or other publication where the release could not possibly get lost.) Remember that in large organizations mail addressed to the organization generally is usually opened in the mail room, where someone attempts to judge the proper destination within the organization. On a large newspaper your release is likely to wind up on a managing editor's or city editor's desk, or it could even wind up on the circulation manager's desk, if you have not specified otherwise. That individual may or may not spend the time reading your release and deciding that it ought to go to the business editor, food editor, or even the state desk. He or she may simply be too busy to bother and drop it casually into the "circular file" without further thought. Even if he or she decides to pass it on to someone else it is still likely to wind up in the wrong place and eventually find its way into that famous circular file just mentioned, never to be heard from or seen again.

On the other hand, even if you do manage to get it to the individual editor, columnist, or other party you mean it for, it is still necessary that the release be "right" for that party—be of true interest. You do not—should not—ordinarily write a release and then decide where to send it, but you should follow the reverse pattern, along the following line of procedure:

1. Decide who—what reader/viewer/prospect you want to reach.
2. Decide what kinds of media—which periodicals, what columnists, what radio or TV programs, etc—are most suitable for reaching those prospects. What do they read, watch, listen to?
3. Decide what would interest the editor/columnist/producer, etc—how to slant your release.

Slanting Copy

Slanting copy is a simple concept. It means writing the release in such a way as to address the direct interests of a given audience. Suppose, for example, that you are selling computer software services, and are preparing a release to help make your consulting practice more widely known. Suppose that you wish to offer a free demonstration and how-to-do-it seminar as a means for attracting prospective clients and publicizing your practice. You decide to issue a news release announcing that offering to the world. What next?

There are several possibilities open to you. Your release will have to suggest some particular program or kind of program you will be demonstrating. Suppose you have a choice among a new inventory control and inventory management program, a new word processor, or the latest and most popular computer game. Which one is most likely to attract the prospects you want?

Obviously that depends on the kind of prospects you want. An inventory program is going to attract only businesspeople for whom inventory control and management is important. It certainly is not likely to appeal to the owner of a small luncheonette or a high school youngster. The game program will not appeal to the businessperson normally.

That's a rather obvious case. Not all are so obvious. It does point up something: You can create more than one version of a release so that you can attract many people. You must also think in terms of the periodicals and other media to which you slant your material. Even that can vary from one publication to another. What one newspaper calls the "Financial Editor" another may title the "Business Editor," although the dullest mail room clerk may be able to interpret your wishes and direct your release to the right editors. Don't count on it: Always assume the worst ("Murphy's Law") and plan according to that assumption.

This is even more critical when you want to send releases to columnists in the hope that they will become interested in your announcements. These must normally be addressed by name, and since many are syndicated and are not on the staff of the individual periodical carrying the column, you must either determine what the columnist's mailing address is or send your release in care of the periodical. (A chat with your local librarian may guide you to the latest directory of syndicates and syndicated columnists so that you can direct your release directly to the columnist of your choice.)

Not everything can be slanted effectively. It would be difficult to slant a release for a male audience explaining how crocheting is making a strong comeback: Few men are likely to take up crocheting. On the other hand relatively few women are enthusiastic about fly fishing. So an article or release on fly fishing might be slanted to fly fishermen with different interests—some like to tie their own flies, while others prefer to buy them ready made and will try every new one they can find—but they have to have that common interest in fly fishing. (In fact, perhaps the most common factor among fly fishermen is their almost legendary zeal, which borders on fanaticism, according to many stories.) On the other hand it is entirely possible that you might be able to slant material on fly fishing even to women who have no direct interest in fishing at all if you address the wives and significant others of fly fishermen with an appeal to buy fly-fishing gear or accessories as gifts to the zealots they love.

Many products and services lend themselves to multiple uses and users, and each potential use and user suggest the keys to a slant. In writing releases to publicize my own newsletters, books, and reports on marketing to government agencies I found many ways to slant them to different audiences. The most obvious and most basic slanting opportunities were these:

- To companies already doing business with the government. The theme was how to do more business with the government.

- To companies who had done little or no business with the government. The theme here was how to break into the government market most effectively.

It is easy to double the number of opportunities, in this case, by splitting your targets into small and large companies, and even to quadruple them by addressing a special category of "mini-small" businesses—those that are home-based and operated as "independent" enterprises. That is, in fact, a rather large and fast-growing element of today's business society.

There are even other possibilities: I can slant releases to small businesses, minority-owned businesses, very small businesses (such as freelancing individuals), businesses by the nature of what they sell, businesses by the nature of the kinds of customers they pursue, and even more possibilities than these. (These are also known as "niche markets.") With an active imagination and a bit of introspection on possible uses and users, slanting offers a great many possibilities and is usually not especially difficult.

This idea of slanting is not for releases only. It is equally useful in writing advertising copy, sales letters, brochures, magazine articles, and just about everything else that might be addressed to the public generally or to any specific class or group of people. The key is simply finding the links between the various readers' interests and what you wish to publicize.

Within every specialty there are more specialties, and sometimes these offer profitable niches that have been overlooked or neglected by others. Investors, for example, often specialize in the types of investments they make and are good prospects for only services relevant to those types of investments. When I sold my services to government contractors, I found small software consulting firms to be my best prospects as those most conscious of a need for help in pursuing government contracts. That does not mean that they were the only group, of course, but only that they were an especially responsive group, a niche market I pursued with great success. I also pursued other niche markets that were well worth the effort.

Product Releases

Many periodicals carry a regular section in which they report on new products. However, any periodical is likely to report on a useful new item—product or service—that is brought to their attention. These notices generally include the price and specifications, and often include a photograph or drawing of the item, if it is a product best presented graphically.

Using Releases in Your Direct-Mail

The release is a versatile promotional piece. It has many other uses that help in promoting your services and related products. Those who use the mails for promotion find their press releases to be useful as mailing pieces, and generally include copies of their releases in all promotional packages, whether mailed to clients and prospective clients, handed out as press kits, or distributed to groups via literature tables, as in the case of seminars, trade shows, and conventions. They can be used with almost as much versatility as you use business cards and brochures, and with the extra advantage that they imply new and special information.

NEWSLETTERS

Another mainstay of PR activity for many entrepreneurs is the newsletter. The newsletter is a promotional tool of great and growing popularity in this era of computers and DTP (desktop publishing) software programs. These modern high-tech tools make it rather easy for anyone to turn out professional-looking publications. Most of the technical skills one might otherwise need to do the job well are furnished in the software. Even so, there is more to turning out a first-class newsletter than choosing from among the many attractive format options offered by sophisticated DTP software programs. From that vantage point, newsletter publishing looks simple enough, but like many other things, publishing a newsletter—or publishing any periodical, for that matter—involves many functions not apparent to the casual observer. It involves those many and complex editorial functions that so many shrink from as strange and difficult. Before we get to those, let's have a general look at newsletters, focusing on two points:

1. There are many, many thousands of newsletters published. In the United States, estimates range from 30,000 to 100,000, depending on what one includes in the definition of a newsletter. They are produced by individuals and organizations of almost every possible descrip-

tion—companies and corporations, associations, government agencies at federal, state, and local levels, and sundry other groups, organized for sundry other purposes. They are written for profit and for promotion. Because the omnipresent modern PC makes it so easy to produce a newsletter, their numbers are growing rapidly.

2. There is one striking truth about newsletter publishing: The editorial functions necessary in newsletter work are relatively simple, as compared with those necessary to produce proposals, manuals, and many other publications with which we are sometimes unavoidably involved. That is not to say that there are no editorial problems in newsletter publishing, but they are different and usually simpler kinds of problems.

Given that most newsletters are relatively small, only a few pages in size, and produced on relatively leisurely schedules (monthly, most commonly, but still often on bimonthly or quarterly schedules), it might seem at first glance that they are not much more trouble to produce on ordinary office typewriters than on more expensive and more sophisticated computer systems, with their word processors and laser printers. That would be a reasonable conclusion, if one considers the "production" (typing and layout) requirements only. There are many other needs in newsletter publishing which good software and a bit of computer skill can satisfy quite well, which typewriter production cannot satisfy: Good software programs can do many more things than word processing per se. In fact, many busy newsletter publishers have contracted out certain tasks which they could do more effectively and certainly more economically in-house, with the aid of their own systems. Let's first take a brief overview of newsletter publishing to get some appreciation of the many functions and problems.

Newsletter Concepts

There are three broad concepts or objectives on which most newsletters are based:

1. Some newsletters present periodic summaries of news and related information of interest which has appeared in the public and/or trade press since the previous edition, and/or has come in over the transom, usually via releases and other sources. This is intended to serve busy readers by enabling them to keep up with everything of impor-

tance without the impossible job of reading dozens of publications while also attending to their jobs, businesses, and/or careers (i.e., such newsletters serve readers primarily as digests of news relevant to the readers' interests). This approach requires that you read a great many publications and abstract pertinent information from them regularly. It does, however, demonstrate to the readers that you are "keeping up" in the field of direct interest, and is thus an asset to your professional image.

2. Some newsletters cover subjects or aspects of subjects that are not reported on extensively by other publications, usually because their subject is highly specialized and of interest to a relative few (one consultant publishes a newsletter for those interested in electrical batteries and their development), or is "news behind the news." Readers of these newsletters, having such specialized interests and belonging to a relatively small community of people with that special interest, would have a rather difficult job, presumably, of gathering that information for themselves. Again, this kind of coverage reflects well on your professional image.

3. Some newsletters are primarily opinion- and advice-giving journals, and are based on either the authoritative expertise of the editor and staff (if there is an editorial staff) or access to "inside" information. Financial advisory newsletters, for example, would fit this category. It is easily conceivable that many newsletters published by consultants would fall into this category, and many do. Such a newsletter orientation offers you an opportunity to demonstrate the wisdom and value of your judgment and counsel in your special field.

Newsletters are no purer than are most things, and many newsletters embody combinations of the characteristics described, while remaining predominantly one of the three types. However, it is only by serving some special need that most newsletters are able to attract and keep subscribers, even though the subscription is complimentary to clients and prospective clients. The newsletter used as a marketing promotion pays its way in attracting new clients and retaining existing ones.

The Promo Newsletter

The promo newsletter is almost in a special class in itself, a fourth category, but it is different only in its objective, and not in its kind of coverage. The premise here is that the three general types of newsletter discussed above are all intended to be distributed at no charge because their primary purpose is to serve as marketing and sales promotion tools. So while they may be structured along the lines of any of the general types, they carry some amount of sales–promotional material in the editorial content and may even carry open and unabashed advertisements.

This does not mean that every newsletter published by a consultant is distributed freely. Quite the contrary, many consultants derive a substantial part of their income from their newsletters. Too, in some cases consultants have begun with a complimentary newsletter and soon found their newsletters so successful that readers were quite willing to pay for subscriptions, resulting in the newsletter becoming a significant source of income. Securities salesman Bernard Gallagher and information guru Matthew Lesko are two examples of newsletter publishers who found their promotional newsletters well enough received to turn them into sources of income.

Typical Newsletter Style and Format Characteristics

In specific content, and recognizing that there are exceptions in every case, the following characterizes most newsletters in style and format matter:

- Four to sixteen 8½ × 11-inch pages.
- 2,000 to 8,000 words of copy.
- Composed by typewriter or computer, and justified or ragged right margin.
- Telegraphic writing style, omitting articles, conjunctions, and other parts of speech not essential to meaning.
- All text; no illustrations except for occasional chart or graph.
- No advertisements; 100 percent editorial copy. (Readers who pay a relatively large subscription fee for a few pages of copy are usually not pleased to find portions of those few pages devoted to paid advertising messages.)

Figure 8-3 illustrates the front page of the promotional newsletter of consultant Dorothy A. Creswell, operator of D C Consulting, Inc., Ankenny, Iowa. It is published every month, printed on white paper, four or more pages normally, and without advertising.

A MONTHLY NEWSLETTER FOR THE CLIENTS OF

d c c ®

Data Communications and Computer Consulting

E X E C U T I V E
COMPUTING

PRACTICAL REPORTS ON BUSINESS COMPUTING

JANUARY 1994

Notebook market full of trade-offs

Few industries are as fast-paced as the computer industry. New hardware and software products are released daily. And within the computer industry, no segment is as fast-paced as portable computing.

Most recently we've seen the arrival of two new classes of computers: subnotebooks and personal digital assistants. Subnotebooks are slimmer, lighter, and in several ways less powerful than full-sized notebook computers. But their light weight and small footprint make them very attractive to business travelers.

Personal digital assistants, or PDAs, are handheld devices not intended to replace computers, but rather, to work as personal communicators and information managers.

Of course, all this innovation means more choices — and more questions. What do you sacrifice when you purchase a subnotebook rather than a full-sized notebook computer? Is a personal digital assistant really worthwhile or just another gadget?

So now it's easier than ever to take computing power with you, but harder than ever to decide exactly what to take.

Dorothy A. Creswell

Portable manufacturers offer you various sizes, features, capacities

Notebooks, subnotebooks, and personal digital assistants — there have never been more choices in the portable computing arena. And there have never been more trade-offs. Each class of computer asks you to sacrifice something, be it portability, expandability or usability.

Here is what you can expect to get, and give up, from the two newest categories of computing devices, subnotebooks and personal digital assistants:

Subnotebooks offer light weight, ample power

Not content with notebook computers that weigh in at six to nine pounds, portable computer makers have created yet another category of portable computers called the subnotebook. On the heavy end, you'll find subnotebooks tipping the scale at five pounds, such as the Compudyne 4SL/25 Subnote. On the light end, you'll find compact computers, such as the Hewlett Packard OmniBook 300, the 425 and the Gateway's HandBook, weighing in at under three pounds.

Most subnotebooks, however, weigh between three and four pounds. If you need to take along an AC adapter and an external drive, you'll be carrying an additional 1.5 to 3 pounds.

Some of these smaller units are called palmtops or handheld devices, but to distinguish subnotebooks from pocket-sized "personal organizers," subnotebooks are generally defined as any computer with a full-sized or near-full-sized keyboard and the ability to run standard software programs, not simply ROM-based look-a-likes.

Subnotebooks offer convenience. They come in packages small enough not to require an extra carrying case for storage. Instead, they fit in most standard briefcases and still give you lots of room to spare. Frequent travelers will appreciate the convenience.

They may be light in weight, but they're not lightweight when it comes to processing power. Many subnotebooks are outfitted with 486SX, DX or SL microprocessors, fast enough for Windows and OS/2 applications.

And while most don't pack unusually large hard drives, you can easily find subnotebooks with hard drives containing 40, 60, 80, 125 or even 170MB of space. That should be more than enough to run personal productivity applications on the road.

Figure 8-3. Newsletter of D C Consulting, Inc.

Dorothy delivers her personal message on the front page and offers news and technical information—but not heavily technical—on the inside of her publication. Usually, the information is slanted toward business applications, since she writes for users of computer consulting services, and those users may or may not have interest in or use for "heavy" technical data.

Figure 8-4 reproduces the front page of *the khera business report*, published by Raj Khera, owner of khera Communications, Inc., of Gaithersburg, Maryland. Raj addresses other consultants in this issue with a subject of never-ending interest: pricing services.

Some newsletter publishers mail their copies out in envelopes, most often folded down to fit into an ordinary number 10 business envelope, but most mail them as "self-mailers," with an address block printed on the last page. (See Figure 8-5.) The newsletter is folded twice to present an envelope sized item. If these have a seal or staple to keep them folded, they generally journey through the machines of the Postal Service safely. Unfortunately, when mailed without some device to ensure that the newsletter remains folded, the newsletter is often mangled in those machines.

Frequency of Publication

By far the majority of newsletters are published on a monthly basis, twelve issues per year. It is not uncommon, however, for some newsletter publishers to omit one or two months—July or August (vacation time) and/or December (Christmas and New Year season), and so publish only ten or eleven issues each year.

A month may seem like an ample period to prepare each issue of a 4- to 8-page newsletter, but the monthly deadline rolls around with astonishing frequency. It always seems as though it was only a couple of days ago that you heaved a sigh of relief to get that issue mailed out. For that reason, you may wish to consider a bimonthly or even quarterly schedule. There are even newsletters that are published on a completely undefined schedule: The publisher produces the next issue whenever he or she finds it convenient to do so. (Obviously, this should be done only with a complimentary newsletter; you can't expect people to pay for something they cannot be sure of getting!)

In that regard, it is much easier to increase the schedule frequency (e.g., from bimonthly to monthly) than to decrease it (e.g., from monthly

APRIL 1993

PROFIT-MAKING STRATEGIES FOR HIGH TECHNOLOGY BUSINESSES

the khera business report

PUBLISHED BY *Khera Communications, Inc.,* GAITHERSBURG, MARYLAND

Quotable Quotes

"The first impression you make with your client should be the very best; you can never overcome the effects of a questionable image in your client's mind."

- William Cohen

"For small businesses, setting prices isn't textbook mechanical...it is usually a sweaty process."

- Ronald Torrence

In future issues:

Productivity Tools: A Guide to Software That Makes a Difference

What to Put in Your Company's Brochures

Writing a Press Release That Gets Published

And More!

If you don't receive *The Khera Business Report*, call (301) 309-0969 right now for free trial issues!

Pricing Your Professional Services

How much are your services worth? How much do you charge for your work? Pricing your services is one of the most challenging aspects of running a business. If you price too high, you might not get many clients. If you price too low, you might not make any money.

$81 per hour. That's what one management consultant calculated for one consultant to earn $50,000 per year. Let's take a closer look.

First, to calculate the yearly billable time, deduct the following days from one year: 15 for vacation, 9 for holidays, 5 for sick, 12 for training, 44 for marketing (one day each week), 104 for weekends, and 28 for administrative activities (one hour each day). In a non-leap year, this leaves 148 billable days, or 1184 hours for a typical eight-hour day.

Now, add the following to a $50,000 yearly salary for overhead:

◆ $3600 for insurance (medical, life, disability, liability, etc.),
◆ $7200 for rent (in a one-room office suite),

(See page 2 - PRICING)

Figure 8-4. Newsletter of Khera Communications, Inc.

D C Consulting, Inc.
P.O. Box 195
Ankeny, IA 50021-0195

Address correction requested

Figure 8-5.   Back Page, Showing Address Block

to bimonthly). The psychological effect—the perception by the client—is an unfavorable one in the latter case.

Some newsletter publishers use serial numbering for each issue instead of calendar identification, as in Figure 8-6, the newsletter of Steve Lanning, director of The Consultant National Resource Center of Big Spring, Maryland. Dave Voracek, who operates his The Marketing Department in Alexandria, Virginia, publishes his own monthly news-

CONSULTING OPPORTUNITIES JOURNAL®

America's Continuing Education Source For The Marketing of Professional Services
Published By **The Consultant National Resource Center**

Vol. 10, No. 4   ISSN: 0273-4613

Horizontal Marketing Opportunities for COJers

[Editor's Note: Vertical Marketing is the sum total of activi ties and strategies you pursue in developing your niche or vertical marketplace in your field. For instance if your field is engineering, all activities that promote your position with clients in engineering would be considered vertical. The horizontal aspect of marketing comes when you earn income from areas not in your target area of expertise.]

Case history 1: Management consultant in the area of safety earns extra cash flow from leads he generates with clients for environmental consulting—and vice versa.

Case history 2: Training consultant in mergers/acquisitions gets invited to be a part of program at several trade shows in unrelated industries. She gives the breakout sessions free and is invited back because she doesn't "hawk her wares" to the attendees—although she is asked for more information by a good portion of the audience because she gives solid and valuable information thereby making her tradeshow host look good.

Case history 3: Computer consultant introduces CEO/owners to strategic planning/marketing

See Horizontal on page 2

International Opportunities On The Rise

In 1983, J. Stephen Lanning, the Executive Director of Consultants National Resource Center (CNRC) started taking note of the consulting audiences he spoke to as to international activity. He then did the same for 1992.

Going over the COJ back issues from that period and his notes on his surveys it was noted that in 1983 the highest percentage of the audience doing consulting outside the USA and Canada was 22%. Taking the same survey again in 1992 the highest percentage was 85% (packaging consultants). Averages have risen, too.

What's The Reason?

Activity stems mostly from the former Soviet slave states of Rumania, Hungary and so forth with Southeast Asia running a close second for independent practitioners. New development is the primary reason.

The CNRC has one member who is

See International Oppotunities on page 3

Vertical Marketing Update...
Seminar Marketing Again Takes Lead in Generating Clients

Are seminars effective in generating clients? What do we mean by effective? What are the lasting benefits in developing a seminar, workshop or simply a less-than-one-hour talk? Are there any negatives actual or perceived by potential clients?

Our Famous $100,000 Story...

Just for fun, we went back to the October 1983 issue of COJ where we answered those questions with the lead story, "Consultants Sell Over $100,000 in Services In One Day..." (Vol 3. No. 3.) Well that was then. Has anything changed?

The total volume from that one day venture for the consultants in the article exceeded $160,000—granted, very unusual for a firm of just four employees—

with one being full time support. But nonetheless not all that rare today in the world of seminars and backend selling in this age of targeted database marketing. [CNRC does have a few copies of that issue left @ $10. postpaid from CNRC on a first-come bases.]

It's true that today's audiences are more sophisticated than in 1983, but from what the Center has been hearing, seminars DO continue to produce clients. In fact so

See Seminar Leads Again on page 2.

> **Don't miss the next issue for what may be at least one, possibly two of the biggest announcements in consulting history!**

Figure 8-6. Serially Numbered Newsletter

letter, 12 months a year, with serial numbers to identify the issues. (See Figure 8-7.)

"Canned" or "Private Brand" Newsletters

Manufacturers of many kinds of products will "private brand" them for quantity purchasers. Every major supermarket chain, drug store chain, and other such retailers have their private brands, usually manufactured by the major corporations but packaged with the chain stores' labels. Labels on merchandise today, from soup to television sets, may or may not identify the real or original manufacturer.

Much the same thing is possible for the consultant who wants to publish a newsletter. There are many newsletter publishers who will produce a special version of their newsletter for you in whatever quantity you require, with provision for you to insert your own name, logo, and copy. Usually, the original publisher will allow you up to a full page, or simply insert your name, whichever you wish. The newsletter illustrated in Figure 8-3 is one of that type. It is the product of Executive Computing of Berkeley, California. The newsletter is monthly, and the costs vary, in proportion to the quantity ordered.

Newsletter Content and Editorial Problems

The major problem of a newsletter editor is (or should be) sorting available material to decide what to use—in effect, deciding what material is indispensable and must be published somehow, so the rest is to be screened out. If the editor/staff is doing the job well, there is usually far more material available at each editorial deadline than can be fitted into the space available. Typically, the editor has been gathering material steadily since the previous edition, storing it somewhere until the time comes to begin making up the next edition. At that point, the editor decides which items to use and which to discard.

There are different ways to do this. Some editors will simply store all the raw source data until some predeadline date, and then begin making all the decisions and preparing the copy that will go into the next edition. Others will decide that certain pieces are "must" items, and will prepare the copy well in advance of the deadline, leaving space open and other material stored until the time arrives to make final decisions. (I kept a special in-basket into which went everything that arrived at my

Management, Marketing & Design News Highlights
Compiled for clients and friends of The Marketing Department by
Dave Voracek • P.O. Box 3525 • Alexandria, VA 22302 • (703) 824-8787   Volume 11, Number 1

**TOP
BRANDS**

What are America's "Cadillac" product brands? Sad to say, that car didn't make the cut. But an EquiTrend survey of 2,000 men and women over age 15 found these to be the top products that signify "quality" to the public...

1.	Disney World & Disneyland	6.	AT&T long-distance
2.	Kodak film	7.	Mercedes automobiles
3.	UPS package delivery	8.	Arm & Hammer products
4.	Hallmark cards	9.	Chiquita bananas
5.	Fisher-Price toys	10.	Levi's jeans

The bottom of the list included both Diet Coke and Diet Pepsi, U.S. Sprint and MCI long-distance, Lillian Vernon mail order items and Sanka ground coffee. Interesting.

**ODDS ARE
GETTING
BETTER**

Four out of five U.S. businesses fail within five years. That's the old rule of thumb. But a new study by the New Jersey Institute of Technology paints a more optimistic picture. They tracked 814,000 new businesses from 1978 to 1986... a period including the 1982 recession...and discovered that more than half made it past the killer fifth year. Economist Bruce Kirchhoff reports that 28% of the companies survived with their original owners, along with an additional 26% who continued on under new owners. Of the rest, 28% were shuttered voluntarily sometime during the eight-year study period, and only 18% of the firms failed in the sense that they left outstanding liabilities. The study also noted that roughly 400,000 people take the plunge into new businesses each year...with the odds in their favor, it now seems.

**THEY
CREATE
CHANGE**

What is the "mind style" of an entrepreneur? A revealing story in the April issue of *SUCCESS* magazine interviewed Harvard professor of business administration Howard Stevenson. "Successful entrepreneurs know their business," he says, "but they don't get married to the previous concepts of the business. It's a curious challenge, because to be successful, you have to understand every detail about your business and your customers. But that doesn't mean you can be locked into things as they are." There are three attitudes Stevenson believes entrepreneurs must have...

- Behind every situation is an opportunity. Successful entrepreneurs try to figure out a way to do things better.
- Entrepreneurs take personal responsibility for bringing about the needed improvement.
- Many times successful people were told by the experts that they were crazy. The mind-set of entrepreneurs is that maybe the experts are wrong.

One of the lessons the professor stresses to his students is that "No success is permanent and no failure is final." Now those are words to live by.

LOOK/SEE

Send for your free video. We have recently done three campaigns where a 10-minute customized videotape was the feature of the promotion. In two instances, the tapes were the perfect way to demonstrate pieces of equipment and sell their

Figure 8-7. A Marketing Consultant's Newsletter

desk and seemed worth considering. When the preappointed day arrived, I began to sort it out to select that which I would use that month.)

At the same time, most knowledgeable editors of periodicals maintain some backup items (items which are not particularly sensitive to the time factor and can be published at almost any time) as a kind of insurance against times when either there is not enough good material or there is an opportunity to fit in a good item that could not be fitted into an earlier edition. (I recently was one of several guests taping interview segments for a new home-business TV show, the tape to be kept for a bad day when weather or some other calamity prevented expected guests from arriving.)

Where Does the Copy Come From?

One of the great fears of those contemplating newsletter publishing is the fear that they will not have enough worthwhile material to fill the issues on a regular basis. If you have such a fear, it is understandable: You are not, after all a journalist or writer, and so unfamiliar with the matter of writing research and "sources."

That is one reason you may wish to consider a boilerplated newsletter that you can buy, with your own name imprinted, and perhaps even with some space made available for your own brief material in each issue.

That isn't the only way to turn out your own newsletter. There are freelance writers who will do the job for you, and will even dig up information for your newsletter. However, if you do choose to produce your own newsletter, getting material for each issue is not a great problem. In fact, after a time it is more a problem to decide what to use from the abundance of material you have. Here, in general, are the principal sources available:

- Ideas inspired by or abstracts of information in other publications you read.
- Others' press releases and other information arriving in your morning mail.
- Ideas derived from conversations with clients and associates.
- "Lifts" from others newsletters or periodicals.
- Letters from readers and other clients or prospective clients.
- Submissions from freelance writers.

Let us have a brief look at each of these:

Abstracts of already-published information.   This is perfectly legitimate, but unless you have the other publisher's permission to quote directly, you must rewrite the information and publish it in your own language. (The original text is protected by copyright, but the information is not, so it is perfectly acceptable to present the information in your own words.)

Press releases and other material in your morning mail.   Press releases may be quoted verbatim; in fact, that is the idea of a press release. You can get yourself on many distribution lists for press releases. For example, I was once on distribution lists for releases from Congress and many government agencies. Once on a list or two, and once a few issues of your newsletter are in circulation, your name will start popping up in lots of places from which you will get releases, brochures, reports, and other information.

"Lifts" from other periodicals.   Many other newsletter publishers grant permission freely to quote them verbatim—even run standing notices to that effect—as long as you make proper attribution so that your readers know where the information came from originally. Here, you need not rewrite, but may quote verbatim.

Letters from readers and others.   This needs no explanation. You generally publish only abstracts of those letters, but be sure you have permission.

Submissions from freelance writers.   You can also solicit submissions from freelance writers, offering payment. A notice posted in one of the writers' magazines or on a few electronic bulletin boards will bring you submissions, which you may then buy, if they suit your needs.

The Computer as an Editorial Safe

Editors and publishers are human, with typical human failings, of course; sometimes they lose manuscripts. (On more than one occasion, I have sold pieces to magazines which paid for them, but never ran them, having lost or mislaid them somehow, and once my book manuscript, already paid for, was mislaid for over a year before the staff found it again.)

The one major advantage of saving material in computer storage, rather than in a hanging file or desk drawer, is that data on a disk is far less likely or able to wander off and hide somewhere than is hard copy stored in a dusty file somewhere. (Some editors like to call these places "safes," although the "safe" is most likely the bottom of a huge stack of paper in a bottom drawer of a battered old oak desk, where it is far from safe against anything but long-term anonymity.)

The problem of where and how to store raw source data remains, unless the convenient expedient of entering all of it into computer storage is considered a viable solution. It makes a great deal of sense to decide in advance what you find useful, write it up, and then enter that into your computer storage, while material of doubtful value may be saved in its original form, since losing it is not of great consequence anyhow. That was excellent logic just a few years ago, when disk storage was quite expensive. Now, however, disk storage has become rather inexpensive, with even modestly priced desktop computers boasting storage capacities to and greater than 100 to 300 megabytes—the capacity to hold many thousands of pages of copy. Moreover, the computer gives you the enormous advantage of being able to search through what is stored there. If you wish to make each edition of your newsletter linked to a common subject, the search capabilities of word processor or other software facilitates finding related subjects quickly. Or you might have already sorted the raw data and stored it in separate files.

Once you have decided what you will definitely want to use, either in the upcoming edition or in a future edition, the efficient thing to do is to prepare it for makeup by writing it up or editing it into final shape, and entering it into whatever file you have started as the final one. Since you will not know until later how much space you will have or what the piece will compete with for space, it is wise to use the journalistic approach of writing the piece in the classic "inverted pyramid" of journalism to simplify the job of copy fitting.

The journalistic inverted pyramid.   The concept of the inverted pyramid is, briefly, to present the who, what, when, where, why, and how as succinctly as possible in the lead sentence, and then add details gradually in succeeding sentences and paragraphs. Thus, there is the story presented in the lead sentence, and the item may be cut at any time and place, and you have a usable item, without losing the story.

In newspaper practice, dealing with straight news accounts, the practice is to first present the bare facts of the story, and then elaborate, level by level, in succeeding paragraphs. Cutting, then, simply means cutting some of the detail, not cutting out any of the essence of the story. For example, a lead sentence might say, "John Hodgkins, President of Acme Tool & Die Works of Harper City, announced today that his company will merge with Consolidated Metal Works of Bridgeport." Every additional sentence will then add details.

The technique need not be confined to news stories; it can be used to present almost any kind of narrative account because it is readily adaptable to other kinds of items. It offers the greatest convenience in finally making up the camera-ready mechanicals. What this means, in effect, is storing material that is approximately one-third to one-half greater than you can use, not counting the material that you consider to be in the safe. Then, when it is time to prepare the camera-ready mechanicals, the job is principally one of deciding on the relative importance of the stories and their details, and cutting accordingly. Because space is always at a premium in a newsletter, rigorous editing is necessary to cram the maximum amount of useful information into the space available. The style is therefore as clipped as possible, even telegraphic, but certainly "lean."

You should try hard to learn lean writing, writing that captures the essence without the extraneous and the trivial details, but also without the verbiage that lends writing a certain style, but is not absolutely essential to central meaning. For example, let's "lean" this foregoing sentence. Here is how I would do that:

> Learn "lean" writing. Capture essence, omit unimportant detail, drop articles and conjunctions, and keep language lean.

Note the absence of articles (e.g., "the") and, wherever possible, conjunctions too. Good editing reduces word count by one-third, in most cases. For newsletters, you can often cut it to one-half and even less.

Physical Format

Some newsletters use typewritten full measure, which means a single column of copy extending from the left-hand margin to the right-hand margin as in typing a letter. This is probably the most efficient use of the space, but many newsletter publishers prefer to use a two-column format, either justified or unjustified. The ragged-right (unjustified) format with hyphenation is probably a more efficient use of the space, but the justified copy is considered more attractive, and perhaps more professional-looking to some publishers. Probably the two-column format is easier to read, but any argument for the allegedly better appearance of justified copy, as compared with ragged-right copy, runs into some counter-arguments that the typewritten and ragged-right copy appears more spontaneous and timely, qualities regarded as assets for a newsletter. That is, after all, a matter mostly of stylistic preference, rather than practical expediency.

There is probably not a great deal of difference in space usage between justified right and ragged right, for any given type font, but there are condensed fonts that do make more efficient use of the space. You might therefore consider using a condensed font.

In these matters, as in most, there is no unvarying truth. It is doubtful that any newsletter reader spends time contemplating such matters as spontaneity of appearance or the virtues of one format as compared with another. In any case, the now-common use of word processors and related equipment makes such arguments irrelevant, since between the software and the hardware (and especially in the growing diversity of printer capabilities) the newsletter publisher is offered a wide variety of capabilities, such as printers with proportional spacing, which make highly economical use of the space. There are many other considerations in using word processing for newsletter publishing than the editorial ones, which, you may remember, are admittedly relatively minor here, as compared with other publications projects and tasks.

Further Considerations

Newsletter publishing involves a number of related functions and attendant problems, many of which you may have never considered or even been aware existed. Perhaps publishing a newsletter involves commitment to a great deal more obligations than you realize or are willing to undertake. Following are a few "musts" for most newsletters. Although not all may apply to you, consider them.

1. Establishing circulation. For the publisher of the for-profit newsletter, this means soliciting subscriptions, but even the newsletter sent out to a mailing list strictly as a marketing tool (i.e., complimentary) must

have a mailing list of suitable readers, if it is to do the job it is sent out
to do.

2. Mailing copies faithfully to the list at each publication date. This
means addressing labels, envelopes, wrappers, or something that
will bear the name and address, as well as the physical chores of
doing the mailing. Again, the computer, with a suitable database
program, simplifies the task greatly.

3. Keeping records of the status of each subscriber, especially of subscribers who are required to pay subscription fees and whose fees
support the publication.

4. Maintaining the mailing lists (i.e., "cleaning" them of nixies [undeliv-
erable addresses] and expires).

5. Keeping up-to-date status information on customers who have
bought books, reports, cassettes, or other ancillary materials from
you.

6. Maintaining other mailing lists such as prospects for marketing purposes, former subscribers, and buyers of other products or services
you sell.

A Newsletter That Is Not a Newsletter

No matter what frequency you choose as that for your newsletter schedule—monthly, bimonthly, or other—the deadline always comes at a most
inconvenient time, a time when you are preoccupied with other pressing
duties and schedules. You are thus faced with a problem every month,
which you may be able to solve by publishing on a when-convenient
schedule, as explained earlier (Figure 8-6), or resorting to another device
I developed some years ago when I faced that problem: I invented a
newsletter that was not a newsletter.

I decided that the problem was in the expectations I engendered in
the reader. By publishing a newsletter that had a regular calendar identification—usually the name of the month of issue—I was rather clearly
advising my reader that he or she could expect an issue each month at
the same time, with the possible exception of the one or two months of
the year I chose not to publish. I decided to avoid making that promise or
even implying it. I chose to create the non-newsletter periodical, for
which I nevertheless charged a subscription fee based on a span of some
number of issues—twelve for a full year's subscription.

I promised, instead of a monthly newsletter, a series of special reports that I would send out during the year, minimum of twelve, with the probability of more—bonus reports—occasionally. It was successful immediately, and I was able to the establish a production schedule suited to my convenience. I had no difficulty selling subscriptions, despite the lack of a firm deadline to print and mail, and I experienced no complaints that the issues did not arrive faithfully every 30 or 31 days, but might require more than 12 months to produce twelve issues. (So often, our expectations are not borne out by experience. I learn and relearn the lesson of "asking" my clients what they want by testing my assumptions.)

How Sophisticated Must Your Design and Format Be?

On the subject of design and format, I am now going to step on a few toes. I plead guilty to being Mr. Pragmatic and probably coming up rather short in artistic sensitivities. Unfortunately, artistic sensitivities are often directly opposed to business realities: You may find that you cannot afford to worry about art, at least not in the start-up phases of operation.

It is possible to be quite artistic in designing a newsletter, especially in the design of the nameplate—that element that appears at the head of the first page, often enclosed in a box, for one. There are other such devices one may use—blurbs, graphic figures, oversize type, and numerous others.

It is my view that many, and perhaps most, of these are unnecessary refinements that add both unnecessary expense and practical difficulties. I doubt very much that these costly refinements add to the value of your newsletter or to the response it produces. I believe that a simple, businesslike appearance is as effective as the most sophisticated design. I think the preoccupation with the cosmetic elements, beyond that of an appearance of businesslike and professional efficiency, is self-congratulatory, but of little practical benefit. At least in the beginning, I would not be overly concerned with any format beyond that of practical simplicity. Time enough later to refine the design.

In my opinion too many independent entrepreneurs practice excessive self-indulgence in such matters as these. For example, the neophyte entrepreneur, struggling to get his or her newly launched consulting enterprise off the ground, wastes time, money, and energy on the design of a logo, for the enterprise.

A logo—a symbol identifying the enterprise—is a nicety for the business that has "arrived" and can afford to waste a bit of money on its "front." It's a financial burden for the business that is still struggling to build a firm base. Prospects do not become clients because of your logo, even if they note or are conscious of the logo.

Exactly the same can be said for an arty business card or distinctive stationery. Prospects may note these, and even remark on them and remember them, but are not induced to do business with you because of them. The cost and time is much better invested in more direct marketing efforts.

9

FORMAT AND
STYLE ISSUES

Restaurants, hotels, and many other businesses work hard at creating favorable images—at *ambience*—in their places of business. The equivalent for most of us as independent consultants is the impression made by our correspondence and printed materials.

IT'S A MATTER OF PRESENTATION

Since most of what our prospective clients see of us, especially in the beginning, is in our correspondence and printed materials, their appearance represents our own ambience, the aura or the correctness and good taste of the presentations we make. That includes such items as format, type styles, paper, language, and several other elements that inevitably add to or detract from your intended meaning and the impact of your message.

There are many protocols concerning the appearance and language of messages, especially formal exchanges but still including situations of far lesser formality. There are many standards and practices considered to be proper and in good taste. A disregard for these, especially in the matter of salutations and forms of address—even one that is completely innocent—can give offense or convey a general impression that will weaken the message completely. That is inappropriate for any professional person, but especially so in the case of a consultant, for whom image is especially important.

Although some of these matters were discussed briefly in passing, in the earlier chapters, and at the risk of being somewhat redundant in that regard, this chapter is offered as a convenient reference file to save you the trouble of searching through earlier chapters for the answers to questions of formats and special problems related to this. In this chapter you will find those suggested formats not covered in detail earlier for letters and other messages, both formal and informal, including such details as proper methods of address for different addressees and different occasions.

Letter Formats

Letters fall into numerous categories, but as far as style and formats are concerned most letters are either formal or informal, or business and personal (which are not quite the same as formal and informal, but are nevertheless quite close to that), and even then their styles are not greatly different from each other.

Aside from that, much of format and style is a matter of personal preference and choice. Whether you use block style or indent your paragraphs, and whether you follow a salutation with a colon or a comma are minor considerations, and you may follow your personal preference in such matters. Some other matters are not so trivial, and can assume great importance to others. In fact, it can be remarkably easy today to give offense, however unintended.

Forms, Salutations, and References

Obviously, when you send personal letters to friends you use informal salutations, depending largely on your relationship—"Dear Joe" or "Hi, Stinky." (I have two business friends I address as "Dear Steverino.") Addressing a stranger, however, even when your letter is a fairly casual one and not especially formal, requires some thought and some knowledge of what is normally considered proper or, at least, acceptable practice.

In these times of sensitivity to equal rights for all people, regardless of individual or even characteristic differences of any kind, it has become a bit of a problem to know how to address some people when you have no idea of whether you are addressing a man or woman (e.g., when you are responding to someone who uses only initials, such as "R. G. Williams"). Today it is by no means certain that the responsible leaders or executives of a business or organization are men, and it can be hazardous to make such assumptions. Many of today's executives and leaders are women. It is easy to give offense by addressing "R. G. Williams" as "Mr. Williams," when Williams' full name is Ruth Grace Williams. When in doubt, in such situations, use "Dear R. G. Williams" or "Dear President Williams," if you know Williams' title.

In the same vein, whereas we have always addressed men formally as "Mr." without regard to their marital status, we have always had the problem of whether to address a woman formally as "Miss" or "Mrs." when we were uncertain about her marital status. There never was a generic form of formal address to a woman that skirted this problem, so we have had to invent one recently, one that is a less-than-ideal solution but one that has become fairly popular. Today, when you are unsure about whether the woman you are addressing is or has been married or, has a strong personal preference that the question not be considered at all, you may usually use the salutation "Ms." safely, and would be well advised to do so. It is the safest course in those circumstances.

I have found, too, very much to my discomfort and embarrassment, that many women today object strongly to being referred to by such terms as "ladies" or "girls," finding such terms condescending or otherwise derogatory. It is obviously more discreet and in better taste or at least far less likely to be offensive to use the generic term "women" today, although addressing an audience or general population as "Ladies and gentlemen" ought still to be acceptable.

Special Titles

Although we pride ourselves in being a classless society—one in which we are all equal, at least in freedoms and rights—we do confer many special titles on individuals, recognizing special achievements and/or the attainment of special status of some kind. In some of the figures in this book you may have noticed the address to "Dr." Anyone with a doctoral degree of any kind is entitled to be addressed as "Doctor," just as those who gain other titles are entitled to have those terms used in addressing and salutating them too, regardless of gender.

Military ranks are another example of this. There is one kind of special case here: When the rank is one of those with two terms, such as Lieutenant Colonel or Major General, the address is always to the second and higher designation. A lieutenant colonel is therefore addressed verbally and in writing as "Colonel," although addressed as "Lieutenant Colonel John Doe" in writing his or her address. The salutation would normally be, like the verbal address, "Dear Colonel."

Complimentary Closes

Complimentary closes may likewise be formal or informal. "Respectfully" is considered to be rather formal and stiff today, with "Sincerely" and "Very truly" in more popular usage. "Cordially" is relatively informal, used in a letter to a stranger and, of course, "Regards" or "Best wishes" are quite informal and generally used only in letters to friends.

Notice of Enclosure(s)

You may have noticed the term "Encl." or "Enclosure" below the signature in some business letters where there was something else in the envelope. This is designed to be a notice to clerks or anyone else, other than the addressee, who may open the letter that there is something else enclosed with the letter. (The addressee would normally know that as a result of reading the letter and would not need the notice.) Some writers use only the abbreviation "Encl." to remind anyone opening the letter that there is something else enclosed, while others identify specifically the other material enclosed.

The usual practice is to type that notice several lines below the signature on the left-hand side of the letter.

Distribution Notices

In many cases, especially in routine business correspondence, copies of the original letter are sent to others for filing and information purposes. Although today we rarely use carbon paper for making copies—office copiers are far more convenient and less messy—the custom of marking the letter "cc:" (for "carbon copy(ies)" has persisted. The term is followed by the names or other identification of the destinations of the copies. This notice appears, like the enclosure notice, beneath the signature, on the left-hand side.

Signatures

Sales letters and other letters mailed in bulk may have a rubber stamp or lithographed signature, but that is a discourtesy when used in individual letters. Other than the case of letters mailed in bulk or copies sent to others for file and information purposes (those are generally not signed at all), all original letters ought to bear the actual signature (not a facsimile) of the sender.

A Few Miscellaneous Format Matters

Less serious but not less important if you wish your letter to appear truly professional and as if you really cared about how they look, are some mechanical details of layout and format.
Some of these details are optional, as in the case of block style versus idented paragraph styles, but others are not optional at all. There are a few important rules or, at least, principles.

Readability, Real and Apparent.   The physical appearance of the letter is important for more than one reason. Aside from the general impression of professionalism and caring—or the lack of it—there is the matter of readability and apparent readability. There are a great many myths and mistaken notions about this, so that actual readability and apparent readability are sometimes in conflict. For example, many people believe that double-spaced copy is easier to read than single-spaced copy, and in the same vein many believe that copy set in all capitals is eaiser to read than copy set in both upper- and lower-case letters.

Both of these notions are wrong, and the reason they are wrong is quite understandable: They are wrong because we have been trained to read text as upper and lower case letters in single-spaced format, just as we have been trained to read from left to right. While variations from this may appear to be easier to read, actual tests have demonstrated the opposite. If you doubt the effect of our early training in reading, try reading English in the style of oriental ideographs—in vertical columns, in the style of Hebrew—from right to left, or a lengthy text—at least several pages—in all capital letters.

Making Your Letters Appear More Readable. If appearance be-
lies reality in some cases, there are others in which appearances reflect
reality. One of these is the matter of physical balance of text in a letter.

The type should be balanced on the page. This is especially important for short letters, letters of about one-half a page or less, so that the
type is not bunched near the top of the page, with most of the bottom
portion blank.

Text that is "set solid"—large, unbroken blocks of text—appears
formidable and is intimidating to readers. It appears to be difficult to
read, whether it is or not. Here again appearance does not reflect reality.
We have ample evidence that the actual readability of text depends most
of all on how interesting it is to the reader, although the choice of language and sentence structure have some effect. (The Job Corps experience was only one of many that demonstrated the effect of motivation on
reading ability: If sufficiently motivated—interested, that is—readers will
infer the correct meanings of many words that are unfamiliar to them,
and will manage to get the main meanings out of even "purple prose"
passages. On the other hand, the most enlightened use of simple sentence structure and commonly known words cannot overcome the stulti-
fying effect of deadly dull writing.) Ideally, the text ought to be interesting, clearly expressed, and attractively presented, if it is to do its job
at all.

Part of the appearance depends on leaving adequate margins. Margins ought to be at least 1 inch, but margins slightly larger—$1^{1}/_{2}$ inches—
are even better.

To avoid that psychological effect of text that is set solid it is desirable to break up the large passages of text by keeping paragraphs as short
as possible—by starting new paragraphs as often as possible.

Now that is not an entirely arbitrary matter, for the accepted principles of composition dictate that each paragraph be about some topic
which is introduced by the first sentence of the paragraph, and that a
new paragraph must thus be about another topic. That, however, can be
arranged by using a little ingenuity in organizing your letters and making each paragraph highly specialized in the topics it addresses.

GRAMMAR, PUNCTUATION, AND
RELATED MATTERS

There will be no course in grammar here, not even a mini-course, for that
is well beyond the scope of this book, and excellent texts on grammar are

readily available. (A few will be cited in the bibliography later.) Consult one of these if you feel the need for a brush up. However, there are a few related, individual matters worthy of mention in passing, and those will be covered briefly here.

First it ought to be understood that while spellings are usually absolute (although there are many cases where alternate spellings are acceptable), grammar and punctuation "rules" are not really rules for how to express language, but are guidelines reflecting the opinions of certain people deemed to be authorities in the use of the language. So we have the purists who denounce as unspeakably coarse and unacceptable the splitting of an infinitive or the ending of a sentence with a preposition, while we have had such eminent masters of English usage as Winston Churchill who denounced such standards as being unimaginative and divorced from reality. Winston Churchill's famous remark that he used to illustrate the fallacy of unbending rules such as these was "This is an impertinence, up with which I shall not put," in referring to the dictum against ending a sentence with a preposition. He thus illustrated rather dramatically a sensible principle: Do try to observe these principles, such as avoiding the splitting of an infinitive, but not if the alternative to a split infinitive or a sentence ending with a preposition is an ungainly and ungraceful expression.

Another mistaken notion is that there is something wrong in using the personal pronoun "I" in writing. The one-time restriction against using "I" is commonly considered to have been put to rest with the writings of de Montaigne (Michel Eyquem) some time ago (1533–1592). In any case, there is little reason to say "we" unless you truly mean "we."

Rhetoric

Rhetoric is one subject where rules become nearly impossible, for rhetoric has to do primarily with the choice of the right words and their graceful use. It is far more an art than a science, and assaults on the language in this area are quite painful to many.

In my own case I am especially saddened by the growing and expanding misuse of the word "convinced." To be convinced means to be induced to believe something, never to be led to take an action. That is, to say something such as "Joe convinced Betty to meet him" is a horrible assault on the language in my opinion. Here the sentence ought to read either "Joe persuaded Betty to meet him" or "Joe convinced Betty that it would be a good idea to meet him." You never convince anyone "to do" something, but only "of" something.

This is an extreme case, and one that I and others find exceptionally distasteful, but there are many others. "Like" and "as" reflect another case. That tiresome advertising phrase about the cigarettes that "taste good like a cigarette should" was grammatically all wrong, for "like" modifies nouns, not verbs—it is an adjective, not an adverb. Those cigarettes should have tasted "good as a cigarette should," "as" being the adverb necessary to make the sentence grammatically proper.

These two examples point up a common problem. There are many words in English so like other words in sound or spelling that it is difficult to remember exactly what their differences are in meaning and so to remember how to use them properly. To further complicate the picture some of these words can be used as more than one part of speech—effect can be both a noun and a verb, for example. Some of the common and most troublesome such pairs of words are the following (respective meanings follow the words to enhance the illustration):

affect, effect: influence; bring about or result

principal, principle: chief, school official, or investment capital; basic truth

accept, except: receive, agree; leave out

allusion, illusion: reference; false image

appraise, apprise: evaluate; advise or inform

biannual, biennial: twice a year; every two years

calendar, calender: chart of days/months; smoothing device

compliment, complement: praise or commend; complete

continually, continuously: repeatedly; without stopping

council, counsel: board of people; advice

its, it's: possessive of it; contraction of it is

lead, led: a heavy metal; showed the way

reign, rein: to rule; check or control

stationary, stationery: fixed in one position; writing supplies

your, you're: possessive of you; contraction of you are

Punctuation

Punctuation falls into the same class of "rules" that are really not hard and fast rules at all. There are at least three schools of punctuation: closed, open, and mixed. Again, it is Samuel Clemens who left us a memorable remark on the subject. He protested violently when editors tampered with his punctuation. He insisted that no editor—no one— knew as well as he just what he was trying to say and therefore no one had the right or the competence to alter his punctuation.

That may be a bit extreme, given that many writers are not professional writers nor especially well qualified to punctuate their own work, but it does point up the arbitrary nature of so-called rules for punctuation. In my own case I went to school before there was such a vogue as open punctuation (or perhaps it was before I had the opportunity to learn that there was such an idea), and I have consequently had to adjust my thinking to this idea of relatively little punctuation, especially with regard to the sparse use of commas. (The adjustment did not come easily, after years of believing that there was only one set of rules for punctuation!)

In any case, the whole idea of grammar and punctuation is to try to help the reader perceive your whole meaning, with all its nuances and accents, and you should try to achieve that.

Spelling

If there is any overwhelmingly common weakness among writers who are not professional writers it is a sharply pronounced weakness in spelling. We are, too many of us, poor spellers.

One reason for this problem is the nature of English, and the fact that we really speak American here, for English, as spoken in England, is somewhat different in both pronunciation and spelling of a great many words. However, a large part of the problem is due to the fact that we have imported many thousands of words into English from many other languages—Latin, French, Spanish, German, and others—so that we have extremely few hard and fast rules for spelling. Therefore, almost all spelling rules have many exceptions. We are taught as children, for example, that when we spell words with e and i together in them we should remember that the rule is "i before e, except after c, or when sounded as a, as in neighbor and weigh." If you can remember that little verse, you are well along the way to mastering the ei/ie spelling problem. Otherwise it can be difficult to always be sure how to spell such words.

We also often have trouble remembering the plurals of words, especially those words that have come into English from another language and which therefore, do not normally take an s or es to make the plural. Oddly enough, we are usually more familiar with the plural form, so it is often the singular form that we do not know, nor do we even know that we are using the plural form. One of the most common examples of this is a word that has come into widespread use in this computer age: data, which is the plural of datum.

The trouble comes about when we use these terms in sentences with the wrong verbs. One of the most common problems, for example, is that of saying or writing such things as, "The data is being collected," when the correct form would be, "The data are being collected." Try using are and is on the following terms, for example, among which are some of the most troublesome of these pairs:

PLURAL FORM	SINGULAR FORM
agenda	agendum
alumnae	alumna
alumni	alumnus
analyses	analysis
antennas, antennae	antenna
appendixes, appendices	appendix
axes	axis
bacteria	bacterium
bases	basis
crises	crisis
curricula	curriculum
data	datum
diagnoses	diagnosis
errata	erratum
indexes, indices	index
matrices	matrix
media	medium
minutiae	minutia
parentheses	parenthesis
radii	radius
strata	stratum
theses	thesis

Unfortunately, the incorrect use of words can lead to bizarre results, often to the detriment of your image as the writer or, even worse, to the detriment of your organization's image. Here are a couple of examples of what can happen when a writer is not careful to be sure that he or she is using the right words or, conversely, knows the precise meaning of the words:

1. In some types of equipment where the failure of a circuit would be catastrophic the engineers often "back up" all the critical circuits with duplicate circuits that will be switched on automatically, should the original circuit fail. A technical writer preparing a user manual for such a piece of equipment confidently assured his readers of the complete "duplicity" of the circuits in the computer he was writing about, which was not exactly the quality customers wished their computers to have.

2. In another case of technical writing the engineer-writer wished to explain how all the connections in the system (of which there were a great many) were assigned to the rows upon rows of numbered terminals. He headed this discussion, "The Assignation of the Terminals," raising a few eyebrows as a result.

Words and Expressions to Shun

One of the hallmarks of the inexperienced writer is the use of trite and hackneyed cliches, such as "the bottom line," "a breakdown in communications," "sweet as sugar," and "slow as molasses." Another writing sin is the repeated use and overuse of some favored word or term, until it becomes trite and hackneyed in the context of whatever you are writing. (One individual I encountered was so enamored of "adept" and "expertise" that he worked overtime at dragging these into every possible paragraph, until readers begged for mercy!) A third symptom is the use of redundant expressions, such as "past experience" and "past history." What else can those things be but "past?" Then there's the term "wealthy millionaire," it is not an unheard-of redundancy either.

Occasionally we run into oxymorons, too, which are expressions consisting of words or ideas that are incompatible with each other because they negate each other. "Honest thief" and "little giant," for example, are oxymorons, and some people insist that "military intelligence" is also an oxymoron. If you wish to make a specific point by using such a term for its special effect, be sure that you do so in such a context that the reader knows that you are doing so deliberately and not in ignorance.

HOW TO MAKE WRITING (AND READING) AN EASIER TASK

"Writing" is not concerned with words alone. In fact, words are actually rather poor tools for communication, for they are only symbols, and each writer and reader must undertake the chores of translating images and ideas into those word symbols and re-translating those word symbols into the images and ideas they are supposed to represent. Unfortunately, the original images and ideas almost always lose a great deal in those processes. Writing is an act of communication and should utilize all devices that aid communication, including photographs, drawings, and charts.

Illustrations makes life easier for both the writer and the reader. Every good illustration (more in a moment about how to judge how good an illustration is) relieves you of struggling with words alone to get a message or image across to a reader, and in many cases it is far easier to convey what is in your mind with a graphic illustration of some kind. The reader benefits equally, for understanding also becomes easier with good illustrations: Using good illustrations is a win-win situation for both writer and reader. While writing and illustrating are more art than science, there are some guidelines to consider when using such illustrations.

How to Judge the Quality of an Illustration

A good illustration requires little explanation, and that is the way to test the quality of any illustration: Does it require explanation, and if so, how much? Is the illustration clear or is it "clever?" Forget about clever devices and artistic considerations; the purpose of an illustration is to communicate information accurately and efficiently. If the reader has to puzzle over the meaning or study the illustration at great length to understand it, the reader will probably sigh and go on. The basic rule is to always make it as easy as possible on the reader. Cleverness is all too often the death of meaning and understanding, and therefore the death of the writer's effort.

RESEARCH

Inadequate research—which means not having enough information and/ or not knowing the subject well enough—is far more often the root cause of bad writing than is any inability to use the language skillfully enough. An important key to writing well is, then, knowing how to research properly.

Logically—and unfortunately this is not nearly as obvious as it ought to be—the first and most important step in research is one that must be taken before the research effort begins. It is knowing what you want to know, setting a clear and specific objective of the research.

That can be a simple or complex task. If you are answering a customer complaint, it is important to research your own files and be sure that you know exactly what the facts are before you attempt to evaluate the customer's claims and allegations. On the other hand, if you are writing a report or a manual, you must be absolutely clear in your mind what objective that report or manual is supposed to achieve and what information you need to achieve it. In fact, even before you set out on your research you should have worked up some sort of preliminary outline and a written objective.

That presumes that you know enough about the subject to prepare an outline. Sometimes you may have to undertake to write about something you do not know well enough to draft even a rough or preliminary outline. In that case you may have to do some preliminary research so that you can develop a working outline. Even then—and even when you know your subject rather well—always assume that your outline is preliminary and subject to change as you broaden your knowledge and deepen your well of raw material resulting from your research. (There would be little point in the research otherwise!) In fact, it may be that you cannot develop even the broadest outlines until you have done at least enough research to enable you to write a sensible outline. In that case, your first research objective would be to gather enough information to develop a working outline and design your main research plan.

The Research Plan

The research plan is generally a rather informal plan. It consists primarily of setting down your main objective (sometimes with subordinate objectives, where the task is a relatively large and complex one) and the main sources of information.

Typical sources are people (interviews) and documents (files, reports, books, and other such material). As in the case of research and preliminary outlines, early research often uncovers sources you hadn't thought of or known about, so these should be added to your research plan. Here are a few suggested sources:

- Libraries, public and otherwise (including the extensive specialized libraries many major corporations, government agencies, and others keep and sometimes make available to the public).
- Company records (your own company, that is). Often the information you need is in your own files!
- Associations: There are thousands of associations of all kinds, from trade associations to professional societies, and many of these can and will help.
- Public information offices: Large corporations, government agencies, and many other organizations maintain those public information offices mentioned earlier. They are usually quite eager to help.
- Government publications: The federal government publishes a great many books, reports, pamphlets, and sundry other documents through the Government Printing Office and other federal agencies. There are few subjects that have not been the subject of one or more of these publications.
- Public databases. A great sea of information has been opened by the advent of the personal (desktop) computer and the evolution of online databases that have been inspired by that development. This will be covered shortly in this chapter.
- Other special sources. Quite often the early stages of your research will guide you to other sources. Moreover, there are several publications designed especially to guide you to information sources. These publications will be listed later.

When Is Research Complete?

There is no pat answer to when research is complete, because each situation is different. However, there are some indicators to suggest that it is time to end the research:

- You find that you are getting almost entirely redundant information—information you already have.

- You find that the information you are developing is too trivial or too irrelevant to your objectives to be useful.
- You are convinced, for whatever reason, that you now have all or nearly all the information you need to achieve your objectives.

This does not necessarily mean that your research is truly over and done with, however. It is possible that even after you begin writing you will come across a gap in the information that you had not detected before, and that you therefore must return to your research effort to search out some special area.

WORD PROCESSING: IMPORTANT WRITING AID

The microprocessor, a revolutionary breakthrough in electronic high technology, has had an appropriately revolutionary effect in many fields, not the least of which is in business offices generally. The new device led directly to the rapid development of personal—desktop—computers, for which the most popular application proved to be word processing.

A word processor is not a machine; it is a software program installed in a machine—in a computer. (It can be almost any computer.) That is true even in the case of "dedicated" word processors, computers designed to do word processing only, which machines were never particularly prominent nor dominant in word processing and have steadily grown even less so. It is a rare office today that does not have at least one desktop computer, and in most it is (they are) used for word processing far more than for anything else—often for nothing else. The typewriter industry has been dealt a serious blow by word processing, and typewriter manufacturers have been busily converting to the manufacture of computer printers, high-tech typewriters without keyboards.

One serious problem with word processing has been the abysmal lack of understanding about its most effective application. Unfortunately, too many offices have treated the computer and word processor as a super-typewriter. That is, instead of hiring "typists," they now advertise for and hire "word processor operators." Instead of handing typists sheafs of lined yellow paper covered with handwriting, with instructions to type them up as rough draft, they now hand those sheafs of lined yellow paper over to word processor operators with instructions to word process them up as rough draft. Thus little has changed, except that "typing" is now being done on much more expensive systems by much more highly paid operators at much higher final costs.

This lack of understanding is costly in many ways. Word processing is a much better way of typing and revising copy, but that is the lesser part of the revolution and almost insignificant, compared to what word processing really is. The real significance of word processing is not that it is a better way but that it is a different way. That means that it is not better because it is more efficient as a production tool, but it is better because it is light years more effective as a writing tool and—even more than that—as a thinking tool. That latter is, in fact, the key, along with other enhancements which will be discussed.

The key to proper—most effective and most appropriate—use of word processing lies in recognizing it as the writing tool it is. That means that those who are doing the writing, whether they are or are not professional writers, must work at the keyboard, rather than with pencils and ruled yellow pads. The following illustrates this point.

I resisted turning to word processing for some time after it became a viable option for me simply because it had been represented (or, more accurately, misrepresented) for so long as more efficient and speedier in the mechanics of turning out copy ready for the editor. As a professional writer, highly proficient in the mechanics of turning out copy and even somewhat innovative in developing my own, more efficient cut-and-paste methods, I was sure that word processing would not greatly increase my rate of production.

I was not entirely wrong in that: word processing has increased my rate of manuscript production somewhat, but that is not the truly significant change. The significant change is in the quality of my manuscript; it has grown by some inestimable amount. That is because today I do many times more rewriting, revision, and polishing of copy than I ever did before, producing far better copy (or so I fondly believe!) and still a little more rapidly than before. The revision has become so easy (comparatively) it is almost fun to do.

Revision/Rewriting Methodology

In my own working method I do not ordinarily print out copy until I have done all the self-editing, revision, rewriting, and polishing of copy. It is rather easy to do this on-screen, as compared with doing it on paper, once you develop an easy familiarity with the system. This is only part of the benefit and the reason the writer ought to work at the keyboard.

There are numerous other benefits and advantages that the writer will never experience without doing the actual inputting at the keyboard.

Swipe Files

"Swipe files" (referred to earlier) are files of standard or boilerplate material that you can use over and over, with or without some adaptation. The term takes on new meaning when it is applied to computer files stored on a disk. It is easy to call them up—and you are making copies when you do so, the original still intact—and incorporate them into whatever you are currently writing, with or without modification. These can be text, resumes, drawings, or any other material that can be stored. As you proceed these files tend to grow steadily, so that you have an ever richer resource stored in your bank of swipe files. (Many of the files you modify and adapt prove useful for later applications, and so are added to your bank.) Among the most useful swipe files are those of computer-generated drawings—charts, plots, graphs, and the like. They are a bit laborious to generate the first time, but relatively easy to modify and use again, once they are established in your bank of swipe files. Therefore, they can save you a great deal of time in subsequent uses.

Online Research

With the addition of a modem to your computer you can use your telephone line to communicate with any other computer equipped with a modem. Today there are hundreds of online databases—information banks—you can subscribe to and get information from by "downloading" files to your own computer. For instance, when a client wanted some information about certain government markets I got the bulk of the information from such a database over the telephone by requesting a search of the database files in a computer-to-computer link and printed the data out on my own system. This printout alone constituted the bulk of my report, and the whole project therefore consumed extremely little of my time. For a partial listing of some online utilities see Appendix F.

General Communication

The modem-telephone link offers other benefits. For one, it can put you in touch with others via electronic bulletin boards, where you send and receive electronic mail. I often post an appeal for information on such boards and get help from others, just as I respond to their appeals and supply information when I am able to. You can also communicate directly with another individual's computer, if the other computer is also equipped properly with a modem and communications software, and I have found that a useful convenience too. I have communicated and collaborated with other writers through this link, but you can communicate with anyone for any purpose in this manner.

PD Software and Shareware

There is an abundance of free, nearly free, and low-cost software—computer programs known as "shareware—to be had by downloading them from bulletin boards. These are programs written by hobbyists and enthusiasts who are willing to donate these to public use by placing them in the public domain and programmers who will permit you to try their programs out, on the honor system, and pay for them at modest prices if you like them. Hence the terms "PD" and "shareware." Among those I have found useful in writing are programs that count the words in a manuscript, help with indexing and footnoting, check spellings, do simple outlining, make "fog counts" (measures of clarity), and measure reading levels.

There are many novel programs you can pick up, too, and some of these can be useful in writing. Some examples of programs I use can:

- Enable me to instantly project on-screen any month in any year since the mid-nineteenth century or in any future century.
- Enable me to make up a master file of all my files and prepare a directory.
- Recover any file I have accidentally erased—a true life saver!
- Condense files I wish to store in archives into "libraries" that take up about one-half the disk space they would otherwise require.

Helpful Commercial Software

Although many of the free—public domain—software programs and shareware are quite excellent, you must often buy regular commercial software when you need the more sophisticated programs. One class of software that gained a great deal of recognition and popularity were programs to facilitate developing outlines and planning publications. Today, such programs are included in many of the leading word processors sold commercially.

These programs are a great aid to many writers, even to experienced, professional writers, but especially to those for whom writing is an occasional chore and one for which they have neither trained themselves nor which they particularly relish. Basically, these are programs that have the following general characteristics:

1. They assist you in developing a general outline of your subject.
2. You can expand any item in your outline with either additional subordinate items or with a text passage.
3. You can collapse or expand your outline to get a macroscopic or microscopic view of the outline/subject.
4. You can readily shift items around.
5. You can copy or merge items that tend to repeat themselves.

Depending on which program you are using, you can do many other things along these same lines. The idea is to help you develop ideas, and these programs include manuals of instruction intended to help you learn how to get the most out of these programs.

Of course, there are many other useful programs. One class of these is the key-redefinition program, which enables you to store items that you can call up at will with a single key. You can prepare an entire line, title, paragraph, or even a full page of some boilerplated or standard material and have the computer insert it by pressing a single key. I have my name, address, and telephone number in one such key, and the names and addresses of others with whom I correspond on other keys so I can address letters and envelopes with a single key ("h" for my own name, for example).

Most word processors can do searching to help you find things quickly in a file and to make changes when you have erred somehow—for example, to change (automatically) every "Hetty Green" to "Hetty Greene." That works only within a given file, and you must do it over and over for each file, if you have many files to be so treated. However, I purchased a little program, Electra-Find, that will search all the files on a disk or as many disks as I wish to stipulate, upon a single command! That is an order-of-magnitude improvement over the internal "global search" feature of the typical word processor. It's especially useful when you can't remember whether you did or did not mention something earlier in a manuscript; you can send that little program in quest of the information and you will know within a few minutes.

══════ APPENDIX A ══════

A FEW TIPS ON WRITING COPY

Here are a few reminders, as a checklist of "do's and don'ts" to refer to when preparing copy:

- Always make things as easy as possible for the customer.
    1. Make it easy to understand what you are saying. Use short words, short sentences, and short paragraphs. One thought in a sentence, one subject and one main point in a paragraph. (Be sure first that you yourself fully understand the main point.)
    2. Make it easy for the customer to order, ask for more information, or otherwise reveal interest by providing a return card, telephone number, or other convenient means for responding.
    3. Make it easy for the customer to understand what you want him or her to do by *telling* the customer what to do. A great many sales are lost by advertisers who fail to tell the customers what they want the customers to do (e.g., "Just fill out the enclosed card . . .") or what you propose to do (e.g., "I will call you in a few days). Sounds foolish, but experience proves it to be helpful to do this.
- A direct-mail cliche (which is nonetheless a truism) is "The more you tell the more you sell." Don't stint on copy. Be sure to include a letter, brochure or flyer of some sort, and a response device (envelope and/or order form) as an abso-

lute minimum, and there is no harm in enclosing even more. The experts claim that three-quarters of the response results from the letter, and that a good circular or brochure can increase response by as much as one-third. My own experience bears this out quite emphatically. (Note how many contest forms require the respondent to remove seals from one place and stick them in another place. This is part of getting prospects directly involved and so arousing their interest.)

- Don't tell it all in the letter. Split the copy up among the various enclosures, or at least provide additional details in the various enclosures. Make it clear that additional information and details are to be found elsewhere in the enclosures. Give the reader good reasons—inducements —to read everything, if you want maximum impact.

- Geography makes a difference. Prospects who are nearby tend to respond better than those at a distance. Know your nearby zip codes, and use these, but do test, for there are always exceptions. Example: when it comes to consulting and speaking services, there is some appeal, even a kind of mystique, to the expert from a distant place, especially if you are mailing from a major industrial or business center, such as New York, Chicago, or Washington. If you are, take advantage of it, somehow, by giving it prominence in your copy. If you use envelope copy—advertising and sales messages on the outside of the envelope—do two things.

1. Use both sides of the envelope. If you are going to make a bulletin board of the envelope, you might as well get full use of it; copy on both sides pulls better than copy on one side only—if the copy is powerful.

2. Now that you've served notice that the envelope contains advertising matter, why pay first-class postage? You might as well save money by using bulk mail or, at least, something less expensive than first class.

APPENDIX B

A SUGGESTED PROPOSAL OUTLINE

A six-part proposal outline is offered here. That is, there are four chapters or sections, but there is also front matter in the formal proposal, and back matter in many cases. For the informal or letter proposal, you won't have separate chapters, but you can follow the same philosophy and strategy of presentation recommended here.

This format may, of course, be modified to suit your own preferences, circumstances, or dictates of the client. Some Requests for Proposals (RFPs) mandate a standard proposal format of their own, which you will of course follow, in such cases.

1. FRONT MATTER
   - Copy of Letter of Transmittal
   - Executive Summary
   - Abstract of most important points that demonstrate your best arguments.
   - Table of Contents

2. SECTION/CHAPTER I: INTRODUCTION
   - About the Offeror: Briefly introduce your firm, sketch your company and qualifications, refer to details to be found later, make other opening statement.
   - Understanding of the Requirement: Make brief statement of your understanding of the requirement, in your own language (don't echo the RFP), leave out the trivia and focus on the essence of the requirement, providing a smooth transition to the next chapter.

3. SECTION/CHAPTER II: DISCUSSION
   - Discuss the requirement, analyzing, identifying problems, exploring and reviewing approaches (with pros and cons of each). Include similar discussions of all relevant matters, technical, management, schedule, other important points, including worry items. This is key section in which to sell the proposed program, make the emotional appeals (promises), explain the superiority of the proposed program, and demonstrate the validity of the proposer's grasp of the problem, how to solve it, how to organize the resources, and otherwise *sell* the idea.
   - Include graphics, as necessary, especially functional flowchart, explaining the approach and technical or program design strategy employed.
   - Should culminate in a clear explanation of the approach selected, bridging directly into the next chapter.

4. SECTION/CHAPTER III: PROPOSED PROJECT
   (This is where the specifics appear—staffing and organization [with organization chart], resumes of key people, either here or later in this chapter, but at least introduced here by name.)
   - Project management: Procedures, philosophy, methods, controls; relationship to parent organization, reporting order; other information on both technical and general/administrative management of project. (May be separate chapter or even separate volume, for larger projects.)
   - Labor-loading: Explain major tasks and estimated hours for each principal in each task (use tabular presentation), with totals of hours for each task and totals of hours for each principal staff member.
   - Deliverable items: Specify, describe, quantify, as explained.
   - Schedules: Specify, as explained. (Use milestone chart, if possible.)

- Resumes: Resumes of key staff, including associates and other consultants, if any.

5. SECTION/CHAPTER IV: COMPANY QUALIFICATIONS
   - Describe company, past projects (especially those similar to one under discussion), resources, history, organization, key staff, other resumes, testimonial letters, special awards, and other pertinent facts.

6. APPENDICES (Back matter)
   - Append detailed data, drawings, papers, bibliography, citations, and other material that some, but not all, readers will want to read.

APPENDIX C

TIPS ON GRAPHICS

Graphics—drawings, charts, and graphs—add greatly to clear and easy communication of ideas. By all means, make use of them. With today's computers and software, anyone can prepare professional-quality graphics.

A good illustration requires little explanation, and that is the way to test the quality of any illustration: Does it require explanation, and if so, how much?

Is the illustration clear? Forget about artistic considerations; the purpose of an illustration is to communicate information accurately and efficiently. If the reader has to puzzle over the meaning or study the illustration to understand it, the reader will probably set your proposal aside with a sigh, and go on to the next one. Basic rule: make it as easy as possible on the reader. Artistry is all too often the death of meaning and understanding, and therefore the death of the sale.

For function charts, use the WHY? HOW? technique to generate the chart and to test it. Going from left to right (or from top to bottom, if you prefer that progression), ask WHY? of each box, and the answer should be in the next box. Going the other way—in reverse—ask HOW, and the answer should be in the next box. If the answers are not very clear, consider adding boxes (for more detail) or changing the wording in the boxes. (Charts, like text, should go through drafts, editing, reviews, and revisions.)

═══ APPENDIX D ═══

USING HEADLINES, GLOSSES, AND BLURBS

Proposals are not exciting literature, and at best are fatiguing to read in quantities, as customers are compelled to do. Anything you can do to make it easier for the reader will help you, in the end, in more than one way: 1) it will help you get your own messages across and pierce the consciousness of readers who may be reading mechanically, and without full appreciation, by the time they get to your opus; and 2) you will earn the reader's gratitude, which can do nothing but help your case. There are several devices that will help:

HEADLINES

Use headlines—sideheads and centerheads—as freely as you can and as often as you can. Use them to summarize messages, to telegraph what a paragraph or page is about, what the main message is. Use them also to **SELL.** That is, use the headline to summarize and remind the reader of promises (benefits) and proofs.

GLOSSES

A "gloss" is a little abstract in the margin of a page that summarizes the text next to it. Usually, there is at least one gloss on a page, and often there are several.

Like headlines, glosses can and should be used to help sell the proposal by focusing on benefits and proofs.

BLURBS

A blurb is very much like a gloss, except that it is not used as frequently, and is thus somewhat broader in scope and, usually, of greater length. A blurb generally appears after a major headline (usually a center head) or chapter title. Like headlines and glosses, blurbs should be used to sell, as well as to sum up information and communicate generally.

═══ APPENDIX E ═══

MAILING LIST
BROKERS

There is a great abundance of mailing list brokers, firms from whom you can rent (and in some cases buy) mailing lists. You can find them listed in the yellow pages, as well as in many other media. Here are a just a few of them, many of them branch offices of mailing list firms:

American List Counsel, Inc., 88 Orchard Road, Princeton, NJ 08543

AZ Marketing Services, Inc., 31 River Road, Cos Cob, CT 06807

Woodruff-Stevens & Associates, 345 Park Avenue South, New York, NY 10010

Direct Media, 200 Pemberwick Road, Greenwich, CT 06830

Listworks, One Campus Drive, Pleasantville, NY 10570

Qualified Kists. Corp, 135 Bedford Road, Armonk, NY 10504

Worldata, 5200 Town Center Circle, Boca Raton, FL 33486

The Coolidge Co., 25 West 43rd Street, New York, NY 10036

Jami Marketing Services, 2 Bluehill Plaza, Pearl River, NY 10965

Allmedia, Inc., 4965 Preston Park Blvd, Plano, TX 75093

Dependable Lists, Inc., 950 S. 25th Avenue, Bellwood, IL 60104

═══ APPENDIX F ═══

ONLINE UTILITIES
AND PUBLIC
DATABASES

Following is a brief sampling of just a few of the better-known or more prominent online utilities and public databases, available on a subscription basis, usually with a "connect time" and a monthly minimum charge. The difference between them is principally that while the public database is strictly an information source and usually used only by those who need the information for business and professional purposes, the online utilities offer services many use for entertainment and amusement as virtual public meeting places to seek out others with similar interests for chats and debates via the "forums" or "conferences."

ONLINE UTILITIES

CompuServe Information Service, Inc.
5000 Arlington Centre Blvd.
Columbus, OH 43220
617 457-8600
800 848-8900

GEnie
GE Information Services
401 N. Washington Street
Rockville, MD 20850
301 340-4000
800 638-9636

Prodigy Services Company
445 Hamilton Avenue
White Plains, NY 10601
914 993-8848

Minitel USA
1700 Broadway
New York, NY 10019
212 307-5005

PUBLIC DATABASES

Dialog Information Services, Inc.
3460 Hillview Avenue
Palo Alto, CA 94304
800 334-2564
415 858-3792

NewsNet, Inc.
945 Haverford Road
Bryn Mawr, PA 19010
800 345-1301
215 527-8030

BRS Information Technologies
1200 Route 7
Latham, NY 12110
800 227-5277
518 783-7251

Mead Data Central
9393 Springboro Pike
P.O. Box 933
Dayton, OH 45401
800 227-4908

Dow Jones News Retrieval
P.O. Box 300
Princeton, NJ 08543-0300
609 452-1511
800 522-3567

GOVERNMENT ELECTRONIC BULLETIN BOARD SYSTEMS (BBS)

Many BBS are operated in federal government offices. Some are official organs of the agencies, while others are quasi-official in that an employee operates them under the sponsorship of the agency. One that may be the most important of these, from your viewpoint as a computer consultant, is that of the General Services Administration, which has jurisdiction over computer standards-setting and other matters relating to computer procurement by government agencies. This bulletin board carries important information about requirements, procurements, and major contractors, so that it can be an important source of business leads for you. The BBS number follows:

General Services Administration BBS

202 501-2014

A message on this BBS provides a list of telephone numbers for each of the ten GSA regional contacts for ADP Technical Service Requirements contracts as follows:

Region 1   617 835-5753
Region 2   215 597-5104
Region 3   202 501-2014
Region 4   205 895-5091
Region 5   312 886-3824
Region 6   816 926-5610
Region 7   817 334-1684
Region 8   303 236-7319
Region 9   415 974-7557
Region 10   206 442-2418

Another highly important BBS is that run by the Small Business Administration (SBA). The number for SBA ONLINE was given earlier in this appendix ("Miscellaneous Resources") with a toll-free number for access at 2400 baud, but there are three numbers for SBA ONLINE:

202 205-7265
800 697-4636—access at 9600 baud
800 859-4636—access at 2400 baud

Some of the many other BBS in government offices are listed here:

U.S. Navy
Navy ADA Language System: 703 614-0215

Dept of Agriculture
Library: 301 504-6510/800 345-5785
Nutrition: 301 436-5078
Library of Congress
ALIX II: 202 707-4888

Dept of Commerce
Census Bureau: 301 763-4574
Geological Survey: 703 648-4168

Dept of Education
202 219-2011
202 219-2012

Dept of Interior
703 787-1181

State Dept
U.S.A.I.D./Permanet BBS: 703 715 9806—2400 baud
                         703 715 9851—9600 baud

National Science Foundation
SRS (Science and Research Studies): 202 634-1764

Government Printing Office
Federal Bulletin Board: 202 512-1387

A FEW TIPS ON PURSUING GOVERNMENT CONTRACTS . . .

Individuals can do business with federal agencies, just as major corporations do. (I have personally won and performed on many government contracts.) I believe the advantages of doing business with the government far outweigh the drawbacks. The following suggestions will help you get started learning the ropes of selling your services to the government.

To get on Bidders lists: Ask for Standard Form 129, Application for Bidders List, and make it up in enough copies to distribute to the various agencies with whom you think you can do business.

To learn of outstanding bid and proposal opportunities: Subscribe to the *Commerce Business Daily* (CBD) or to any public database that carries CBD ON-LINE, such as CompuServe or Dialog. Also, visit government bid rooms and monitor the notices on the bulletin boards. Don't depend entirely on the Form 129.

If you are in or near a General Services Administration Business Service Center, take the time to visit and talk to the people there. They are located in Boston, New York, Philadelphia, Washington, Atlanta, Chicago, Kansas City, Denver, Houston, Fort Worth, Los Angeles, San Francisco, and Seattle. If not, write to the one in Denver—Denver Federal Center, Bldg. 41, Denver, CO 80225—and request all available information on doing business with the government.

Write to the contracting offices of major agencies (e.g., the Department of Defense, NASA, Health and Human Services) and make the same request for information.

Watch the CBD for announcements of free seminars on competing for federal contracts. They are held frequently, sponsored by Members of Congress in their districts.

Get acquainted with the contracting officers of federal agencies near you. Personal contact helps a great deal in all marketing, and a friendly contracting officer can be very helpful.

BIBLIOGRAPHY

There are many excellent sources of additional information on subjects related to the various chapters of this book. Recommendations made here are based on my own prejudices as sources that have helped shape my own views, are in my own library, proved helpful to me in some way, impressed me as excellent work, are the work of individuals whom I respect and admire, and/or will be helpful to you. I also unblushingly list my own works when I believe the recommendation to be appropriate.

BOOKS

Arth, Marvin and Ashmore, Helen, The Newsletter Editor's Desk Book, 1980, Shawnee Mission, Parkway Press.

Bly, Robert W., Create the Perfect Sales Piece, 1985, New York, John Wiley, 1985.

Bove, Tony, Rhodes, Cheryl, and Thomas, Wes, The Art of Desktop Publishing, 1986, New York, Bantam, 1986.

Holtz, Herman, The Consultant's Guide to Proposal Writing, 2nd ed., 1986, New York, John Wiley.

—— How to Start and Run a Writing & Editing Business, 1992, New York, John Wiley.

—— The Direct Marketer's Work Book, 1986, New York, John Wiley.

——— Secrets of Practical Marketing for Small Business, 1983, Englewood Cliffs, Prentice-Hall.

Jacobi, Peter P., The Magazine Article, 1991, Cincinnati, Writer's Digest Books.

Lewis, Herschell Gordon, Direct Mail Copy That Sells, 1984, Englewood Cliffs, Prentice-Hall.

Newman, Edwin, On Language, 1980, New York, Warner Books.

Strunk, William, Jr. and White, E.B., The Elements of Style, 1972, New York, Macmillan.

Wilder, Claudyne, The Presentations Kit, 1990, New York, John Wiley.

USEFUL PERIODICALS

Direct Response Specialist, Galen Stilson, P.O.Box 1075, Tarpon Springs, FL 34286-1075. A monthly newsletter of direct-marketing ideas and guidance by a direct-mail consultant.

DM News, 19 West 21st Street, New York, NY 10010, a weekly tabloid on direct marketing.

Home Office Computing, Scholastic, Inc., 730 Broadway, New York, NY 10003. Most directly relevant magazine, found on newsstands, or by subscription.

Sharing Ideas!, Dottie Walters, P.O. Box 1120, Glendora, CA 91740. A bimonthly periodical, that has become almost the bible of the public-speaking industry, but is also of interest to writers and consultants.

Target Marketing, 401 N. Broad Street, Philadelphia, PA 19108, a monthly slick paper trade magazine for direct marketers.

INDEX

USER
INFORMATION

I. About the Independent Consultant's Brochure and Letter Handbook Diskette

This disk contains forms, figures, and checklists from the book *The Independent Consultant's Brochure and Letter Handbook*. The forms can be read easily by your editor or word processor and, can be presented on the screen to be filled in quickly and easily and/or printed out, as you wish. Having filled out all the worksheets and other forms, you will have a computer record of your original letters, brochures, or other documents. You may print them out, store them on disks, or otherwise preserve them as archives. Later, when you wish to review your original letters and brochures to update them or make revisions for any other reason, you may modify the files you created originally or you may start over with the blank forms, as you prefer.

Figures are numbered serially by the chapters in which they appear originally, so that Figure 5-1 is the first figure to appear in Chapter 5. The appendices are a summary of reference data, and are named Appendix A, Appendix B, etc, rather than by serial numbering. These documents are designed to be easily modified and adapted. The information covered in this section can also be found in the Readme.TXT document on the disk.

II. Computer Requirements

This diskette requires an IBM-PC or compatible computer with DOS version 2.0 or later. It can be used in both DOS and Windows environments. The files are formatted in Microsoft Word for Windows 2.0, Word Perfect 5.1 and ASCII, which is a universal text format for DOS computers. The files can be read into your word processing software program using the directions contained in this appendix. If your word processing program is not listed below, you can load the ASCII files by following the directions in your software manual. Using the index in your software manual, refer to the section on *Importing ASCII Files or Loading Documents from Other Word Processors*.

III. How to Make a Backup Diskette

Before you start to use the enclosed diskette, we strongly recommend that you make a backup copy of the original. Making a backup copy of your disk allows you to have a clean set of files saved in case you accidentally change or delete a file. Remember, however, that a backup disk is for your own personal use only. Any other use of the backup disk violates copyright law. Please take the time now to make the backup copy, using the instructions below:

(a) If your computer has two floppy disk drives:

1. Insert your DOS disk into drive A of your computer.

2. Insert a blank disk into drive B of your computer.

3. At the **A:>**, type **DISKCOPY A: B:** and press Enter. You will be prompted by DOS to place the source disk into drive A.

4. Place the *Independent Consultant's* disk into drive A. Follow the directions on screen to complete the copy.

5. When you are through, remove the new backup disk from drive B and label it immediately. Remove the original *Independent Consultant's* disk from drive A and store it in a safe place.

(b) If your computer has one floppy disk drive and a hard drive:

If you have an internal hard drive on your computer, you can copy the files from the enclosed disk directly onto your hard disk drive, in lieu of making a backup copy, by following the installation instructions on the following pages.

IV.   Installing the Diskette

The enclosed diskette contains 70 individual files in a compressed format. In order to use the files, you must run the installation program for the disk. You can install the diskette onto your computer by following these steps:

1. Insert the *Independent Consultant's* disk into drive A of your computer. Type A:\INSTALL and press Enter.

2. The installation program will be loaded. After the title screen appears, you will be given the options shown in Figure 1.

3. The following Menu Selections will be listed: Edit Destination Paths, Select Destination Drive, Toggle Overwrite Mode, Select Groups to Install and Start Installation.

4. The **Destination Path** is the name of the default directory to store the data files. The default directory name is LETTER. To change this

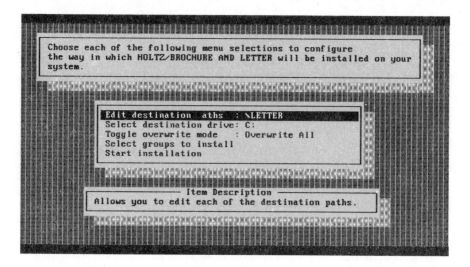

Figure 1

name, press Enter, hit the letter **P,** type in the name of the directory you wish to use and press Enter.

5. **Select Destination Drive** gives you the option of installing the disk onto a hard disk drive C:\ or, if you wish, onto a different drive.

6. The **Toggle Overwrite Mode** pertains to the directories and files you already have on your hard drive. Do not give the default directory the same name as existing directories on your hard drive or the installation program will overwrite or delete any pre-existing directories of the same name. The safest option to protect existing data on your computer is *OVERWRITE NEVER.*

7. The **Select Groups to Install** option, allows you to install each directory on the disk one by one. The files on this disk are in three different formats; Microsoft Word for Windows, WordPerfect for Windows and ASCII. If you wish to install the entire directory at once, tab down to Start Installation and press Enter. To install just one of these word processing formats, press Enter, hit the letter **G,** select the format you do not want to install, and hit Enter again.

The files are now successfully installed onto your hard drive.

V. Reading Files into Word Processing Programs

For your convenience, the files on the enclosed diskette are provided in three formats, ASCII, Microsoft Word for Windows and WordPerfect for Windows. If you have Word Perfect 5.1 or Microsoft Word for Windows, the WordPerfect or MS Word files will be easiest for you to use because they are already formatted. Once the files are loaded into your word processor, you can customize them to suit your individual needs.

If you do not have Windows or you use other programs not compatible with MS Word or WordPerfect, the ASCII files are designed for you. Because ASCII format is standard format for all DOS computers, a number of different users with different word processing programs can read the disk. This means regardless of your particular word processing program (WordStar, MS Word for DOS, WordPerfect for DOS, etc.), you can still use this disk. Once the file is loaded into your word processor, you can customize them to suit your individual needs.

(a) Reading the files into Microsoft Word for Windows

To read a file into Microsoft Word for Windows, follow these steps:
Load the Word for Windows program as normal.

1. When the Untitled document is displayed, select **OPEN** from the **FILE** menu.

2. The **OPEN FILE** dialog box will appear, as shown in Figure 2. At this box, make the appropriate selections for the drive and directory of the document you want to review. For instance, to open the file **1-03** in the LETTER directory, you must select drive **C:** and the directory LETTER and then type **1-03.DOC** under the file name. Click OK to proceed. The file will immediately load into Microsoft Word for Windows.

3. Make your changes and revisions to the document.

4. To print the file, select **PRINT** from the **FILE** menu.

5. When you are through editing it, you should save it under a new name (to avoid overwriting the original file) before you quit.

(b) Reading Files Into WordPerfect 5.1 for DOS

To read a file into WordPerfect, follow these steps:
Load the WordPerfect program as normal.

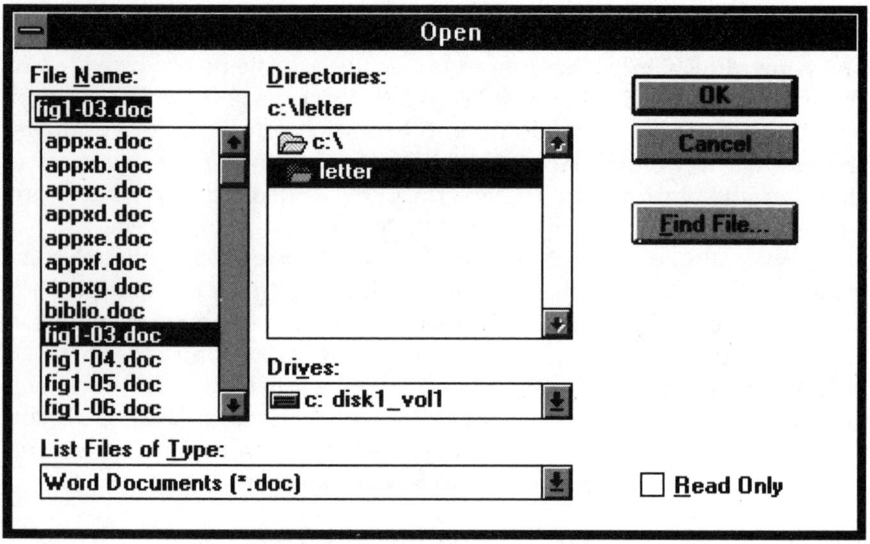

Figure 2

1. When the blank document screen is displayed, press **SHIFT-F10** to retrieve the document.

2. To open the document **1.03,** from the directory LETTER, type **C: \LETTER\1-03.WP.** Press Enter when you have finished typing in the filename.

3. Make your changes and revisions to the document.

4. To print the document, press SHIFT-F7.

5. When you are through editing the document you should save it under a new file name (to avoid overwriting the original file) before you quit.

Reading the ASCII Files into Other Word Processing Programs

To use these files with other word processing programs, refer to the documentation that accompanies your software. Often, the procedure is very similar to those already explained. The two primary steps involved in opening the ASCII files are:

1. Identify the file you want to load from the LETTER directory and indicate the filename to your word processor.

2. Identify the file as a DOS text file.

After these general steps, most word processing programs will immediately load the file.

VI. List of Figures and Filenames

Exhibit Name	Description	Book Page Number

VII.   User Assistance and Information

John Wiley & Sons, Inc. is pleased to provide assistance to users of this package. Should you have any questions regarding the use of this package, please call our technical support number (212) 850-6194 weekdays between 9 am and 4pm Eastern Standard Time.

To place additional orders or to request information about other Wiley products, please call (800) 879-4539.